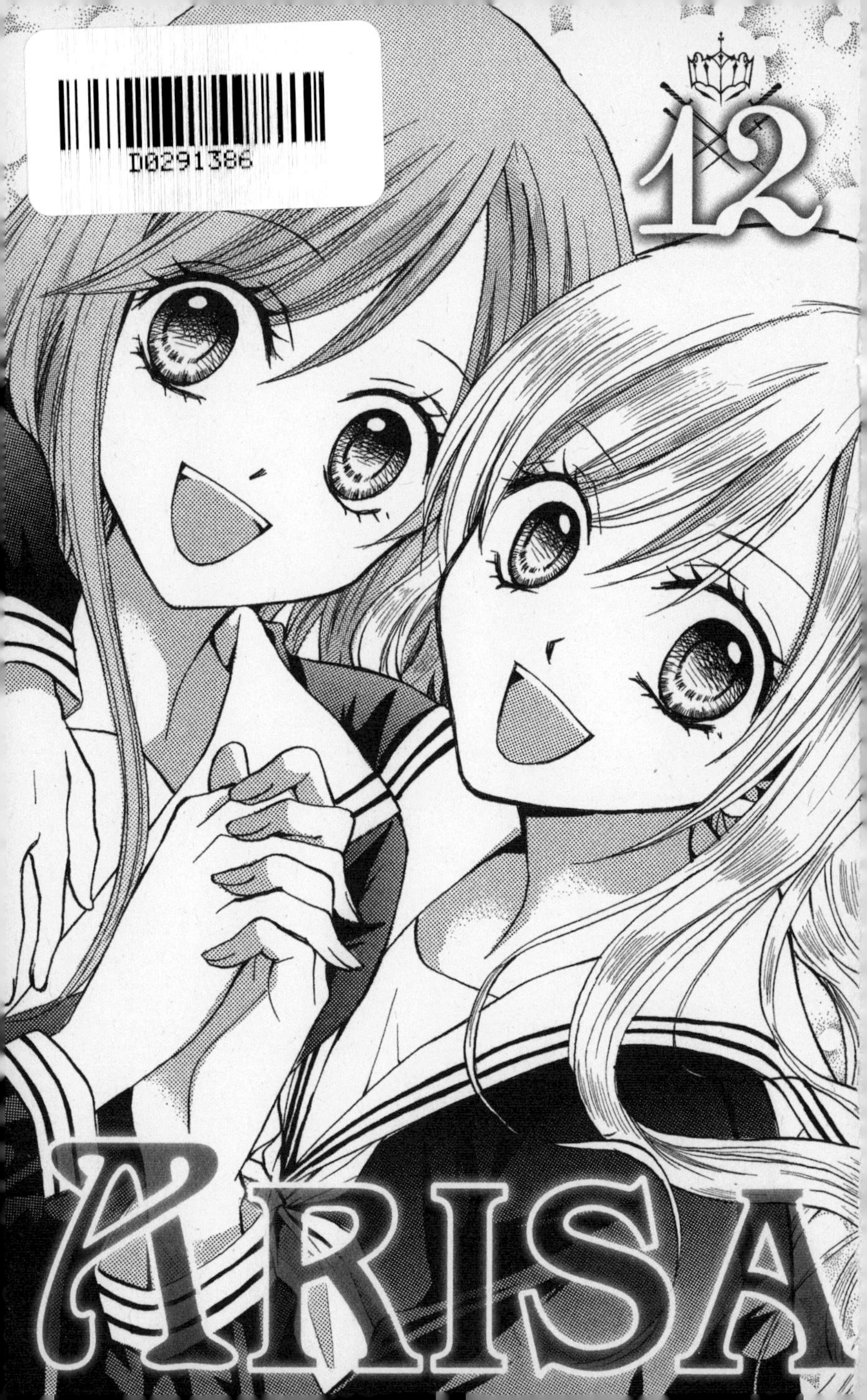
12
ARISA

Contents

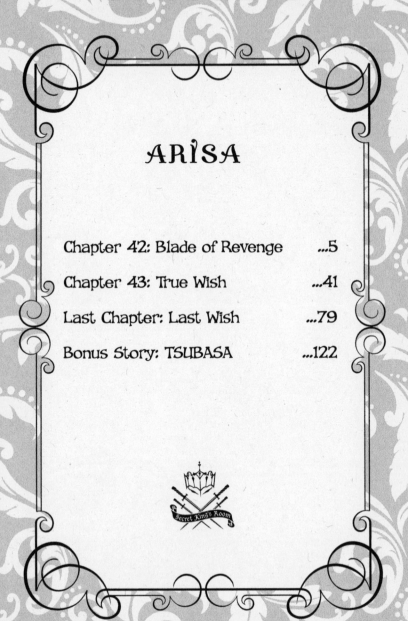

ARISA

Secret King's Room

Character & Story

Tsubasa and Arisa are twin sisters separated by their parents' divorce. They finally reunited after three years of being apart, but their happy time together came to a sudden end when Arisa jumped out her bedroom window right in front of Tsubasa, leaving behind a mysterious card…

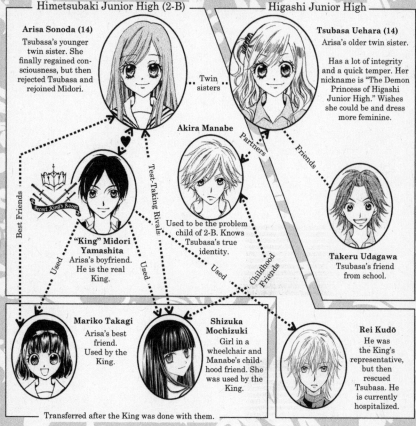

Himetsubaki Junior High (2-B)
Higashi Junior High
Arisa Sonoda (14)
Tsubasa's younger twin sister. She finally regained consciousness, but then rejected Tsubasa and rejoined Midori.
Twin sisters
Tsubasa Uehara (14)
Arisa's older twin sister.
Has a lot of integrity and a quick temper. Her nickname is "The Demon Princess of Higashi Junior High." Wishes she could be and dress more feminine.
Akira Manabe
Partners
Friends
Best Friends
Test-Taking Rivals
Secret King's Room
"King" Midori Yamashita
Arisa's boyfriend. He is the real King.
Used to be the problem child of 2-B. Knows Tsubasa's true identity.
Takeru Udagawa
Tsubasa's friend from school.
Used
Used
Used
Childhood Friends
Mariko Takagi
Arisa's best friend. Used by the King.
Shizuka Mochizuki
Girl in a wheelchair and Manabe's childhood friend. She was used by the King.
Rei Kudō
He was the King's representative, but then rescued Tsubasa. He is currently hospitalized.
Transferred after the King was done with them.

In order to discover the secrets Arisa was hiding, Tsubasa pretended to be her and attended Himetsubaki Junior High. Upon learning that someone known as the "King" on the Internet ruled class 2-B, she braved great hardships to discover that the King was actually Midori. Once Arisa regained consciousness, she chose to go with Midori, even though she knew his true identity. Unable to accept the situation, Tsubasa visited Midori's old orphanage and found out about how he lost his younger twin brother, Akari. When she realized that Midori's true goal was to exact vengeance upon his mother at the Christmas summit Class 2-B was attending, Tsubasa tried to intervene, but...!

Tsubasa!!

ARISA

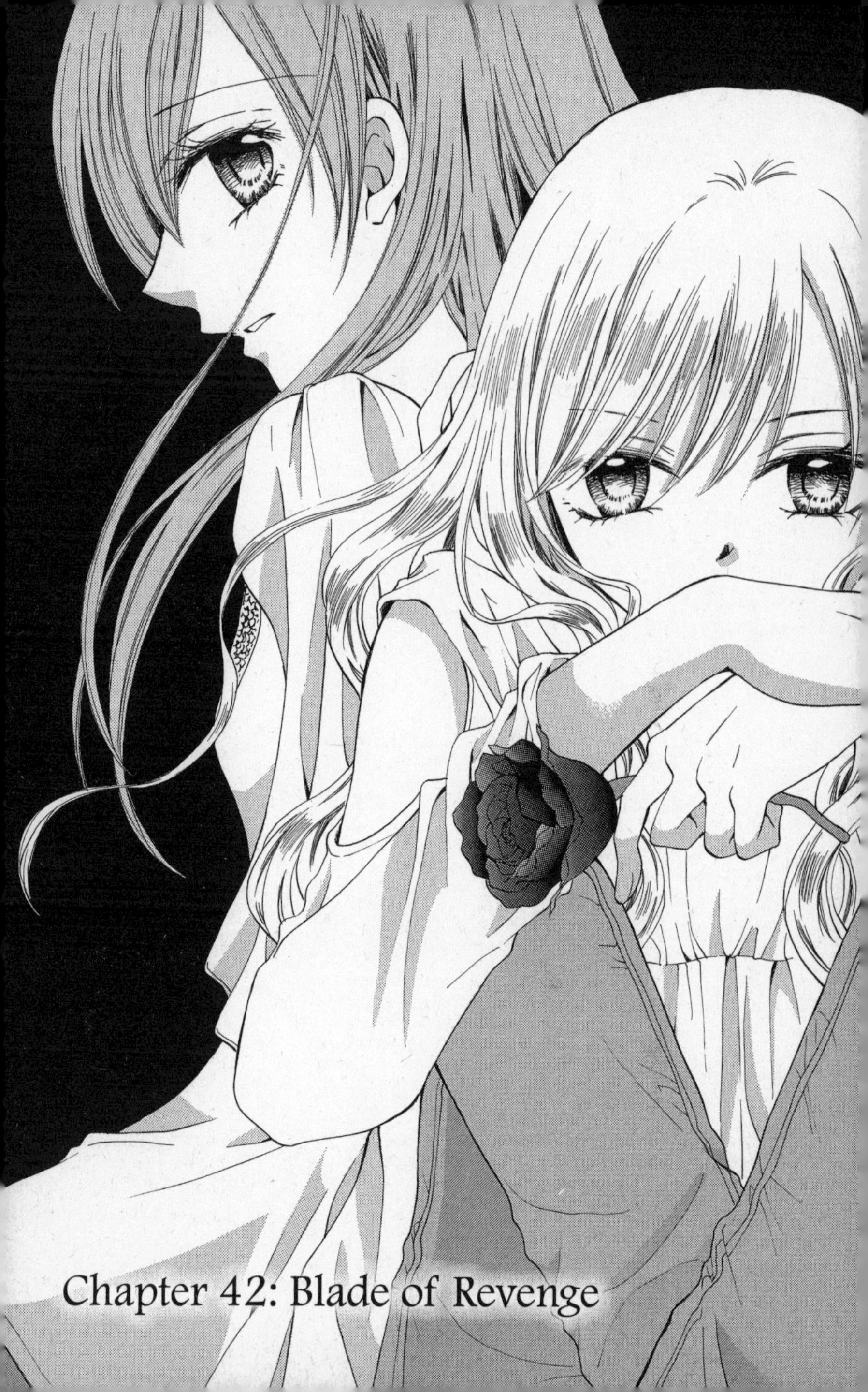
Chapter 42: Blade of Revenge

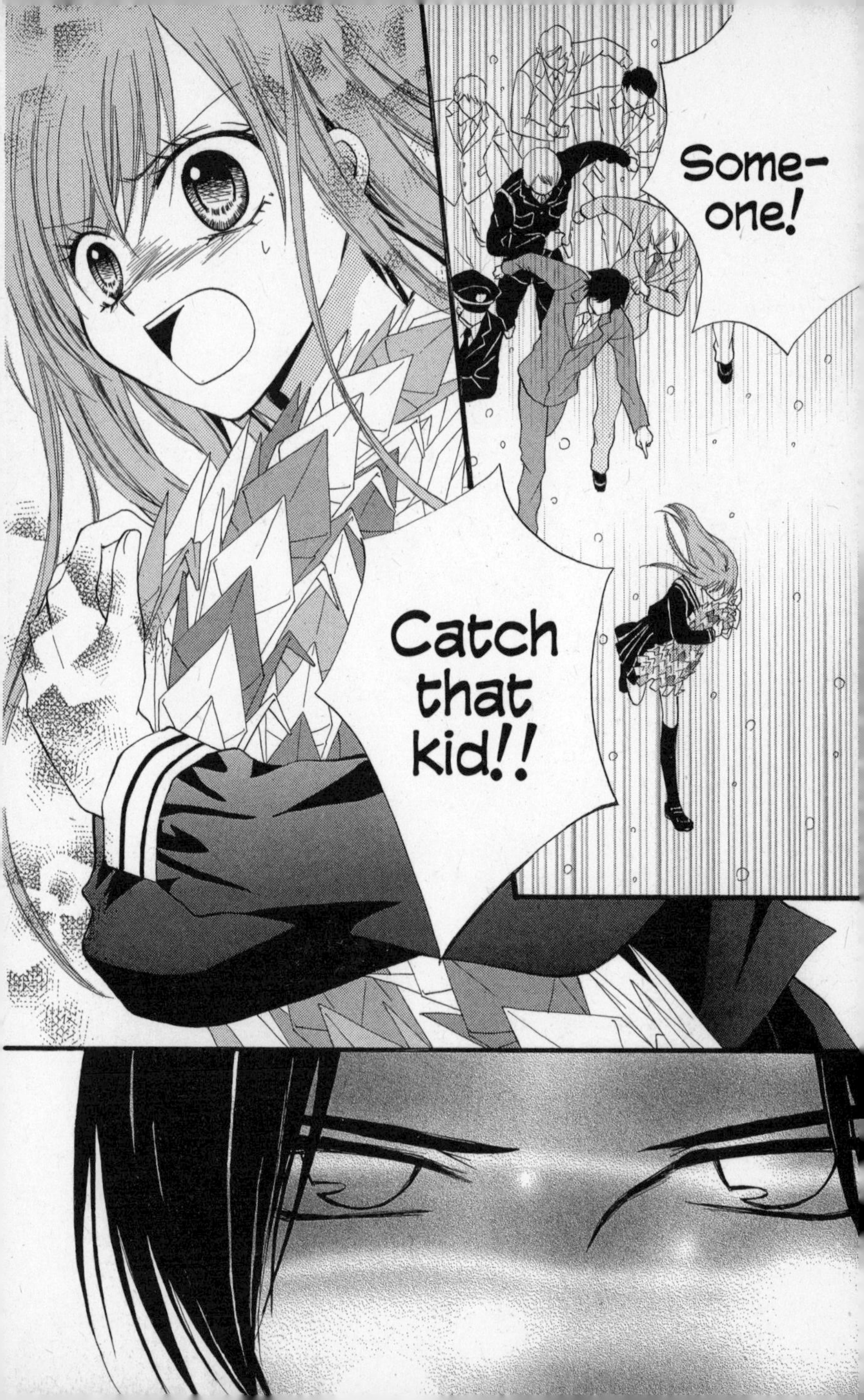
Some-one!
Catch that kid!!

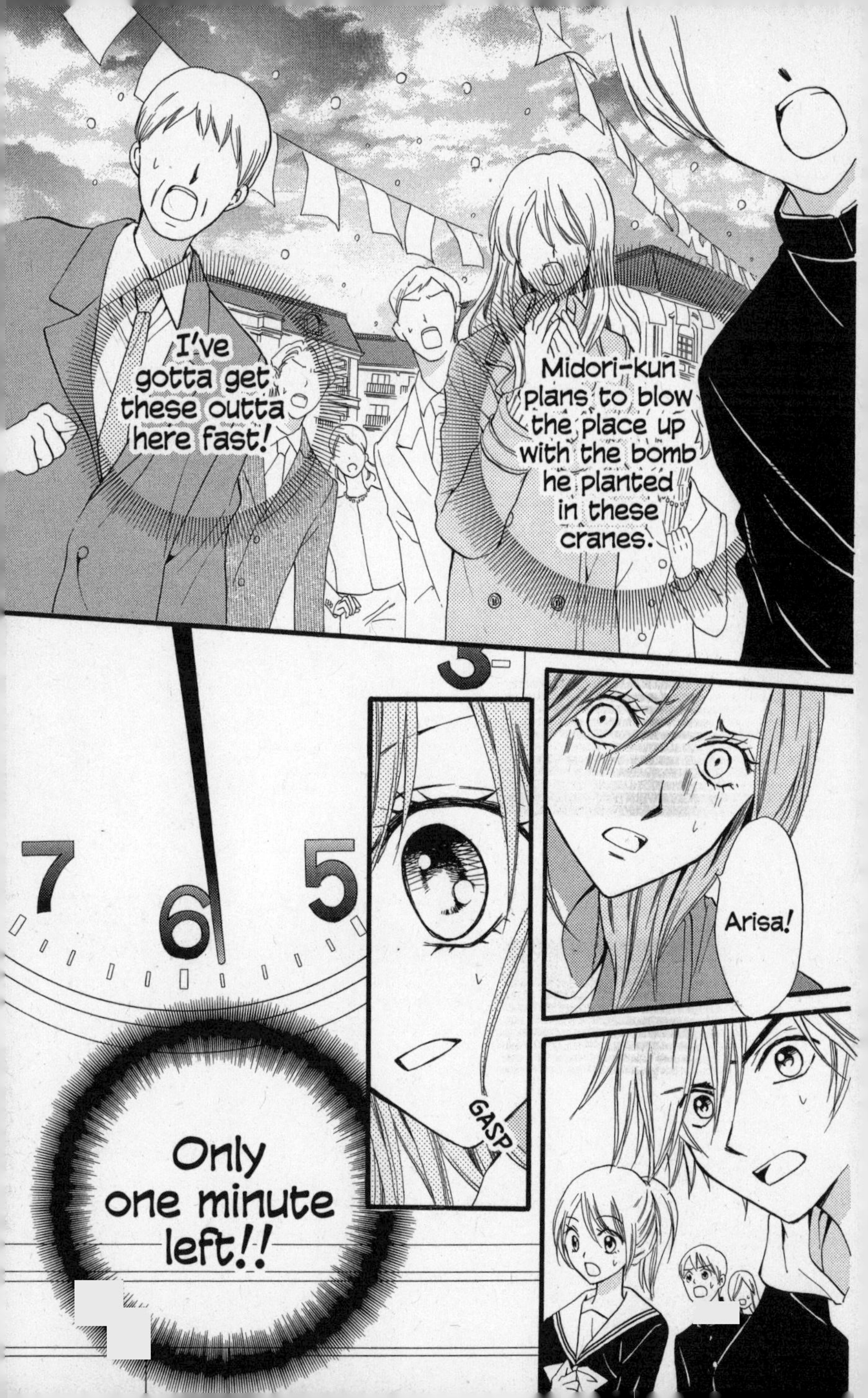
Midori-kun plans to blow the place up with the bomb he planted in these cranes.
I've gotta get these outta here fast!
Arisa!
GASP
Only one minute left!!

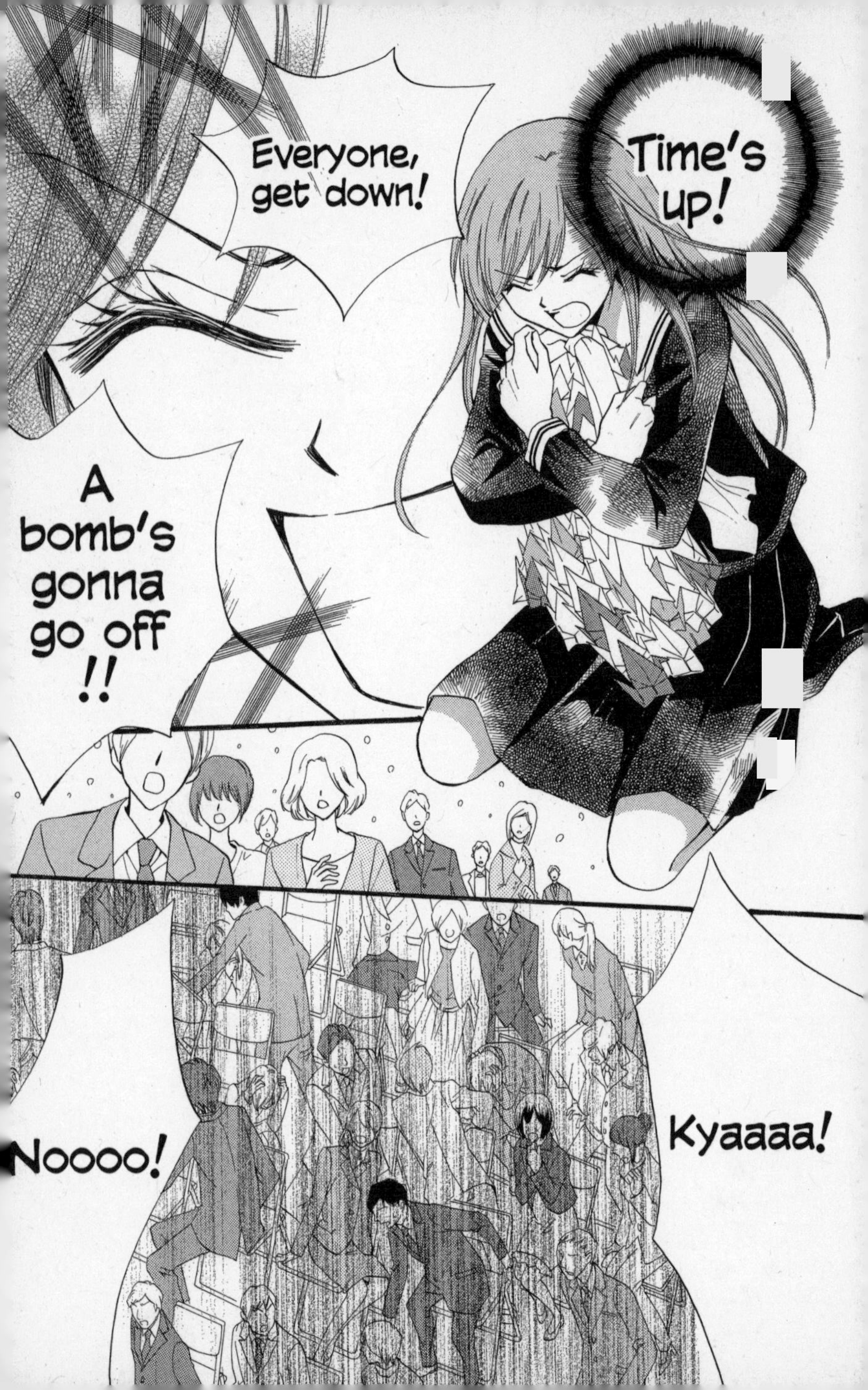
Time's up!
Everyone, get down!
A bomb's gonna go off!!
Kyaaaa!
Noooo!

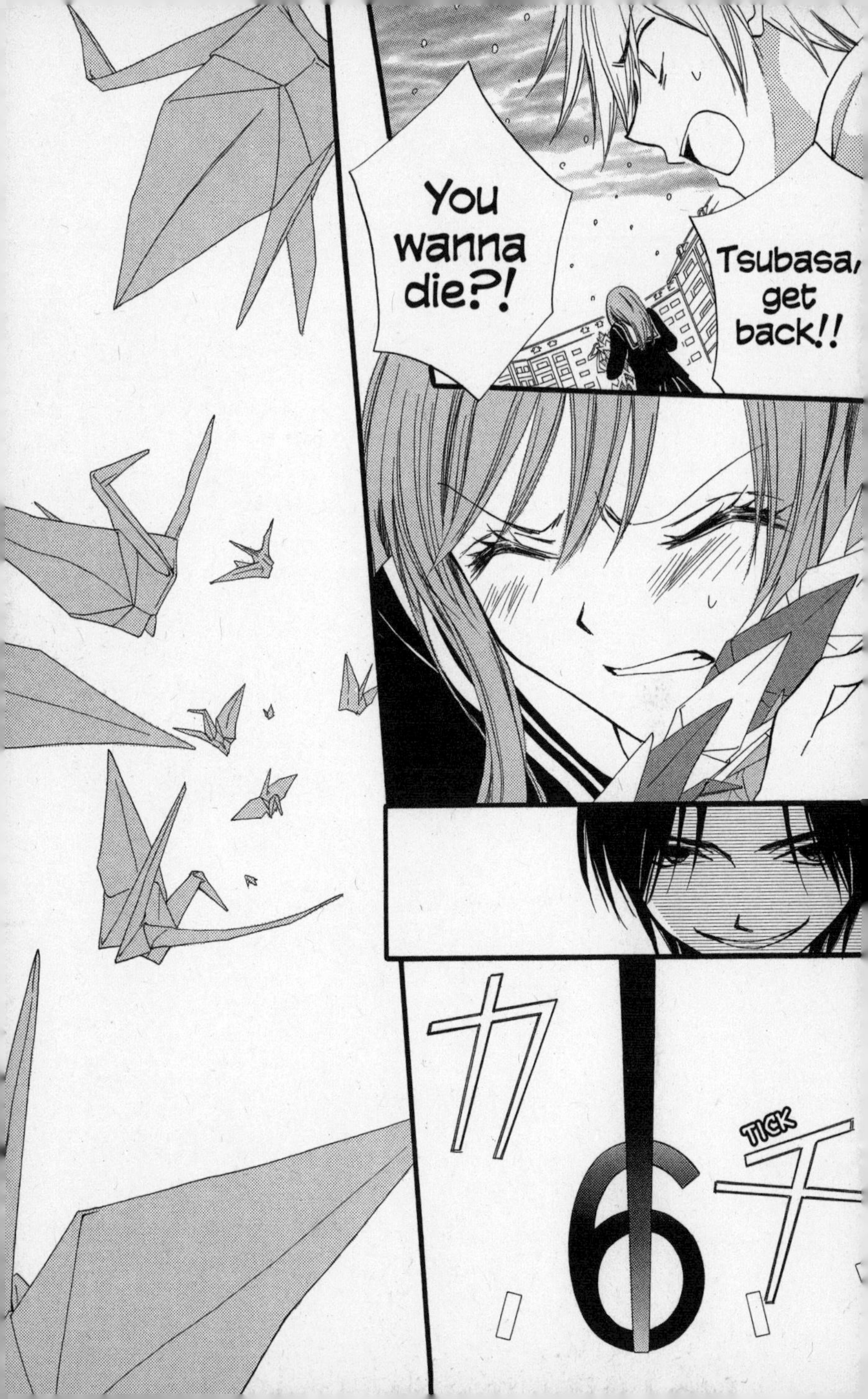
Tsubasa, get back!!
You wanna die?!
TICK
カチ
6

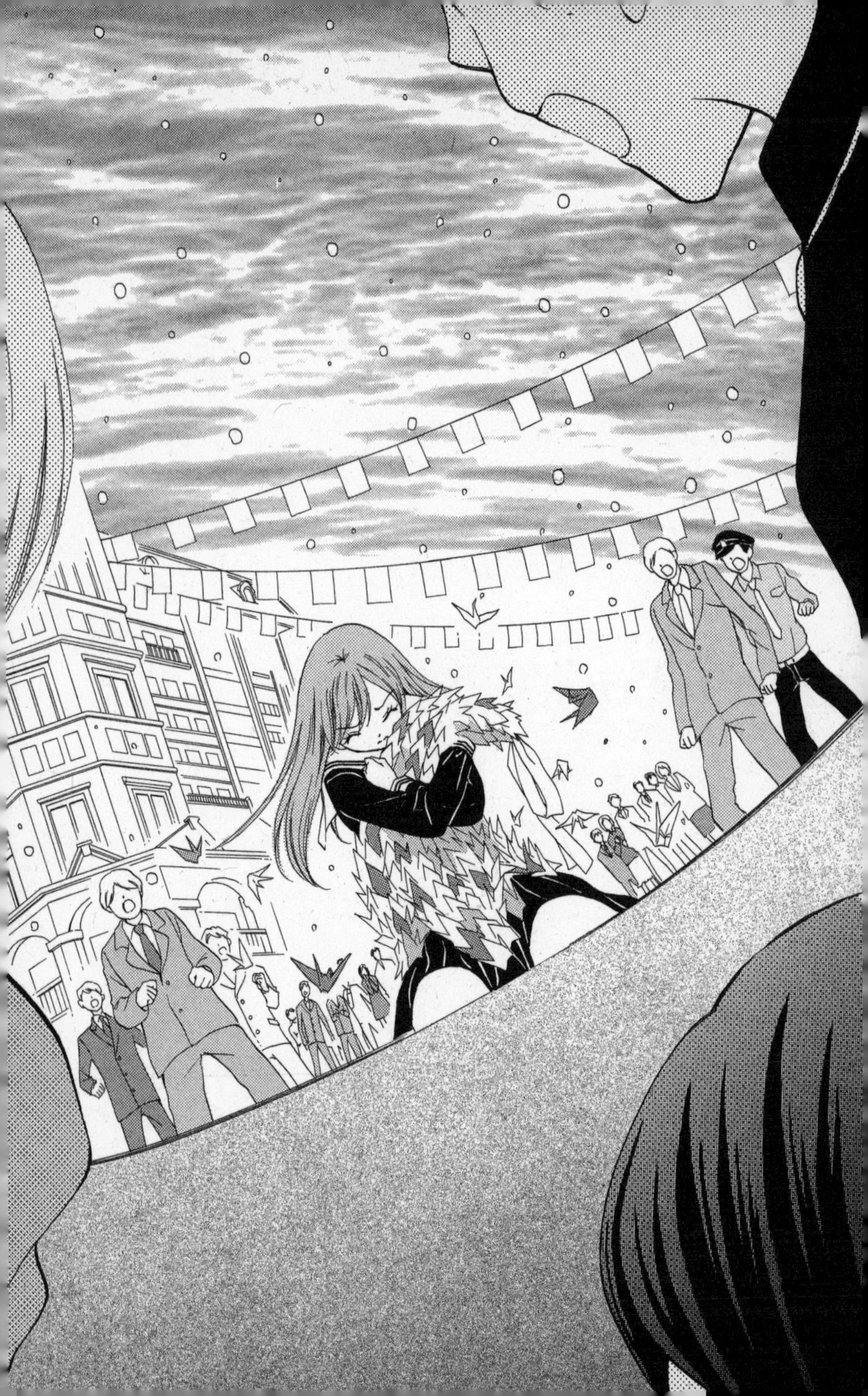

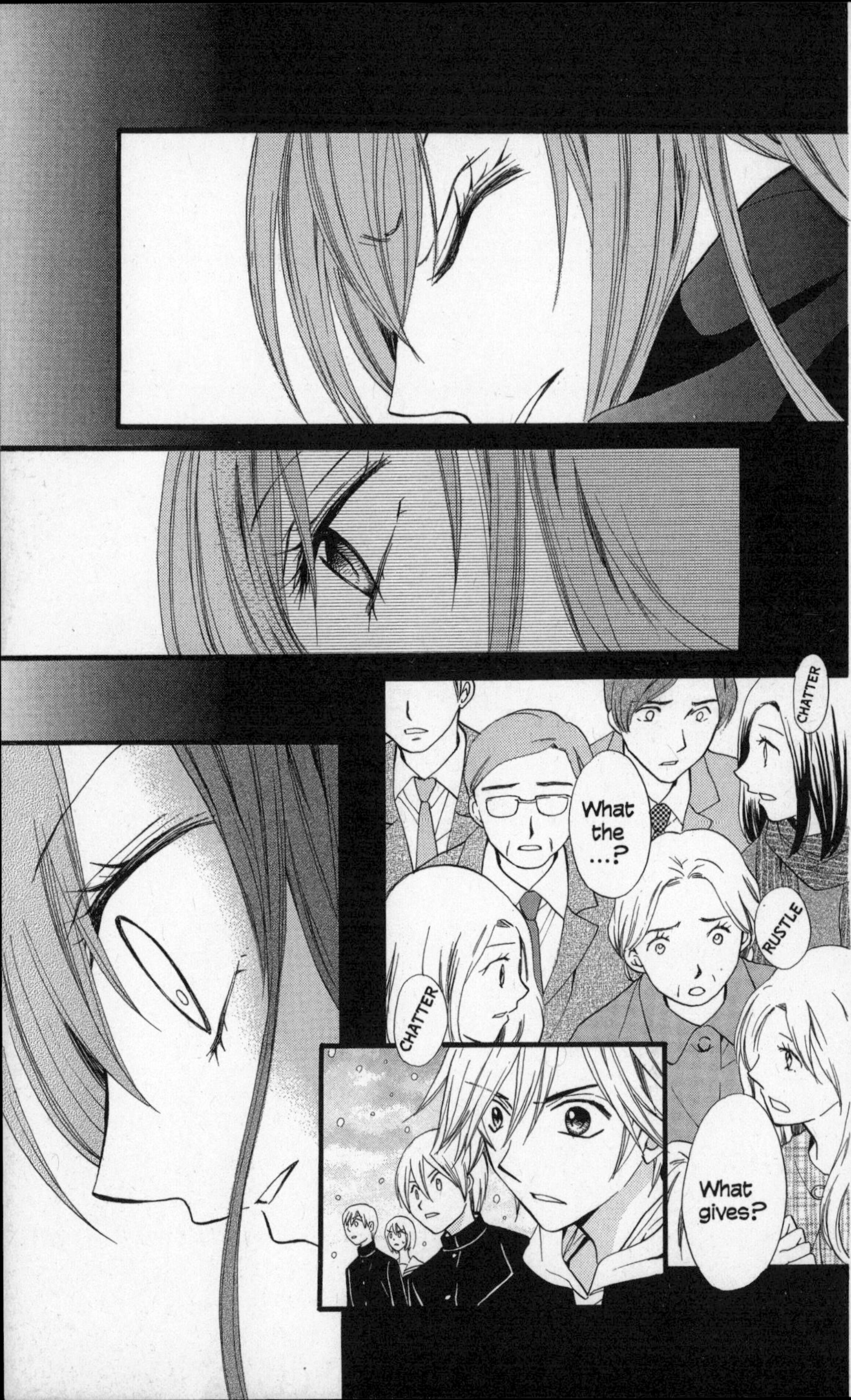
CHATTER
What the ...?
RUSTLE
CHATTER
What gives?

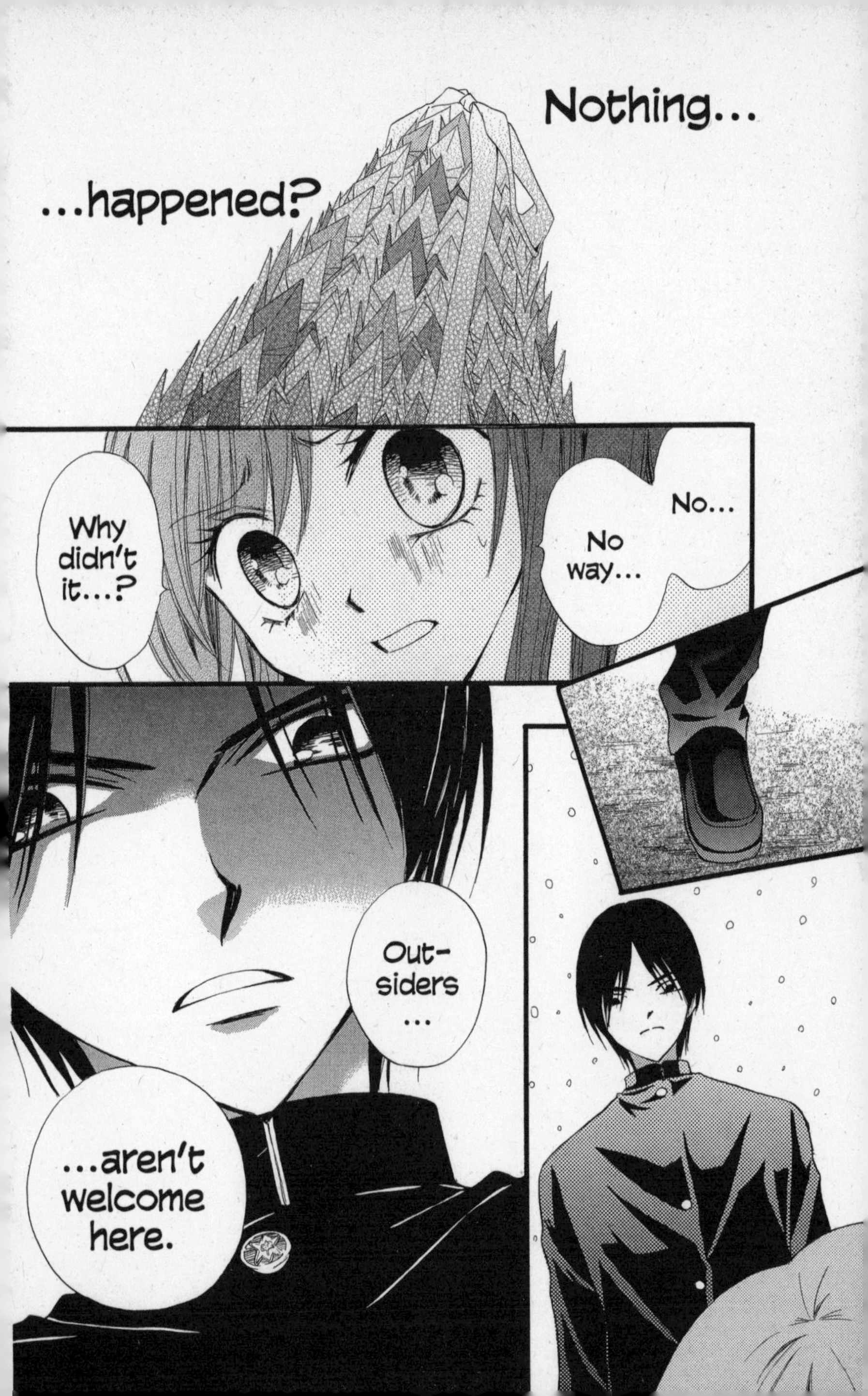
Nothing...
...happened?
No...
No way...
Why didn't it...?
Out-siders...
...aren't welcome here.

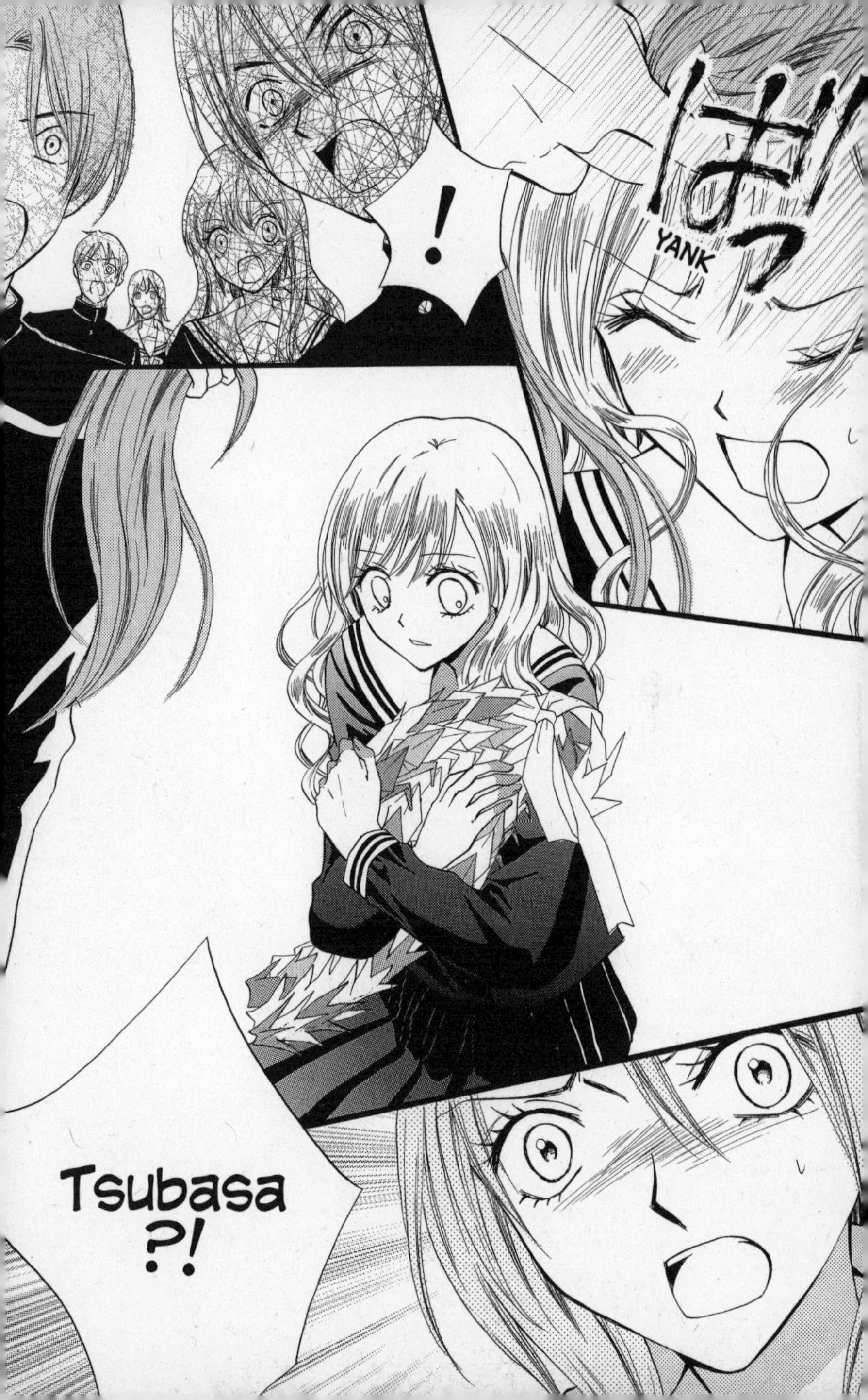

YANK
!
Tsubasa ?!

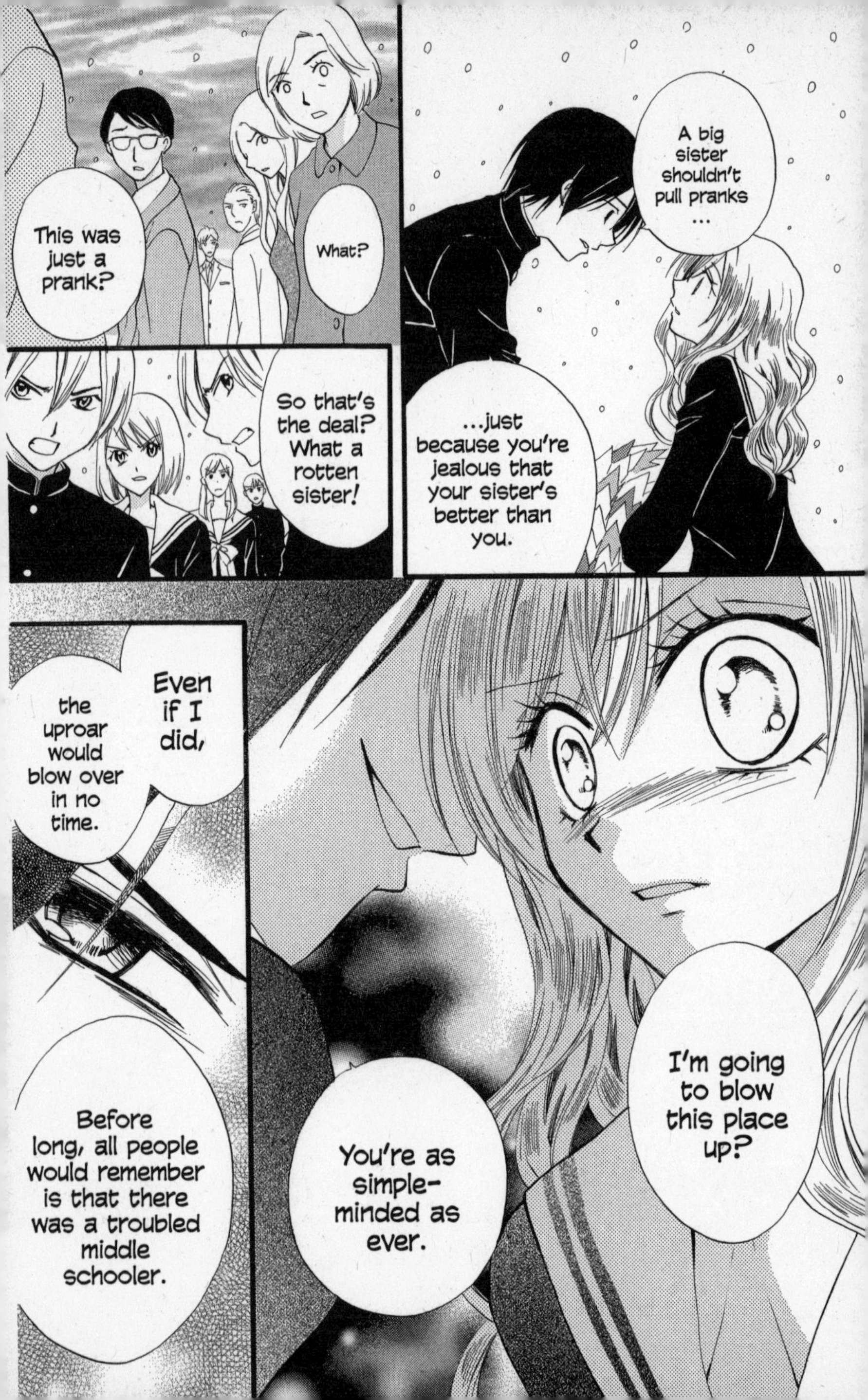
A big sister shouldn't pull pranks ...
...just because you're jealous that your sister's better than you.
What?
This was just a prank?
So that's the deal? What a rotten sister!
I'm going to blow this place up?
You're as simple-minded as ever.
Even if I did,
the uproar would blow over in no time.
Before long, all people would remember is that there was a troubled middle schooler.

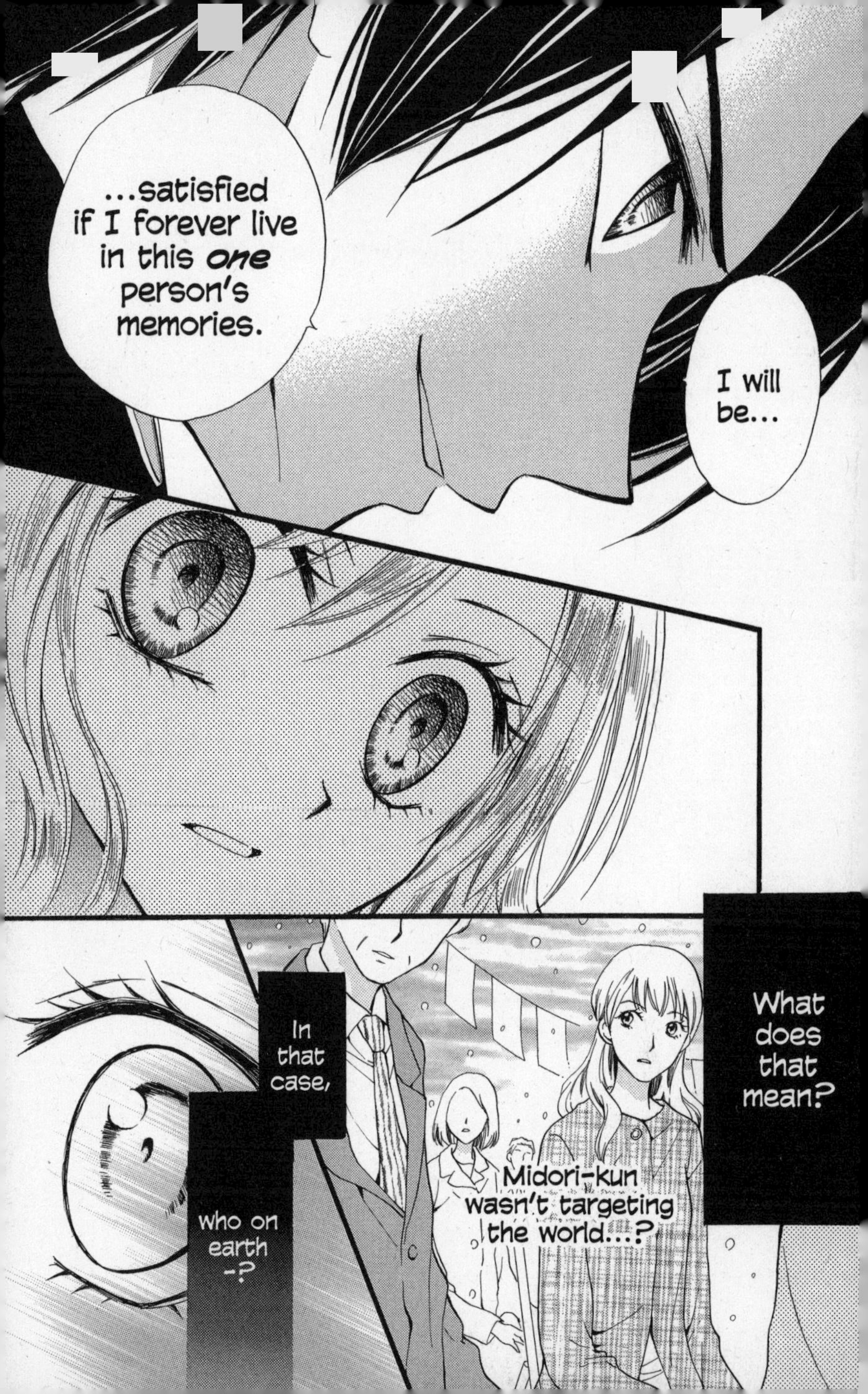
I will be...
...satisfied if I forever live in this *one* person's memories.
What does that mean?
Midori-kun wasn't targeting the world...?
In that case,
who on earth -?

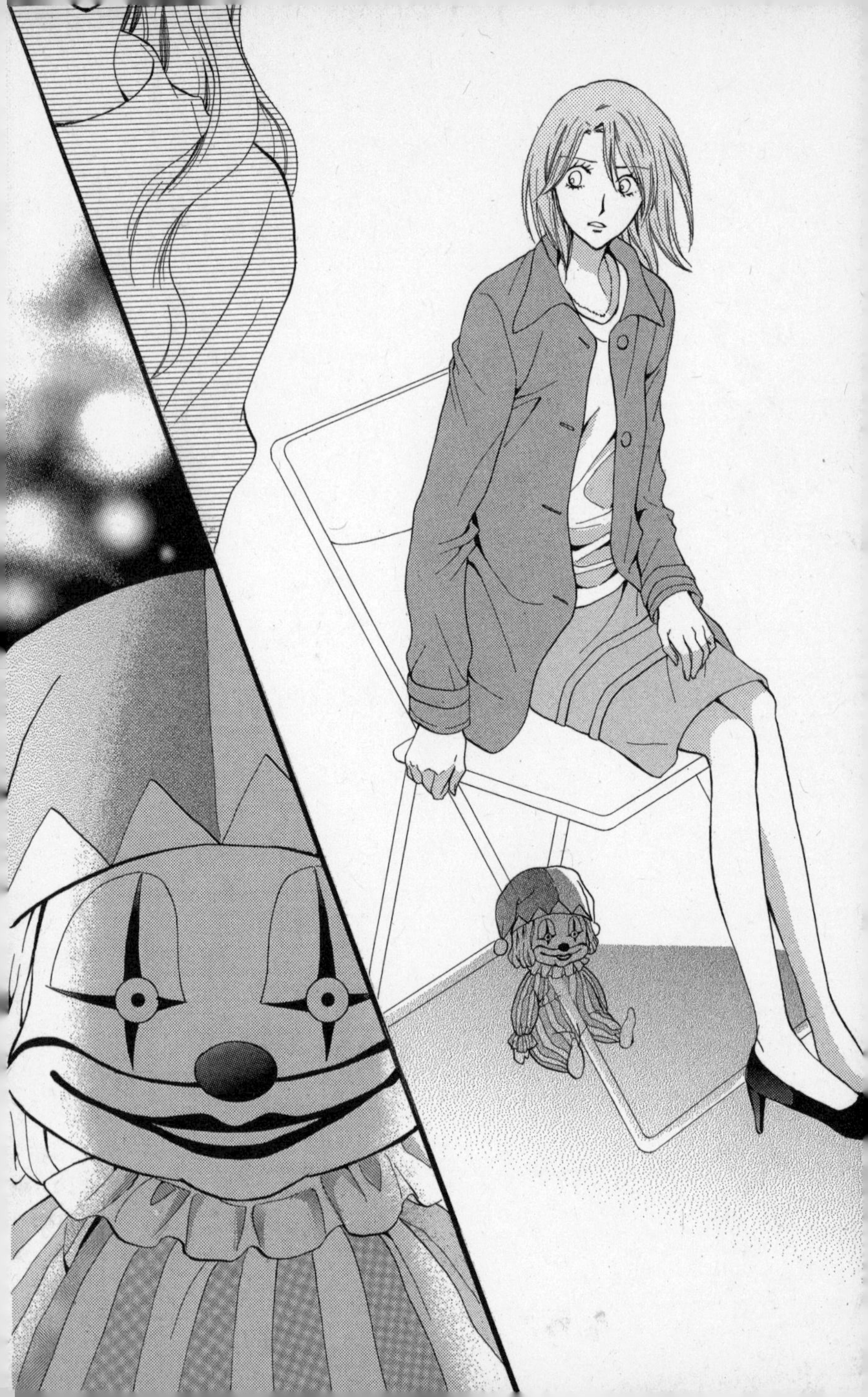

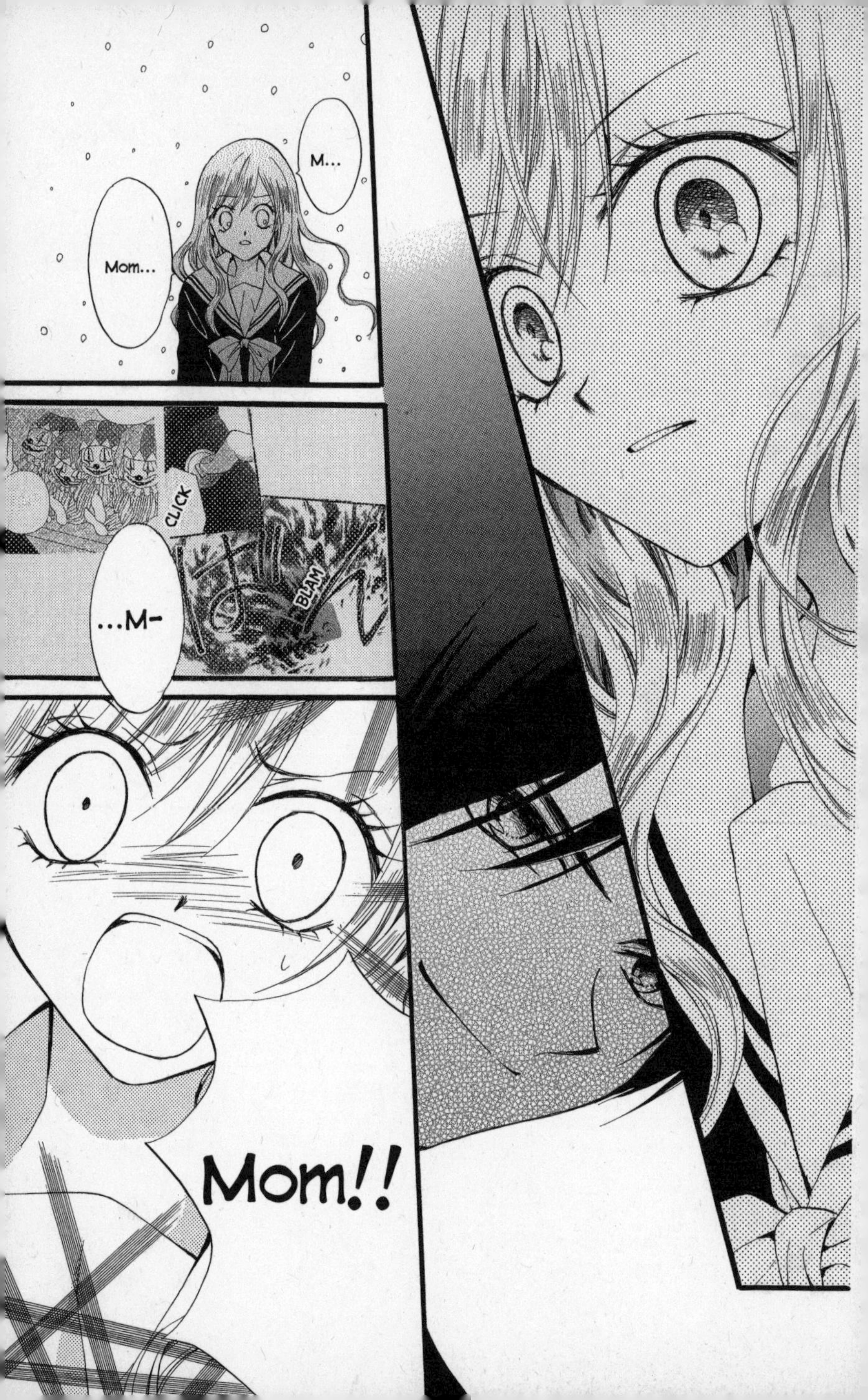
M...
Mom...
CLICK
BLAM
...M-
Mom!!

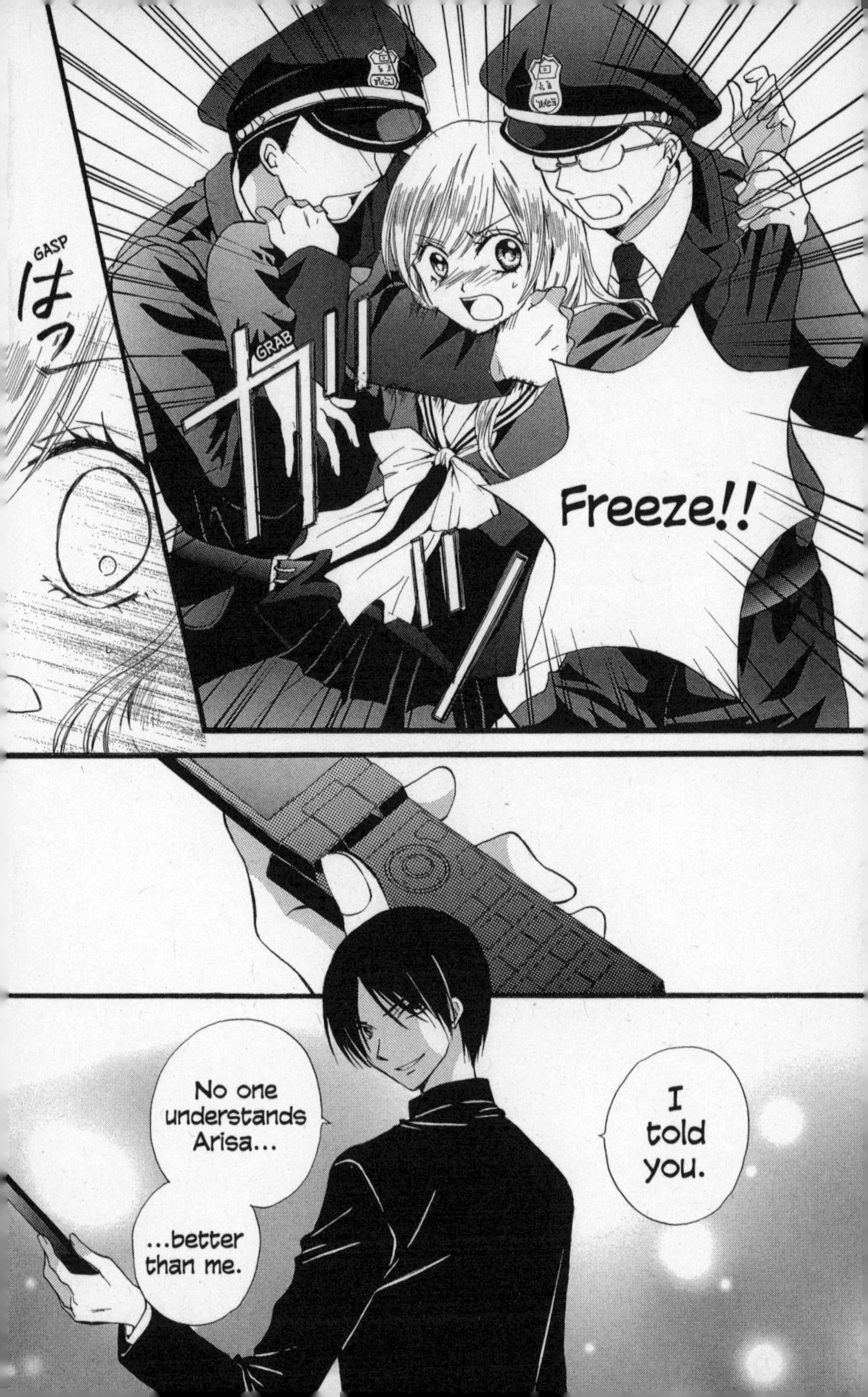
Freeze!!
GRAB
GASP
はっ
I told you.
No one understands Arisa...
...better than me.

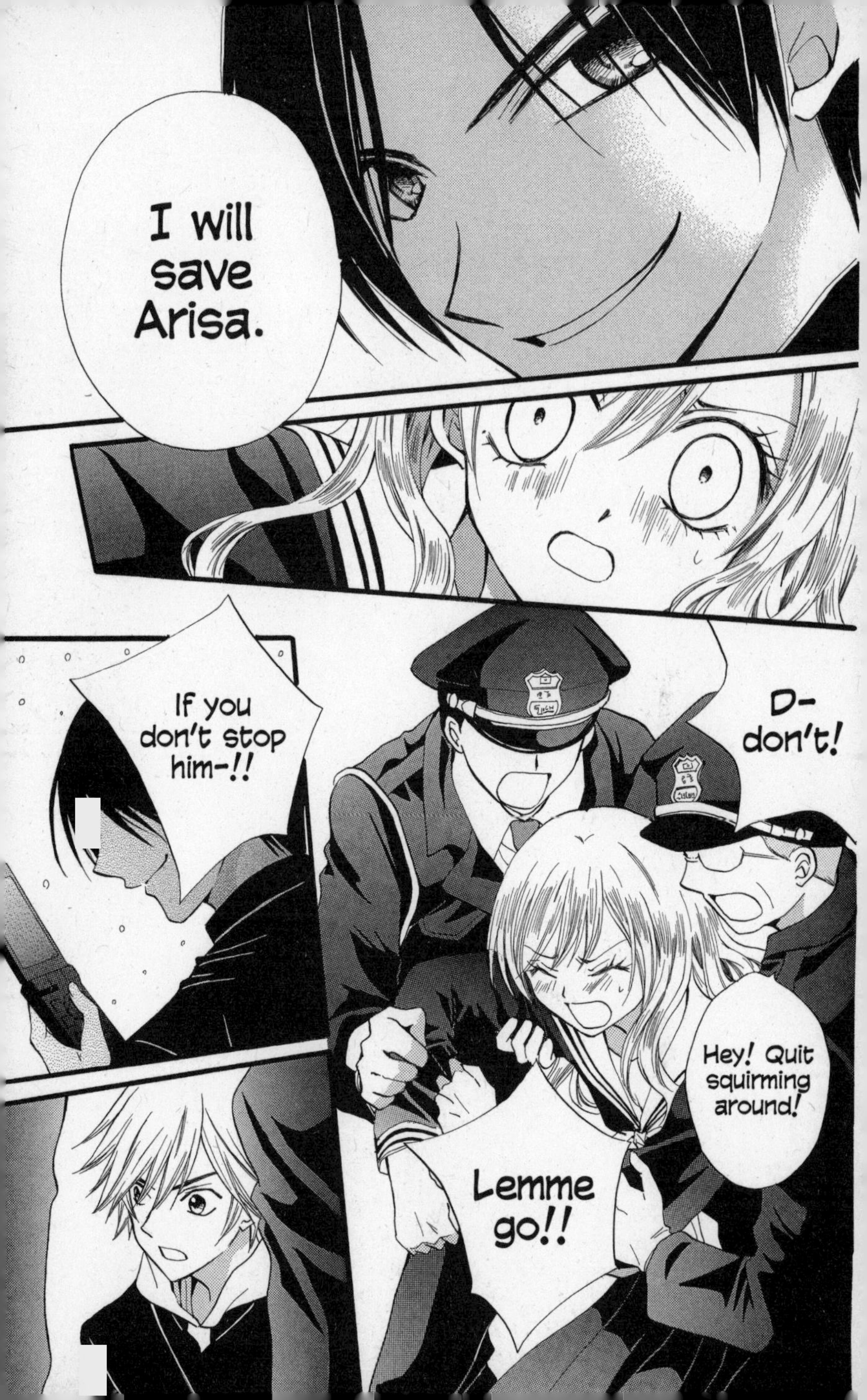
I will save Arisa.
D-don't!
Hey! Quit squirming around!
Lemme go!!
If you don't stop him-!!

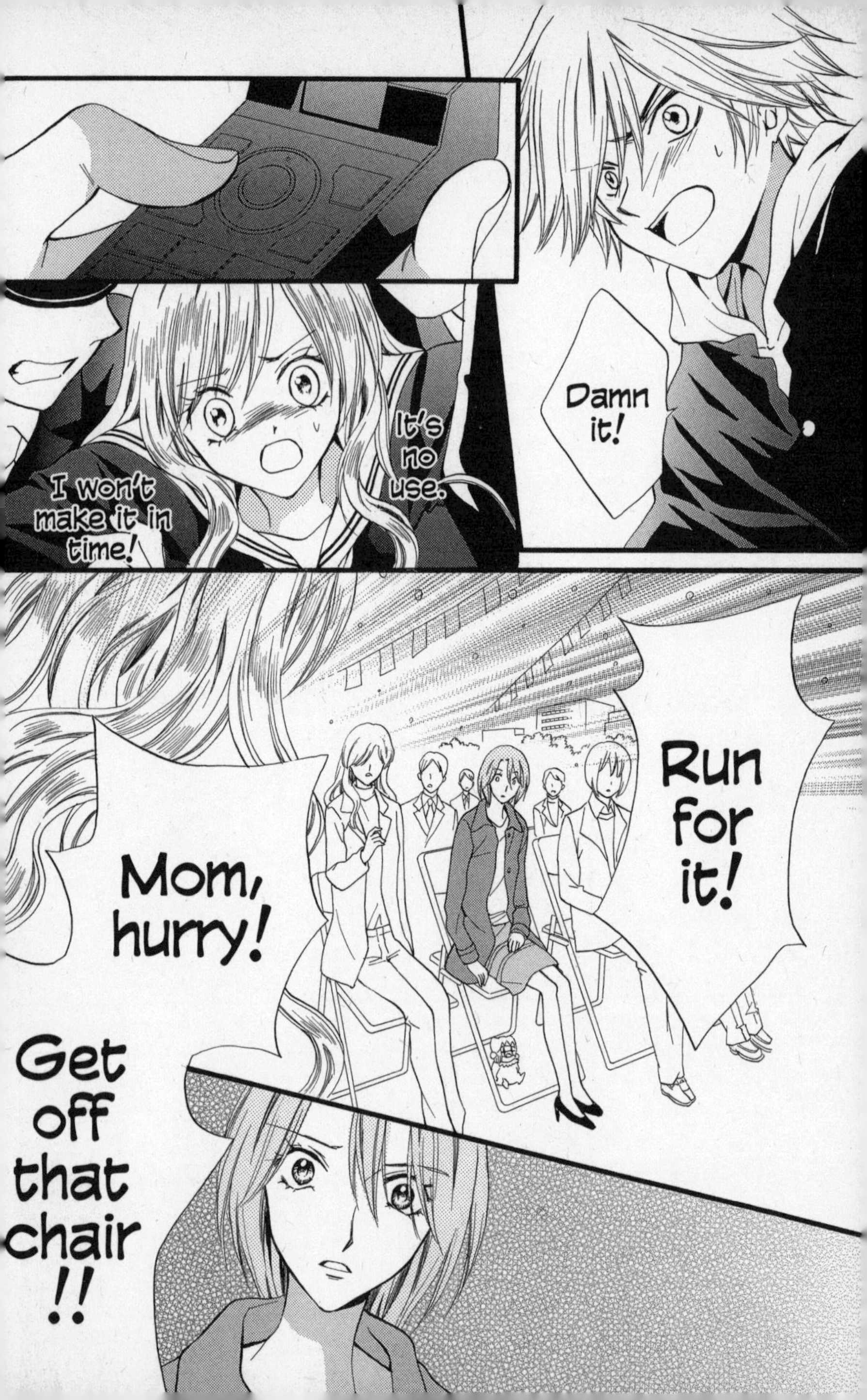
Damn it!
It's no use.
I won't make it in time!
Run for it!
Mom, hurry!
Get off that chair!!

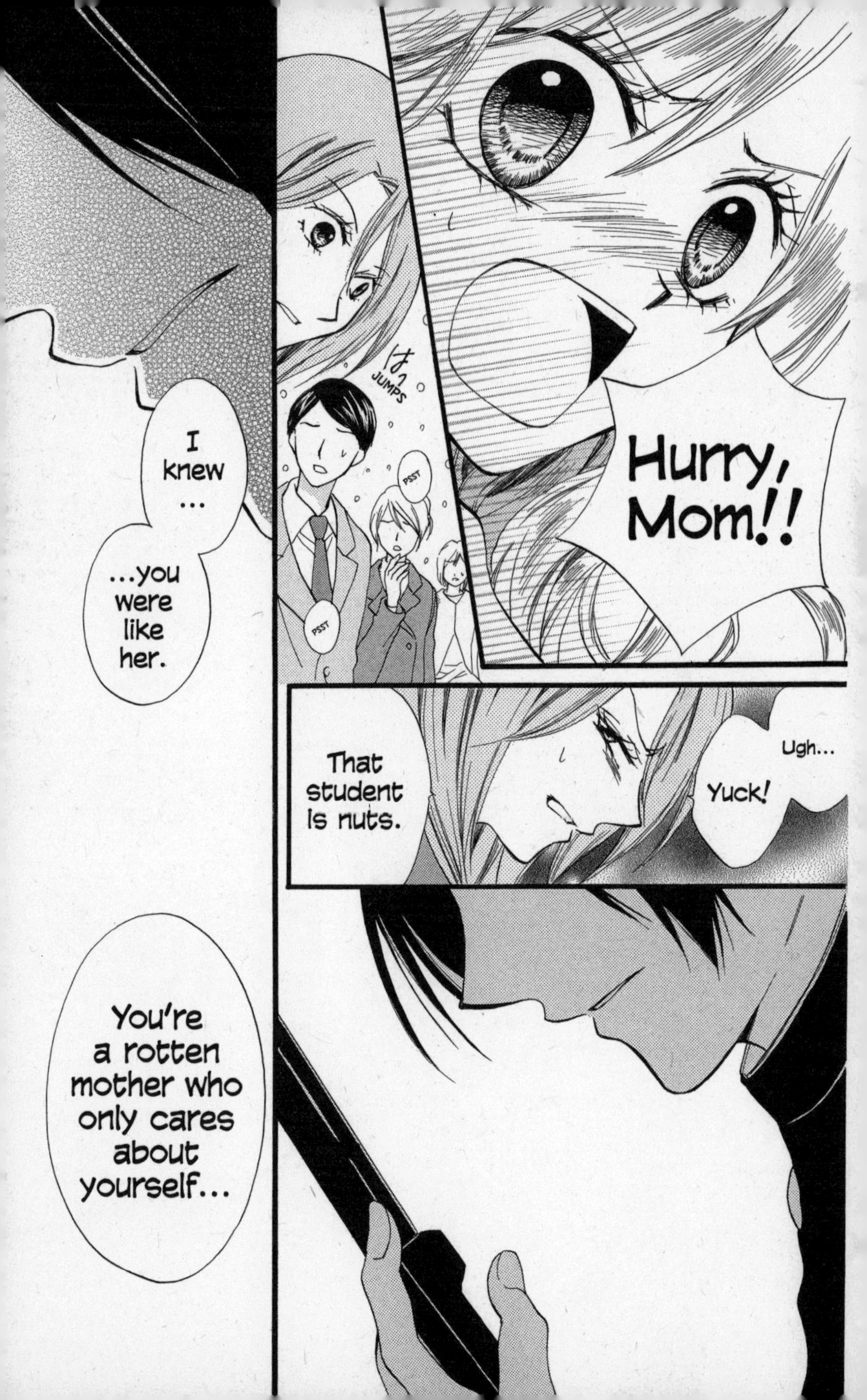

Hurry, Mom!!
は JUMPS
PSST
PSST
Ugh...
Yuck!
That student is nuts.
I knew...
...you were like her.
You're a rotten mother who only cares about yourself...

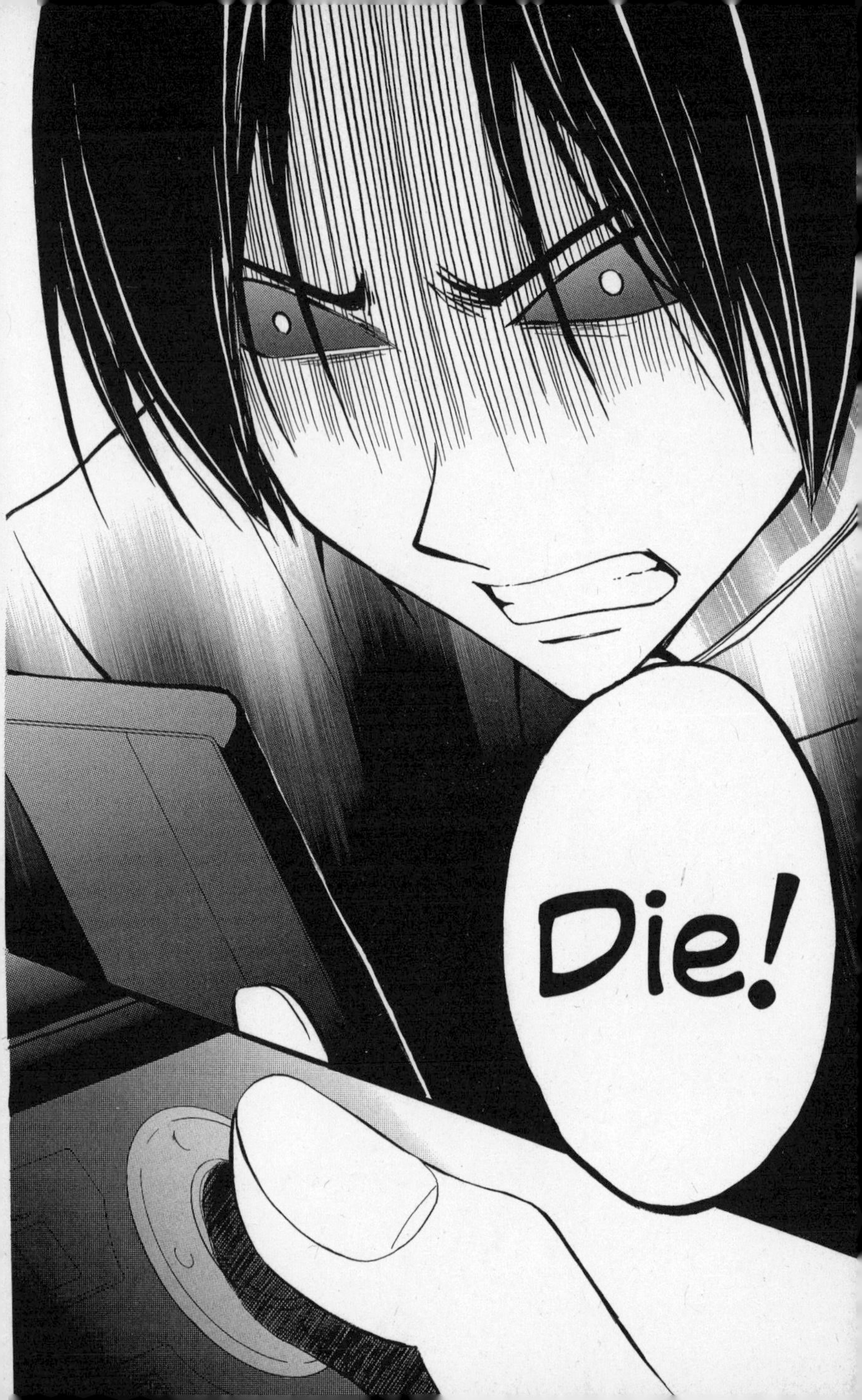
Die!

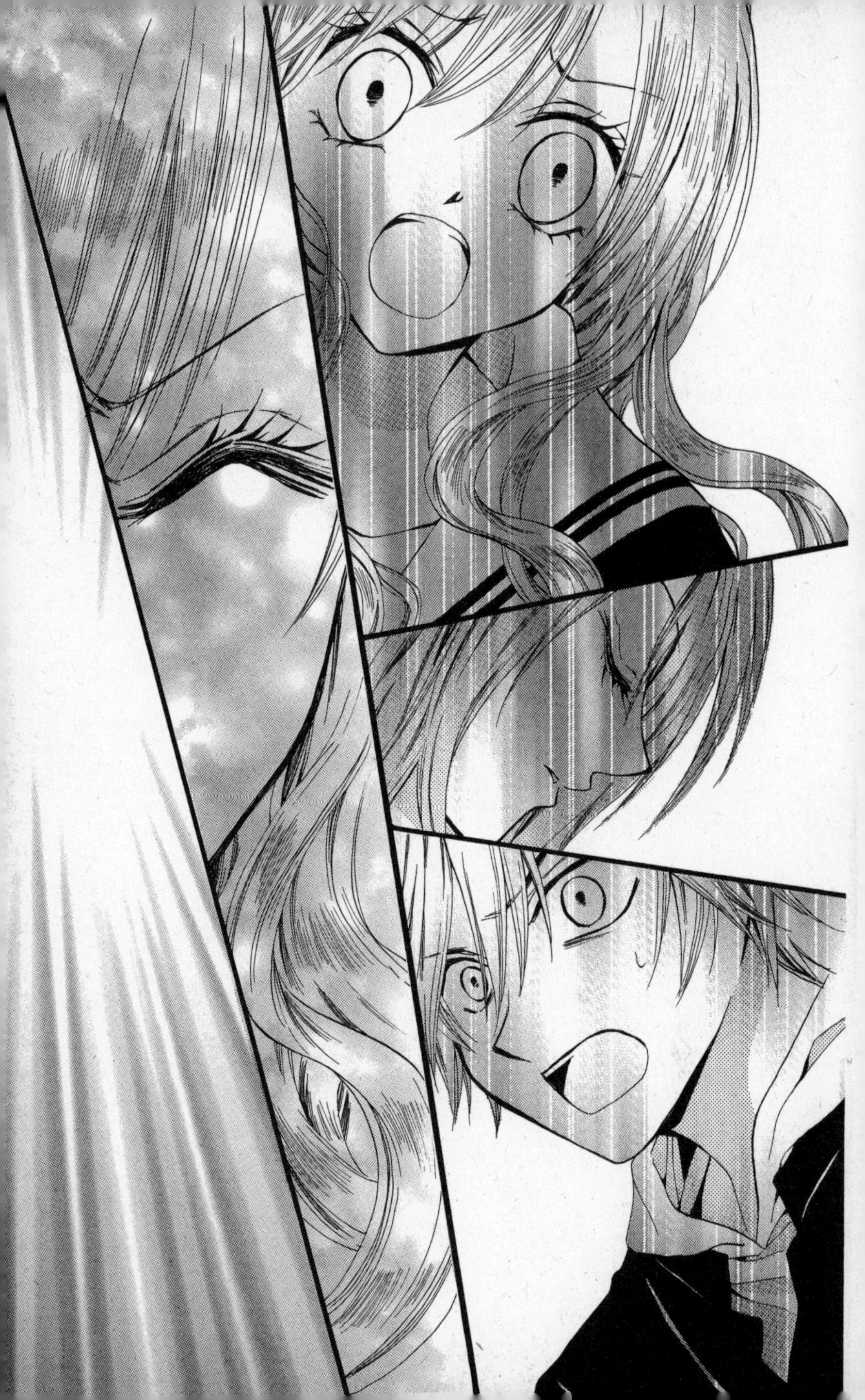

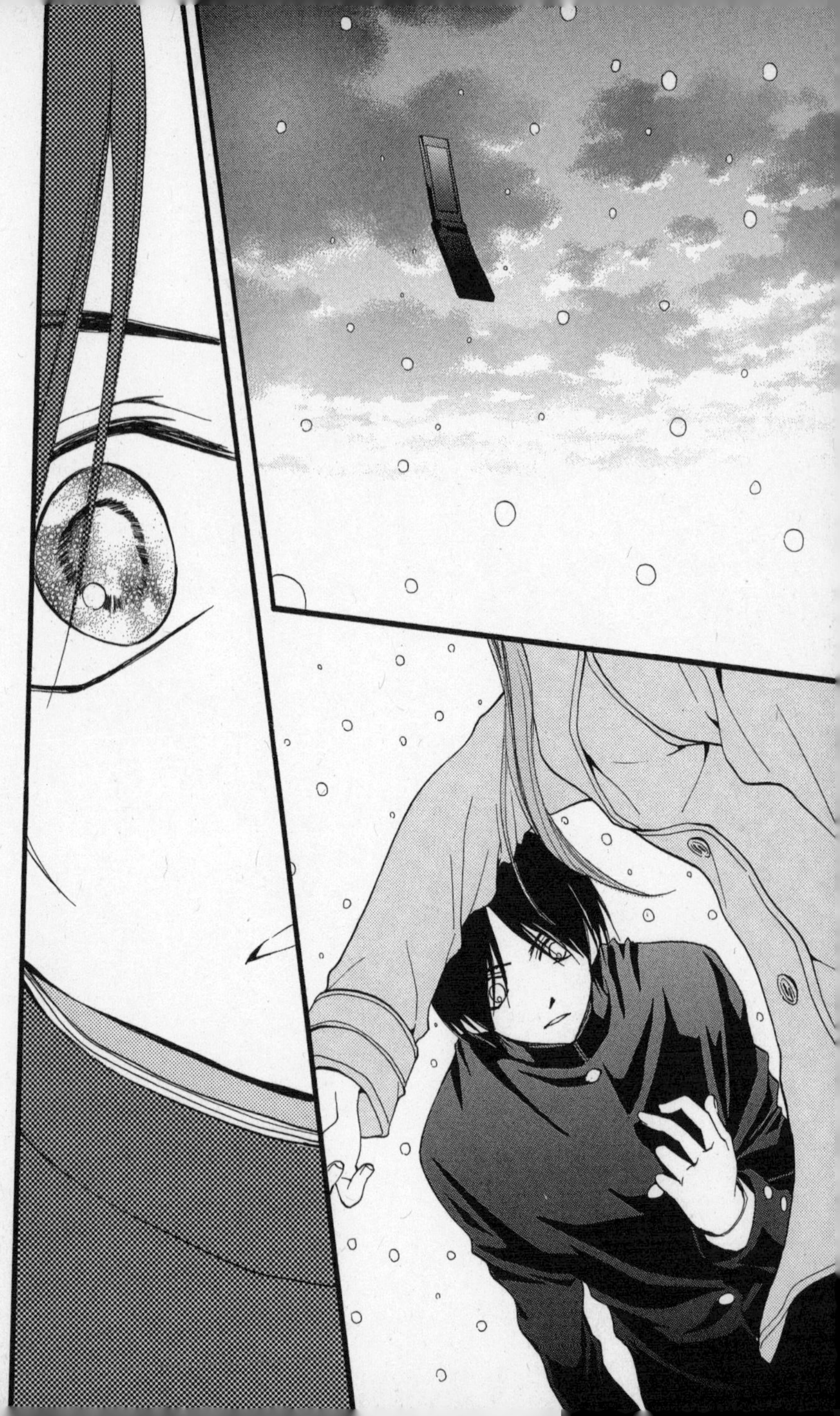

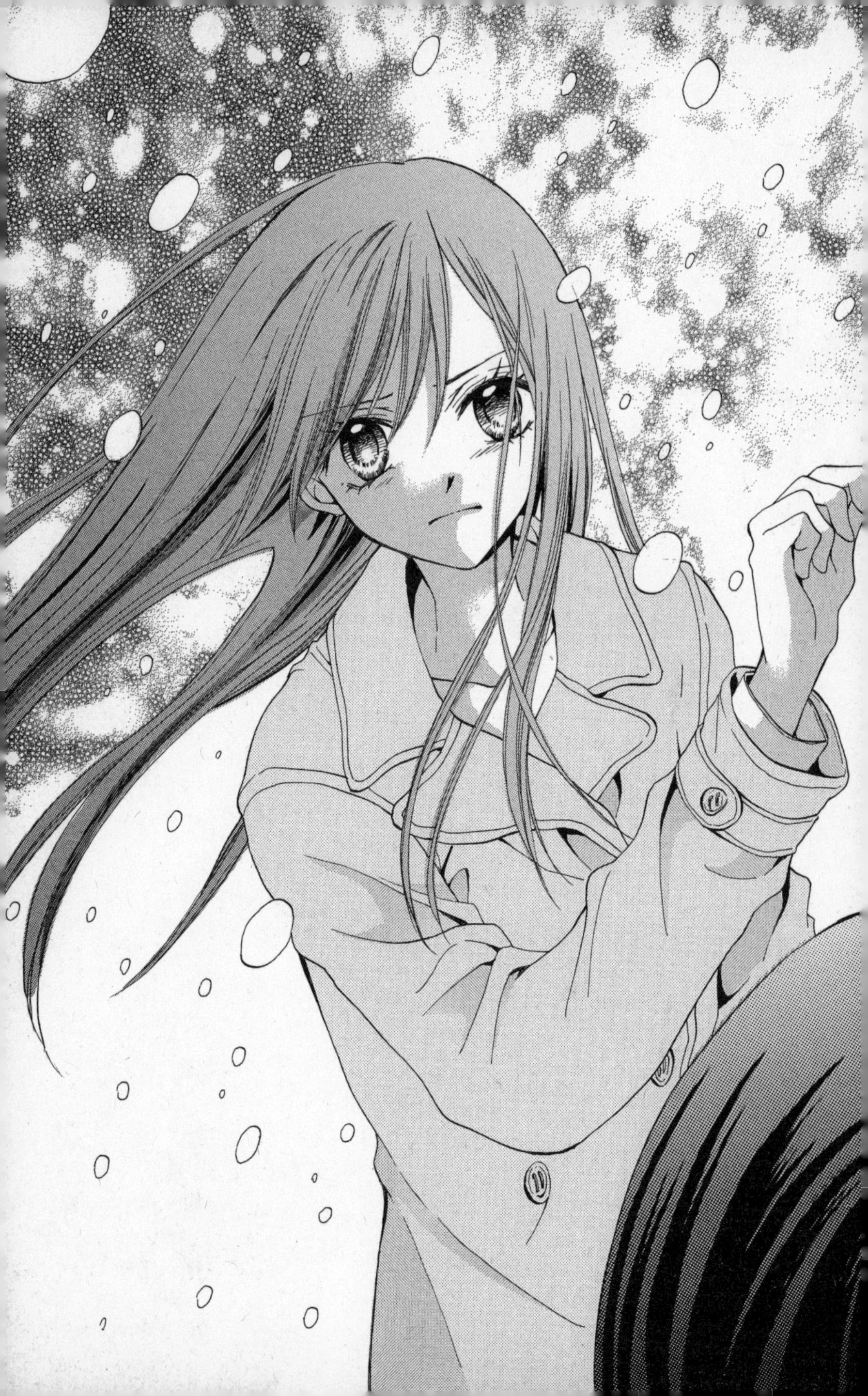

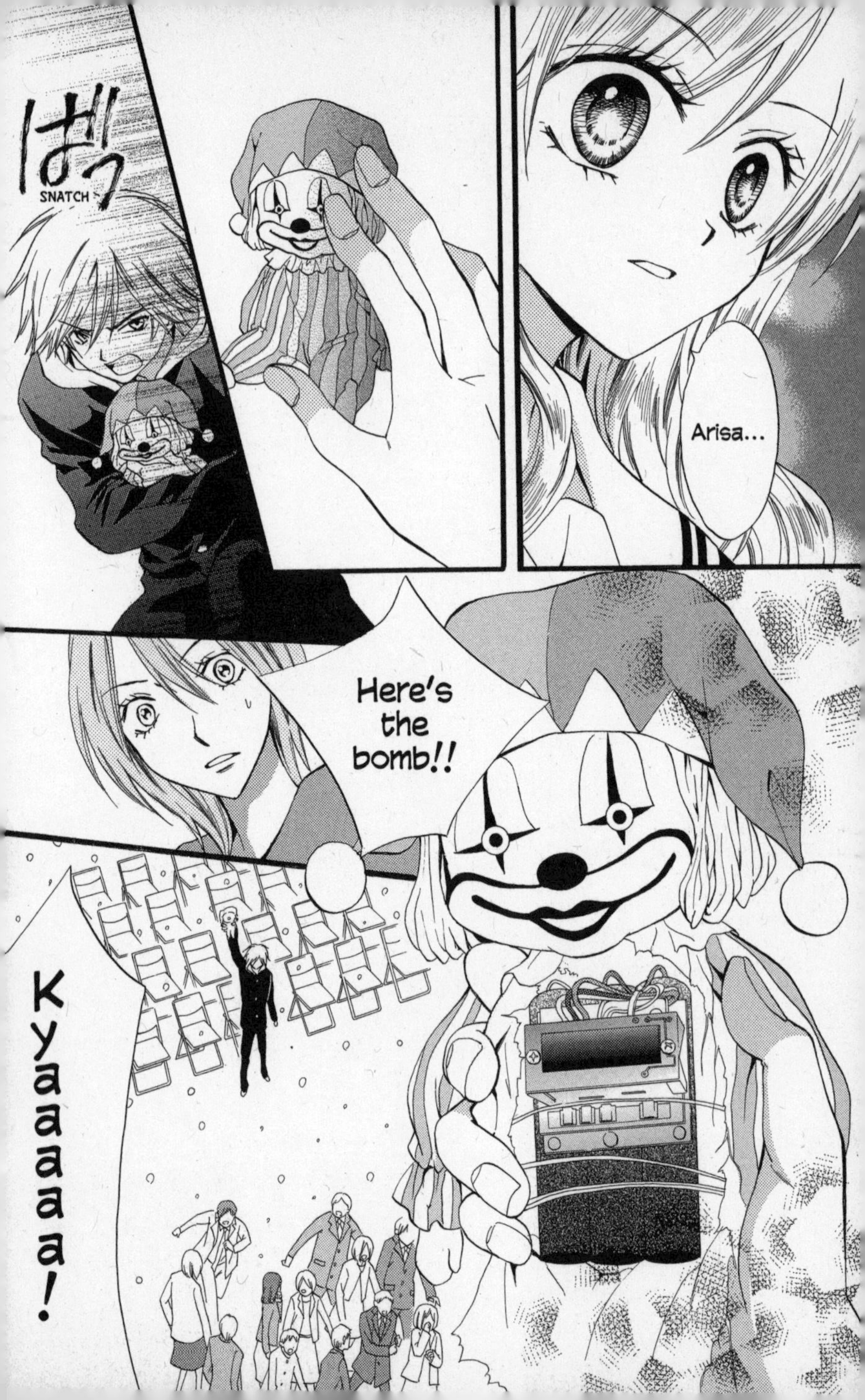
Arisa...
ぱっ
SNATCH
Here's the bomb!!
Kyaaaaaa!

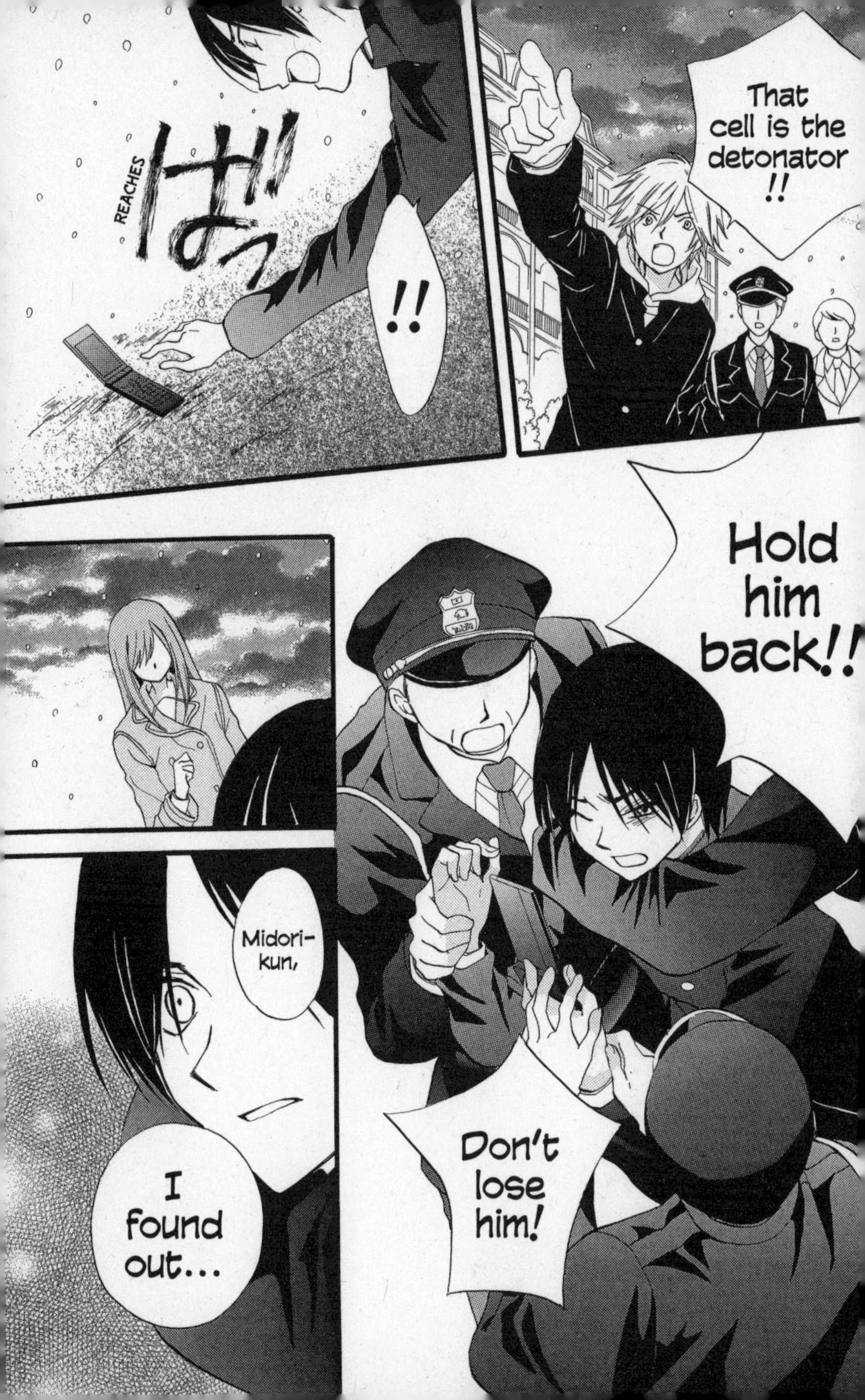
That cell is the detonator!!
REACHES
!!
Hold him back!!
Don't lose him!
Midori-kun,
I found out...

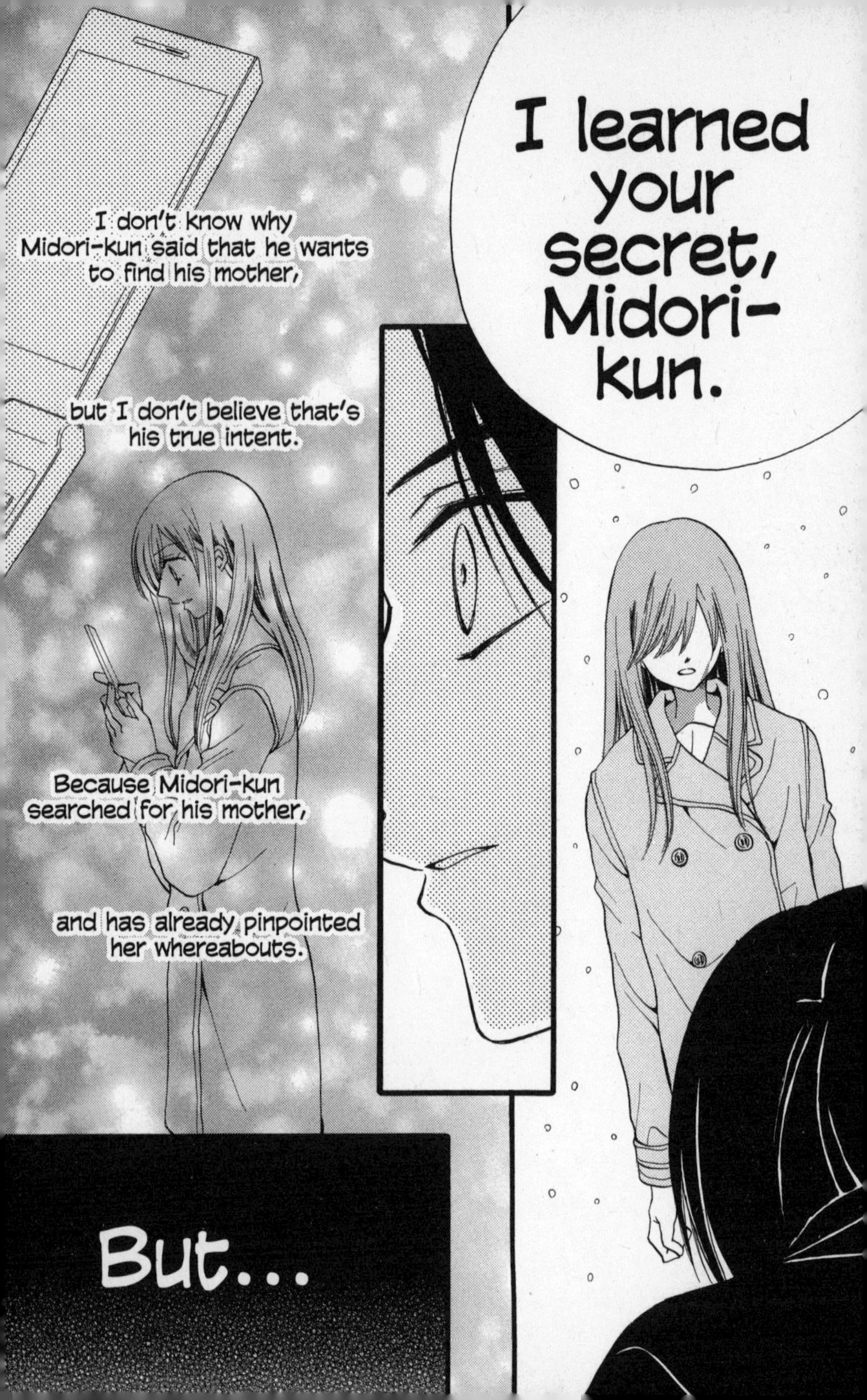
I learned your secret, Midori-kun.
I don't know why Midori-kun said that he wants to find his mother,
but I don't believe that's his true intent.
Because Midori-kun searched for his mother,
and has already pinpointed her whereabouts.
But...

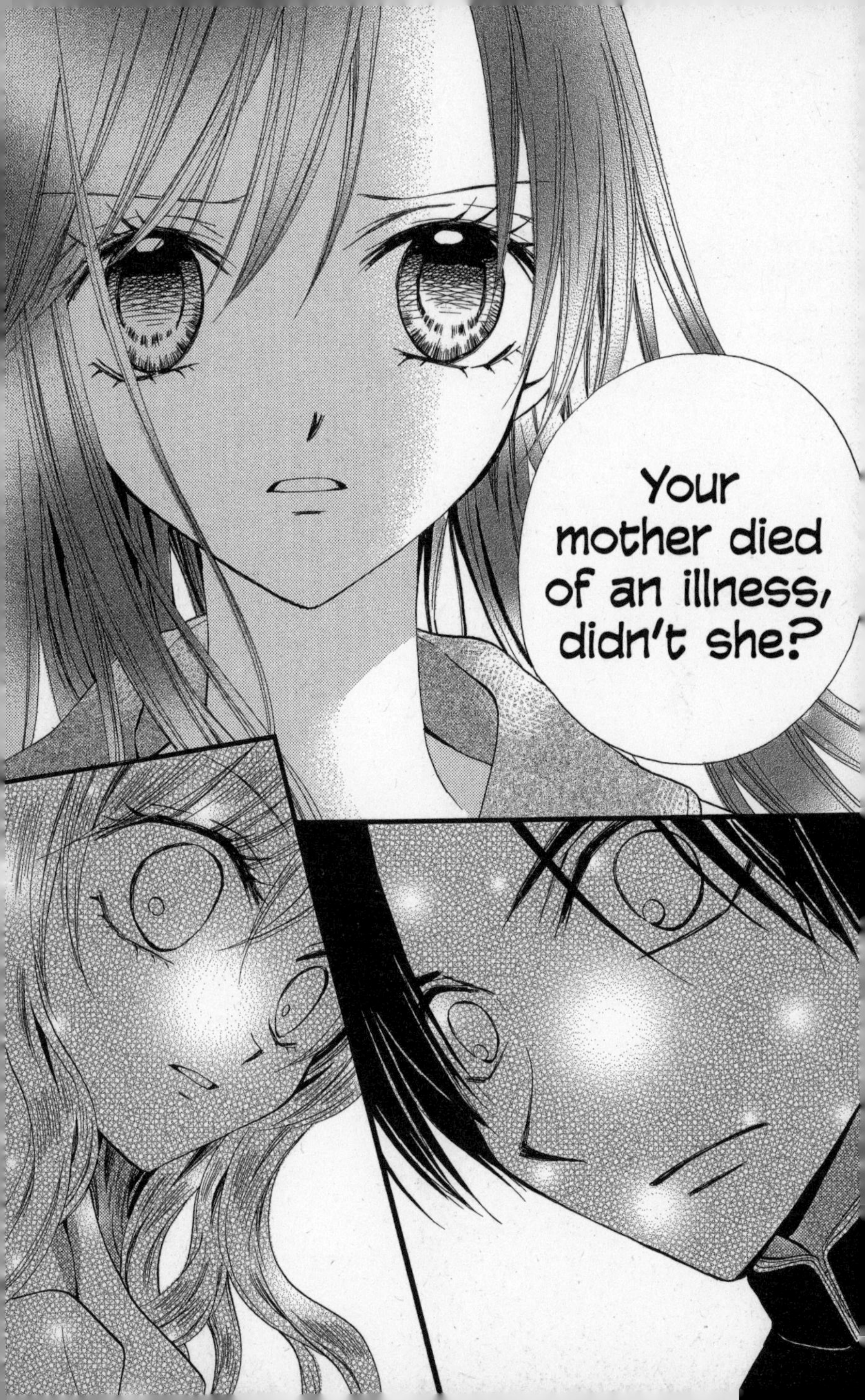
Your mother died of an illness, didn't she?

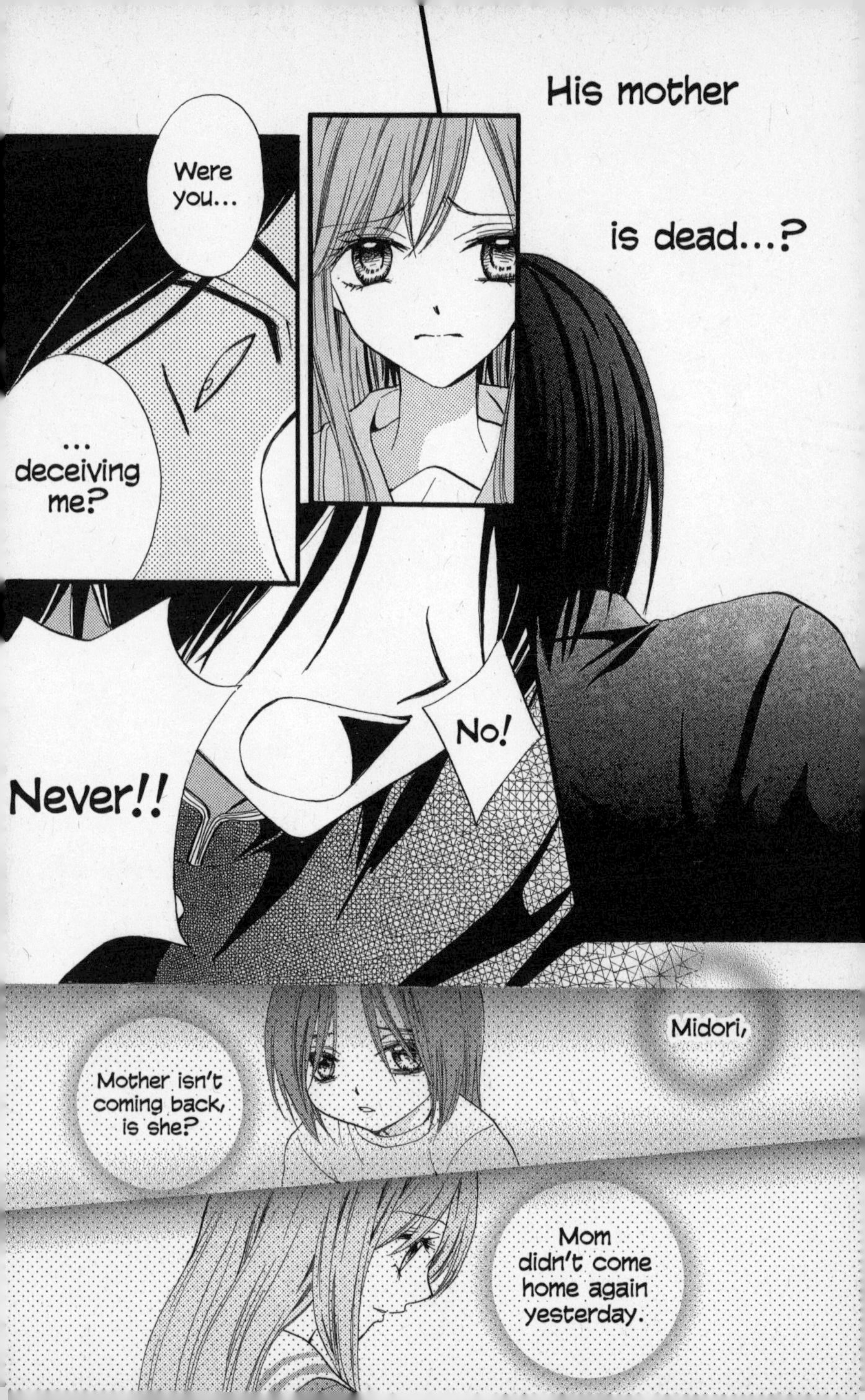
His mother
is dead...?
Were you...
...deceiving me?
No!
Never!!
Midori,
Mother isn't coming back, is she?
Mom didn't come home again yesterday.

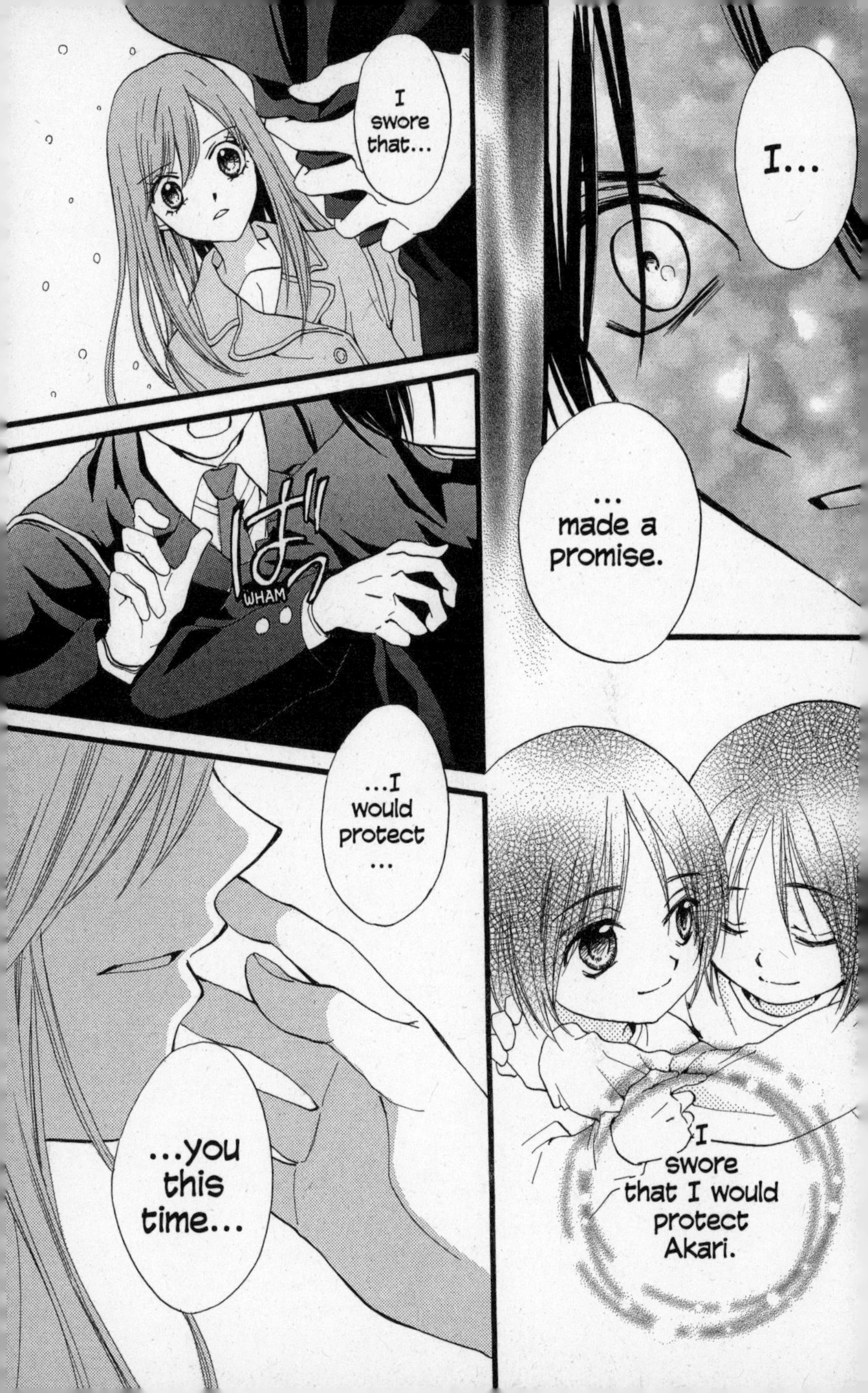
I...
...
made a
promise.
I
swore
that...
ぱっ
WHAM
I
swore
that I would
protect
Akari.
...I
would
protect
...
...you
this
time...

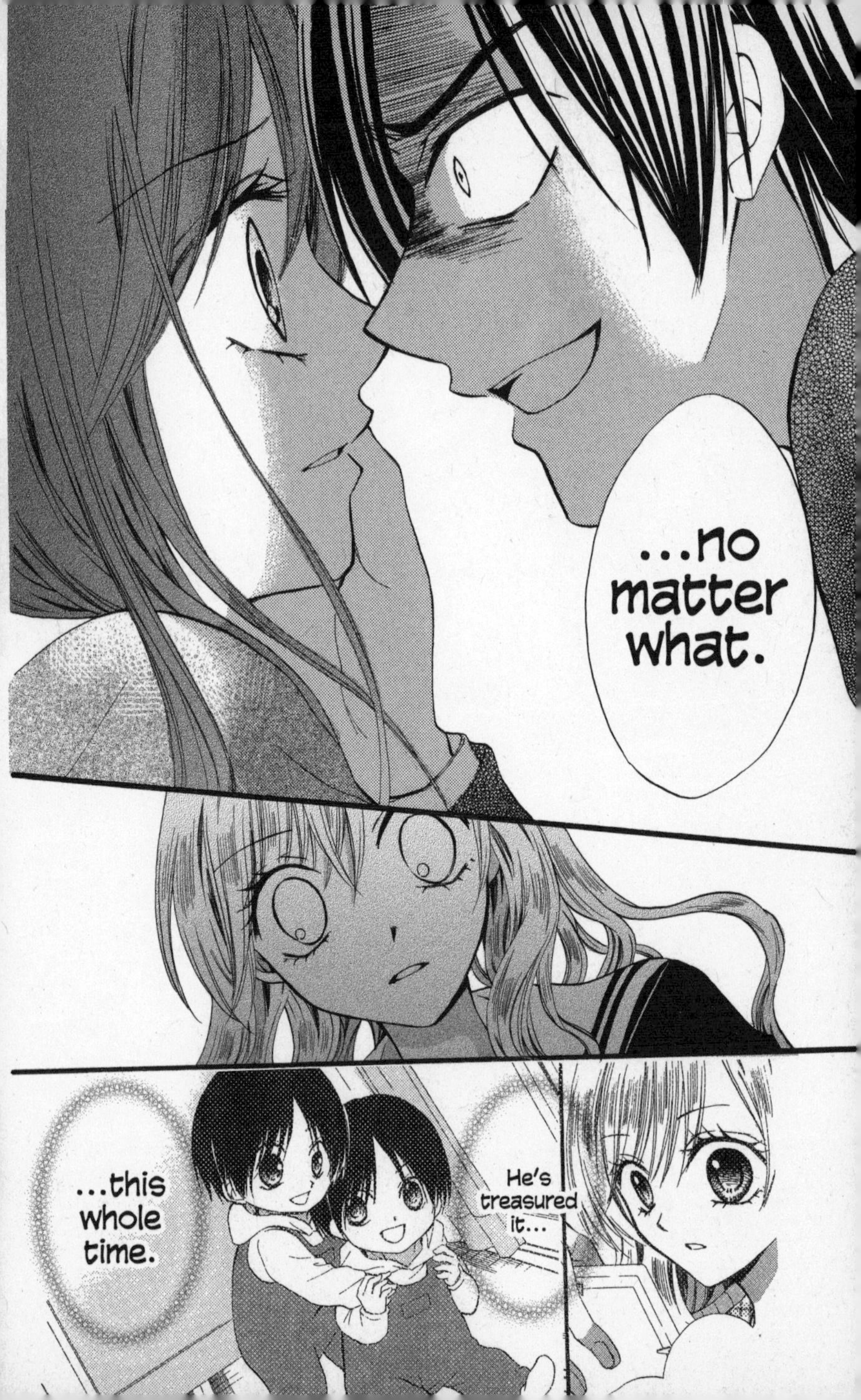
...no matter what.
He's treasured it...
...this whole time.

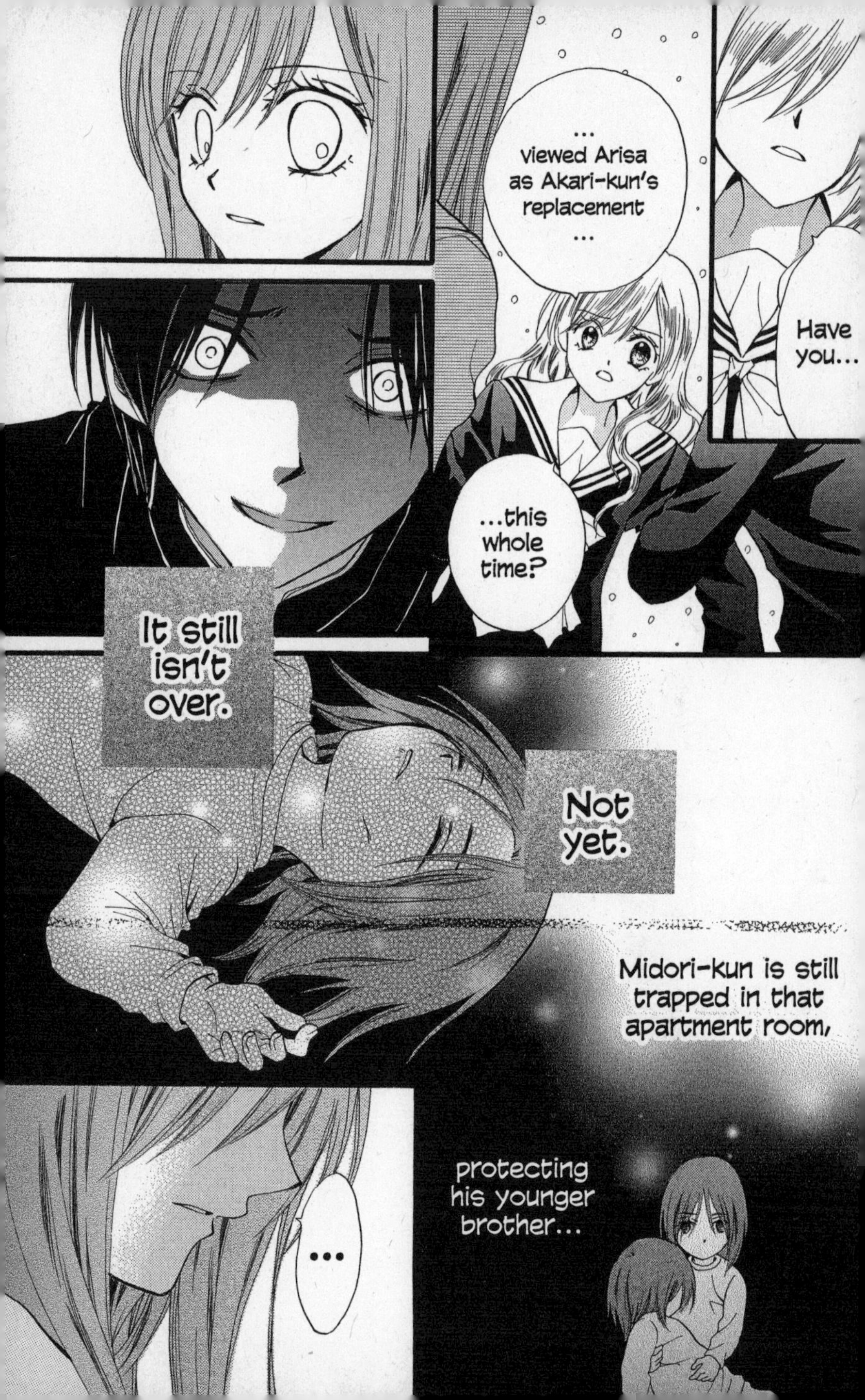
Have you...
...viewed Arisa as Akari-kun's replacement...
...this whole time?
It still isn't over.
Not yet.
Midori-kun is still trapped in that apartment room,
protecting his younger brother...
...

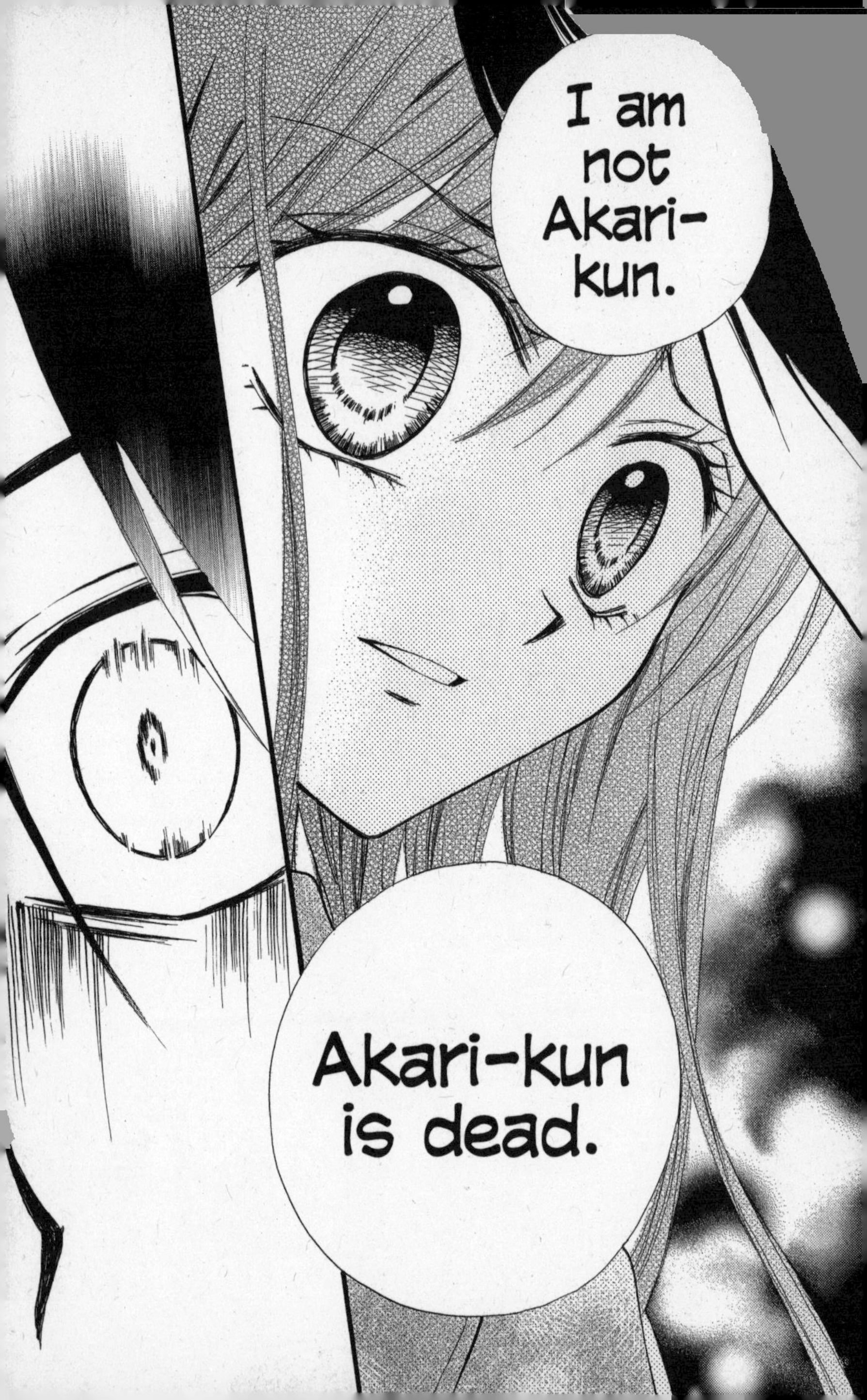
I am not Akari-kun.
Akari-kun is dead.

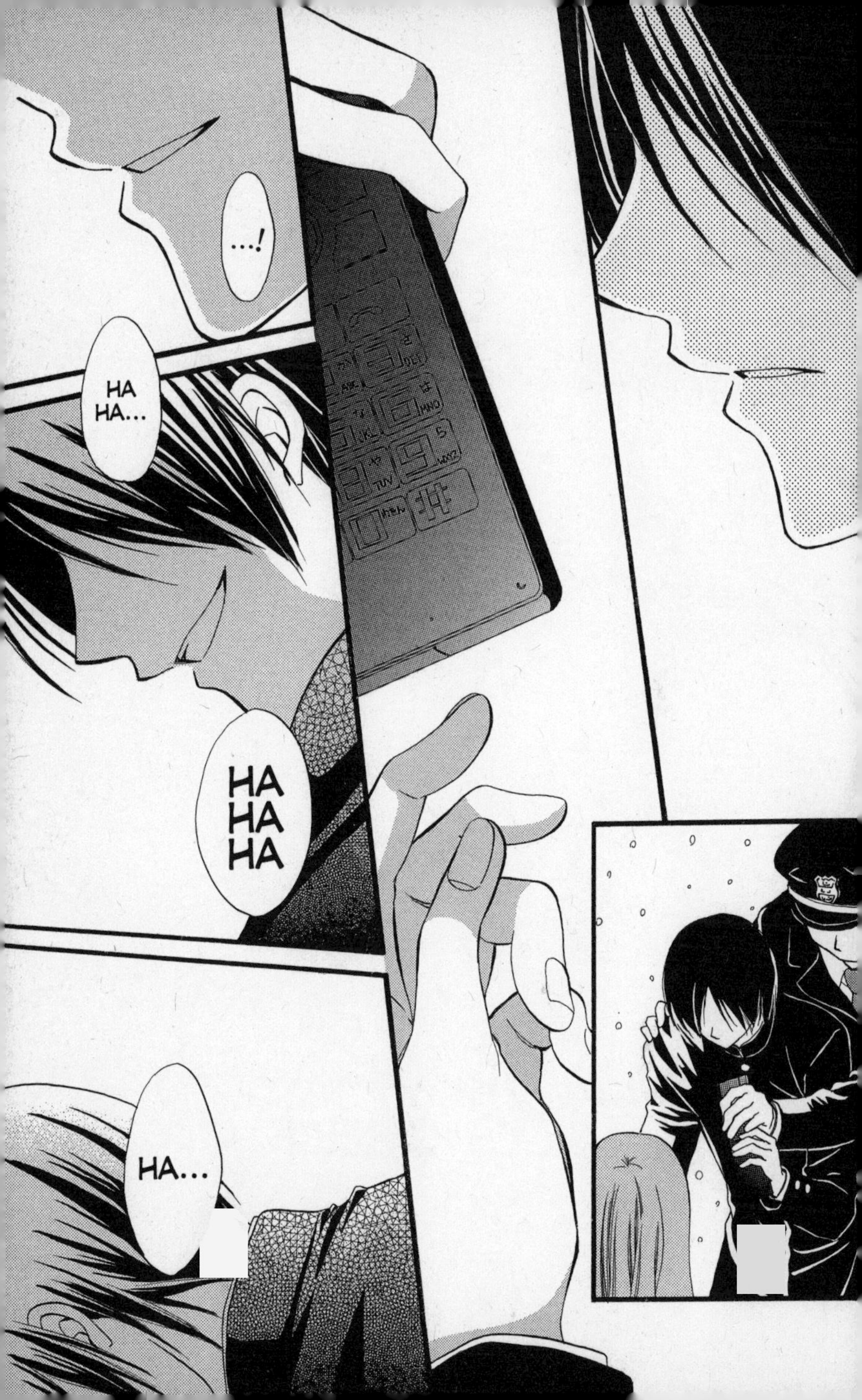
...!
HA HA...
HA HA HA
HA...

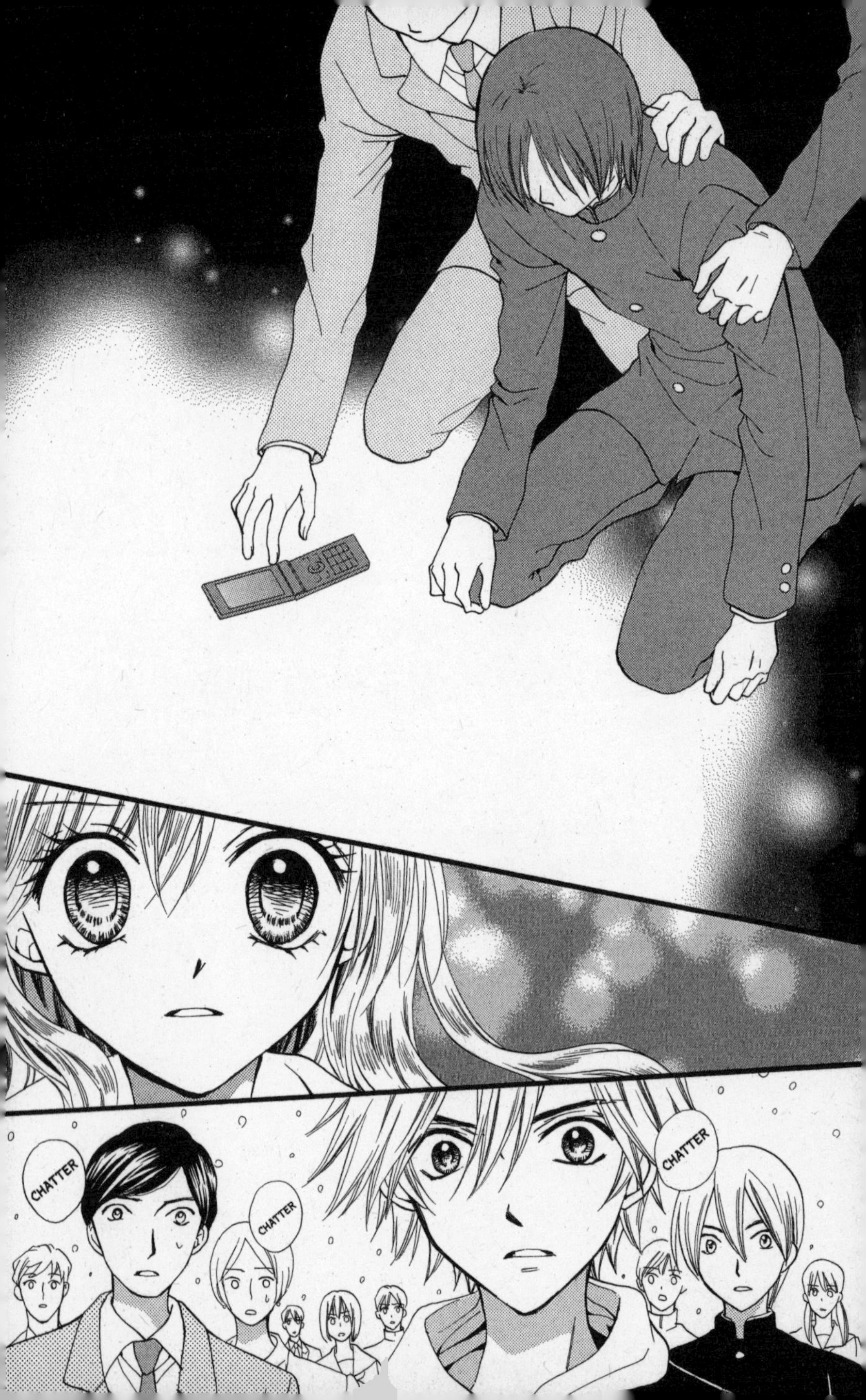
CHATTER
CHATTER
CHATTER

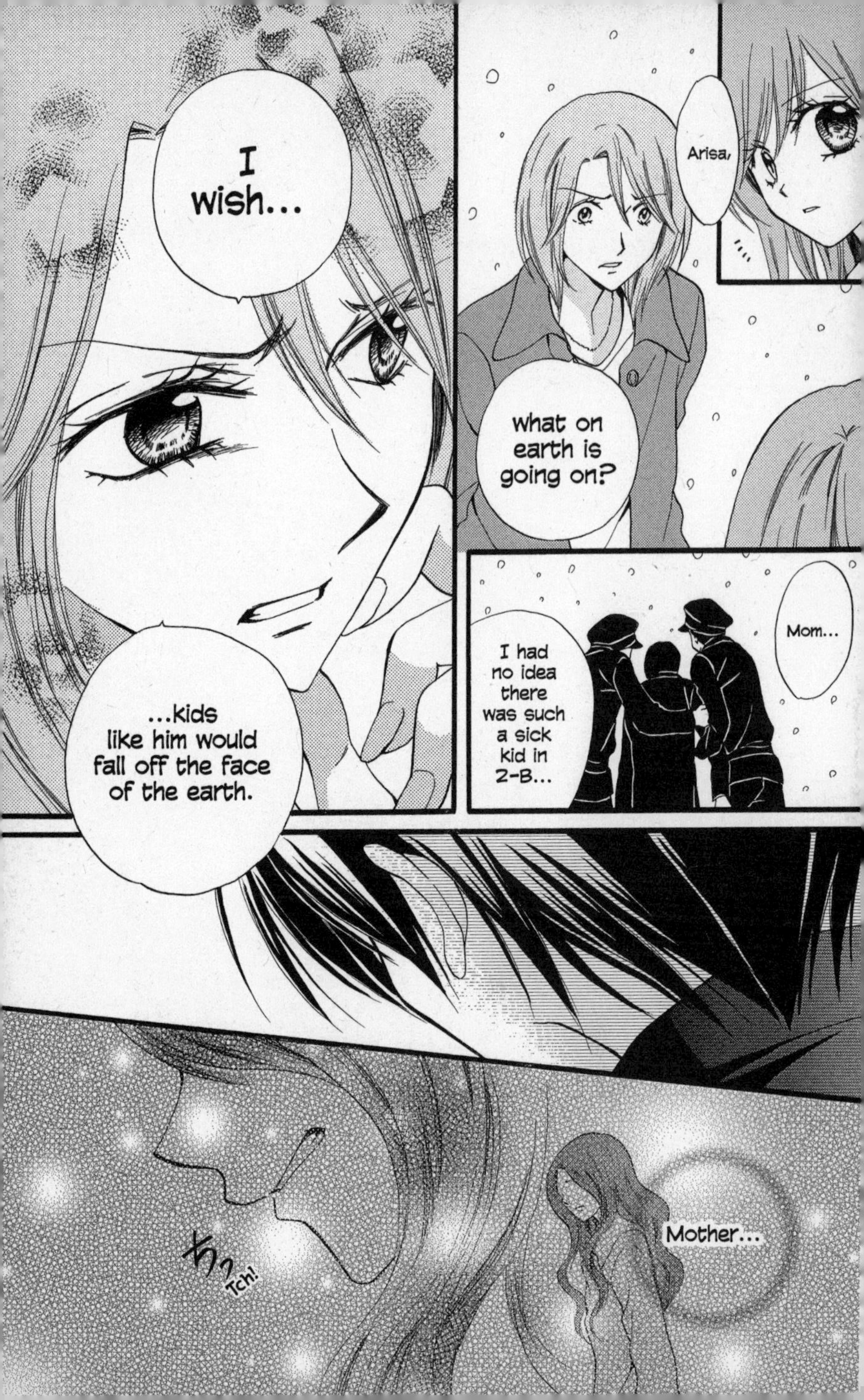
Arisa,
what on earth is going on?
Mom...
I had no idea there was such a sick kid in 2-B...
I wish...
...kids like him would fall off the face of the earth.
Mother...
Tch!

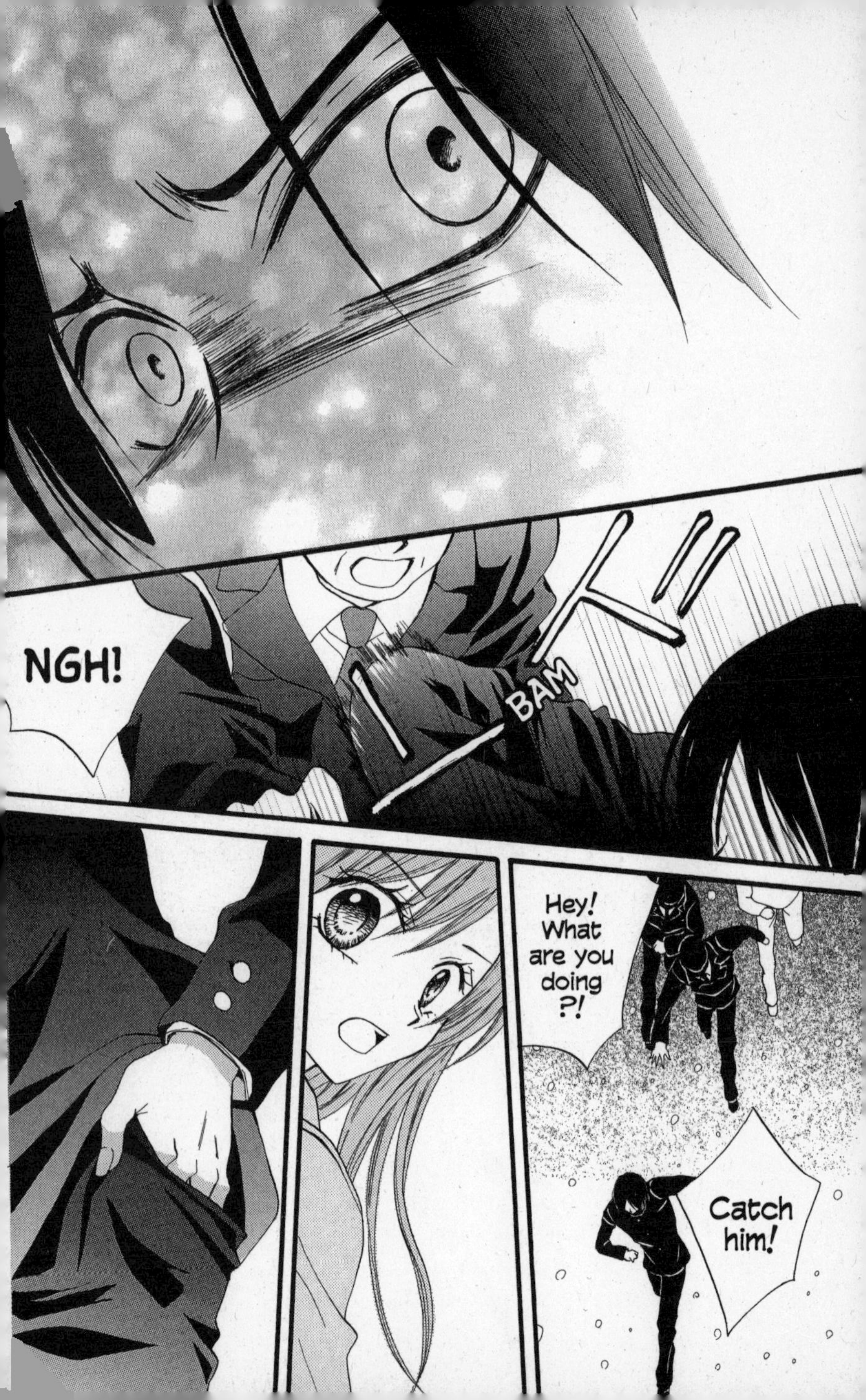
NGH!
BAM
Hey! What are you doing?!
Catch him!

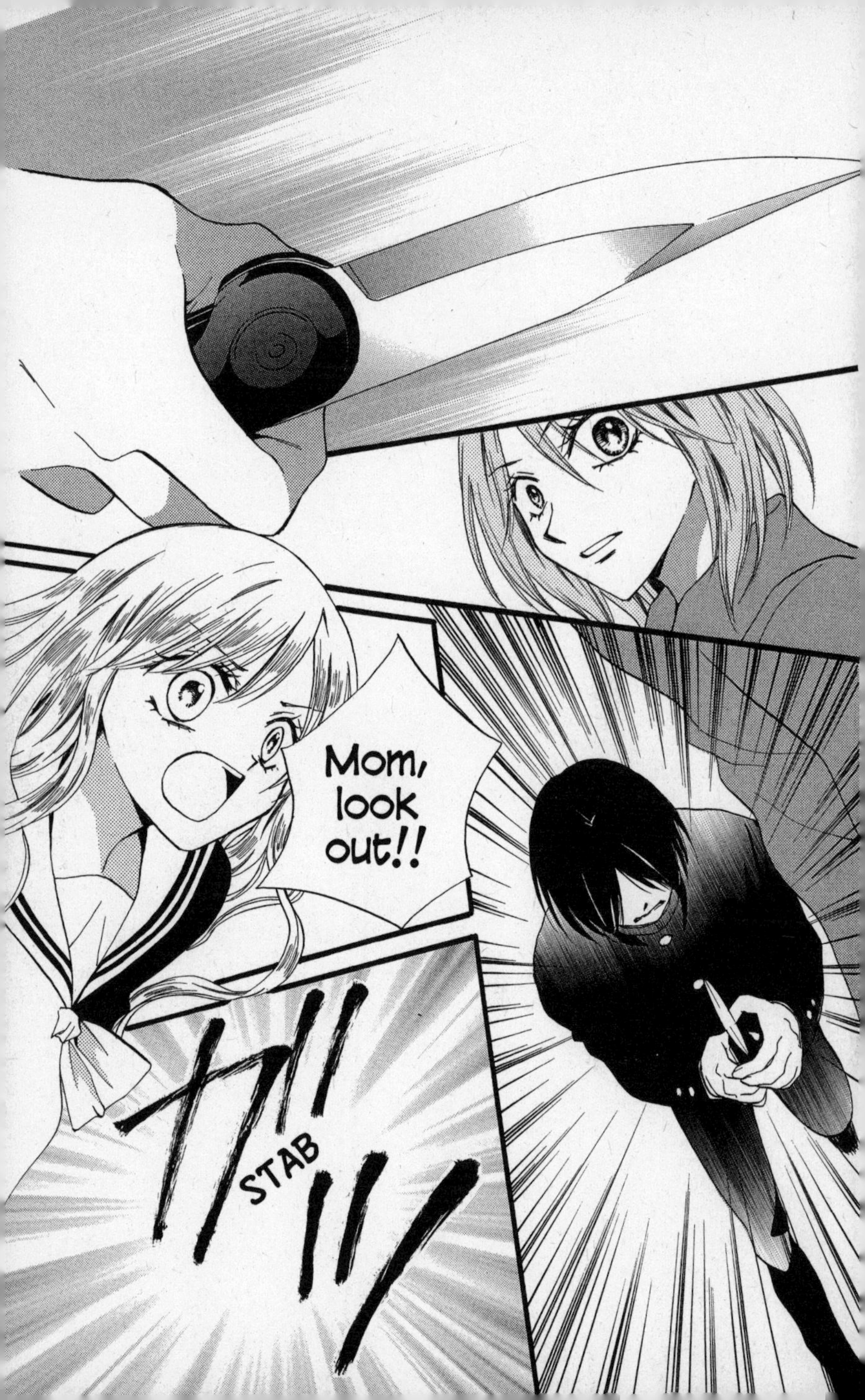
Mom, look out!!
STAB

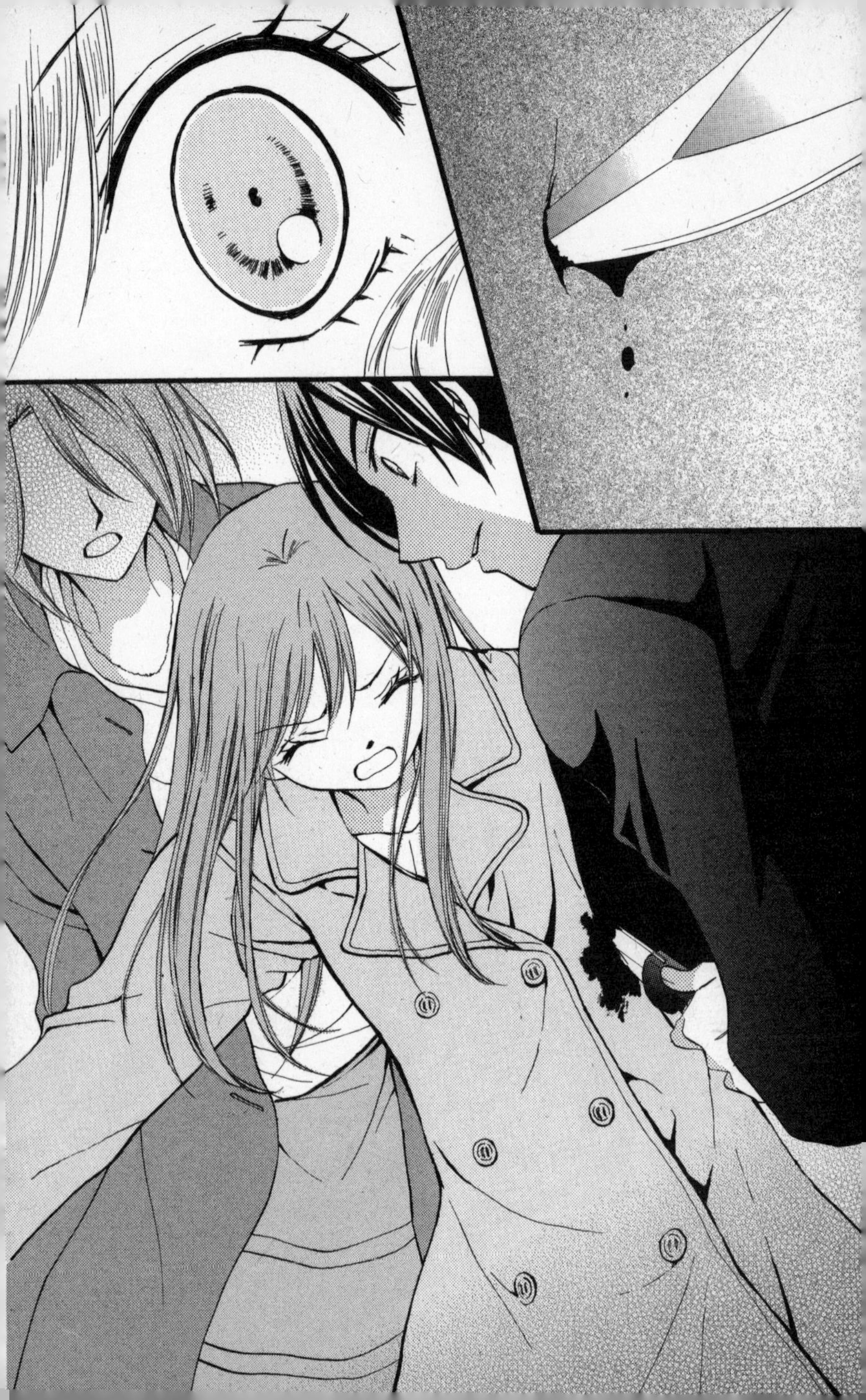

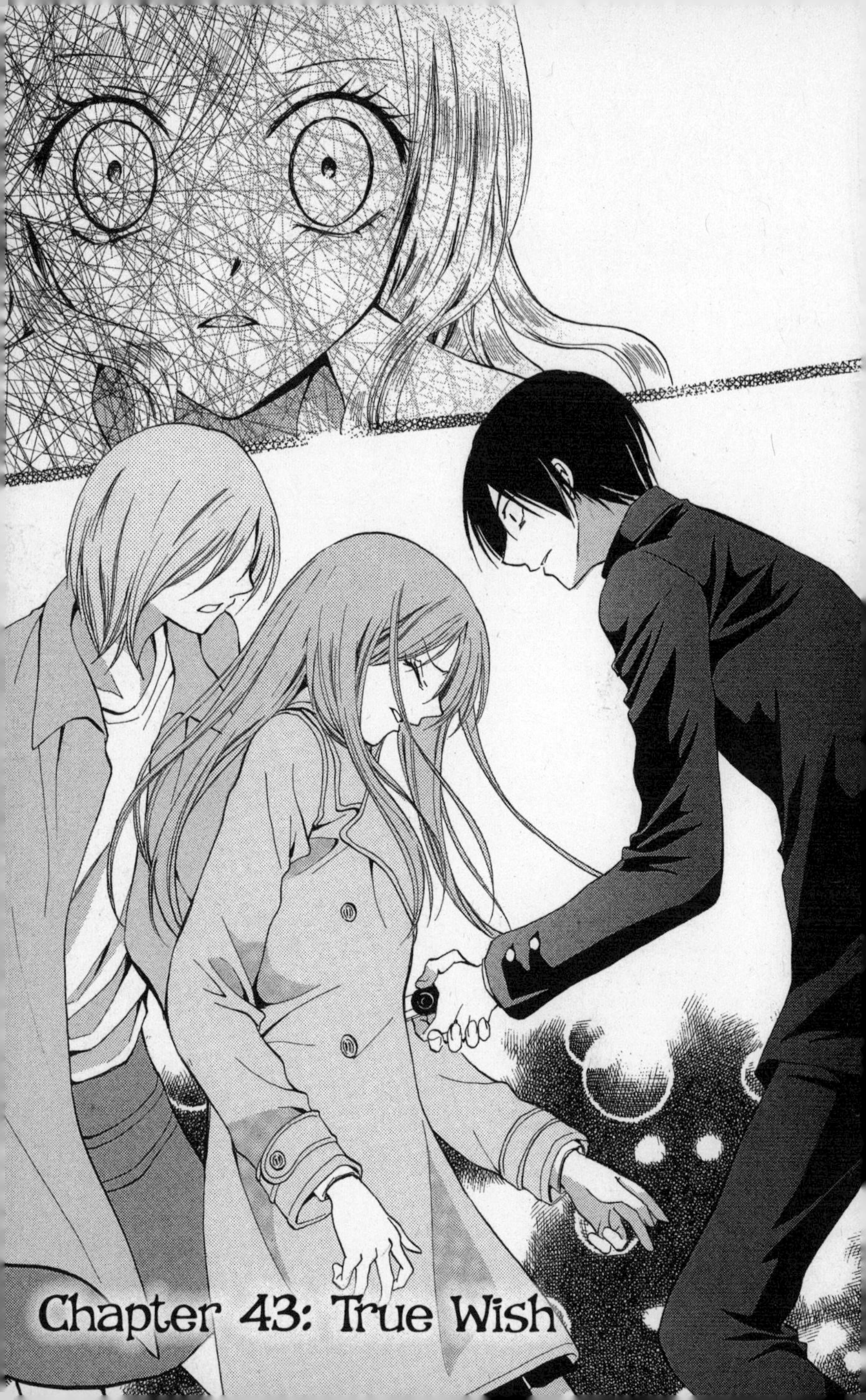
Chapter 43: True Wish

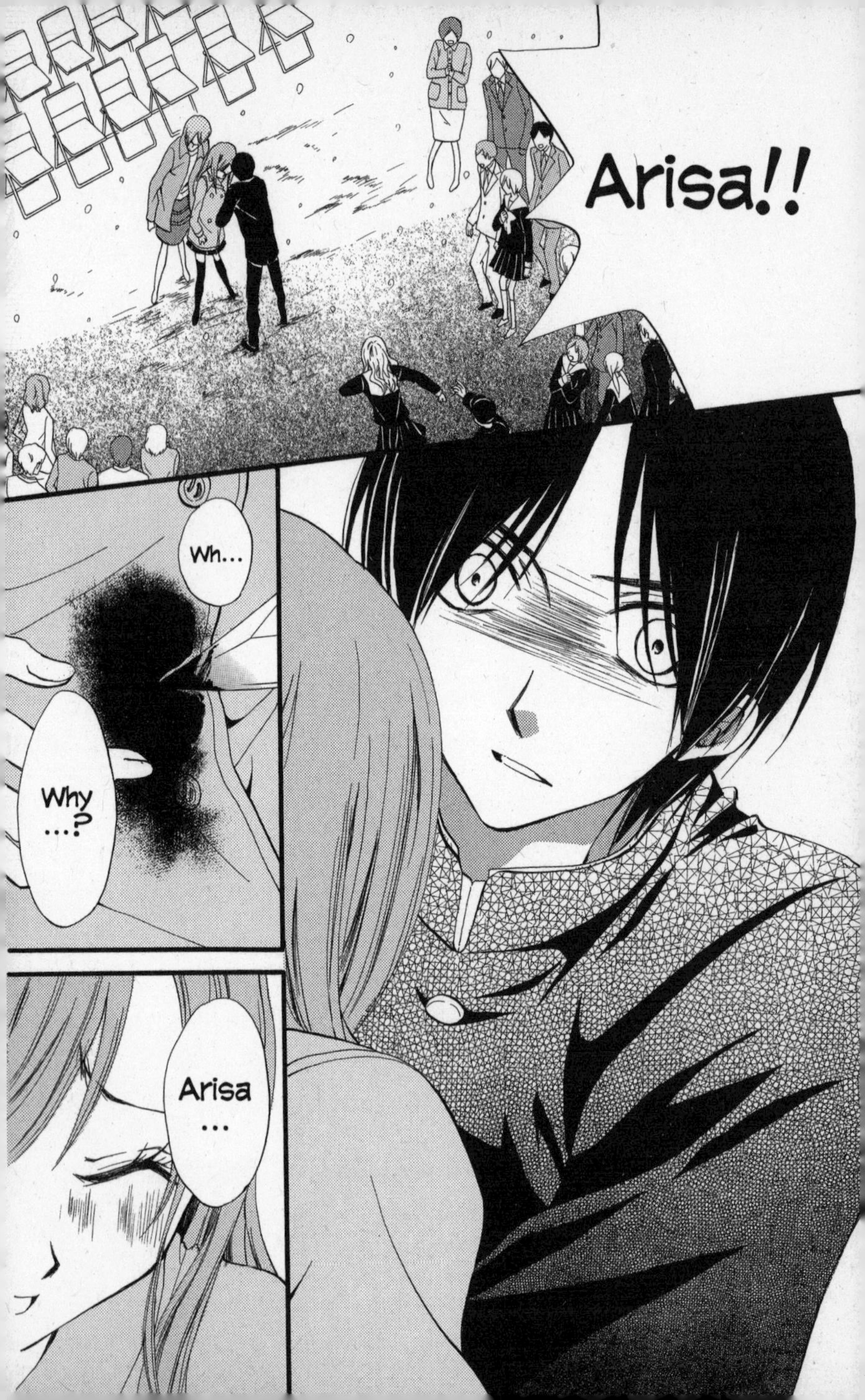
Arisa!!
Wh...
Why ...?
Arisa ...

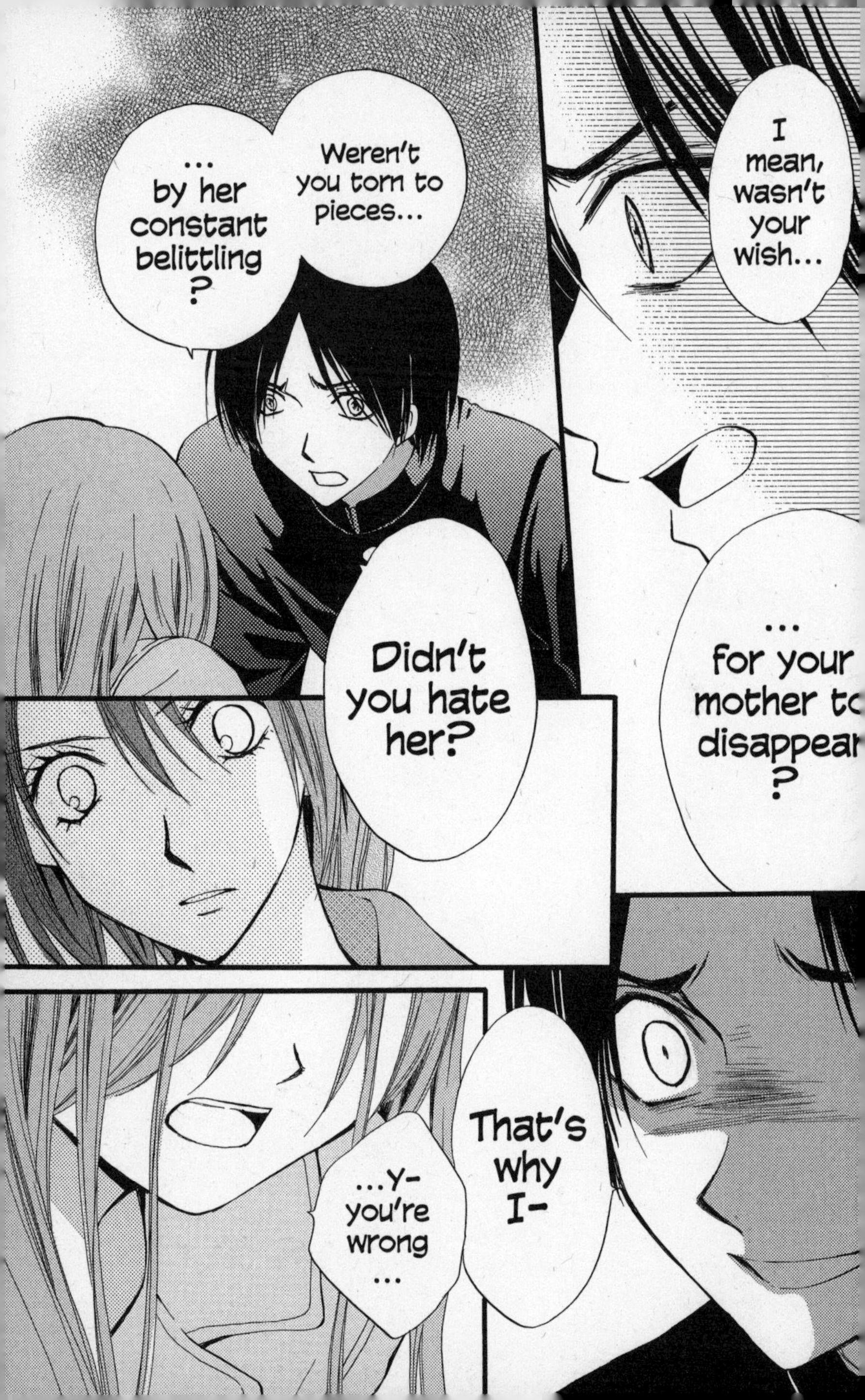
I mean, wasn't your wish...
... for your mother to disappear?
Weren't you torn to pieces...
... by her constant belittling?
Didn't you hate her?
That's why I-
...y-you're wrong ...

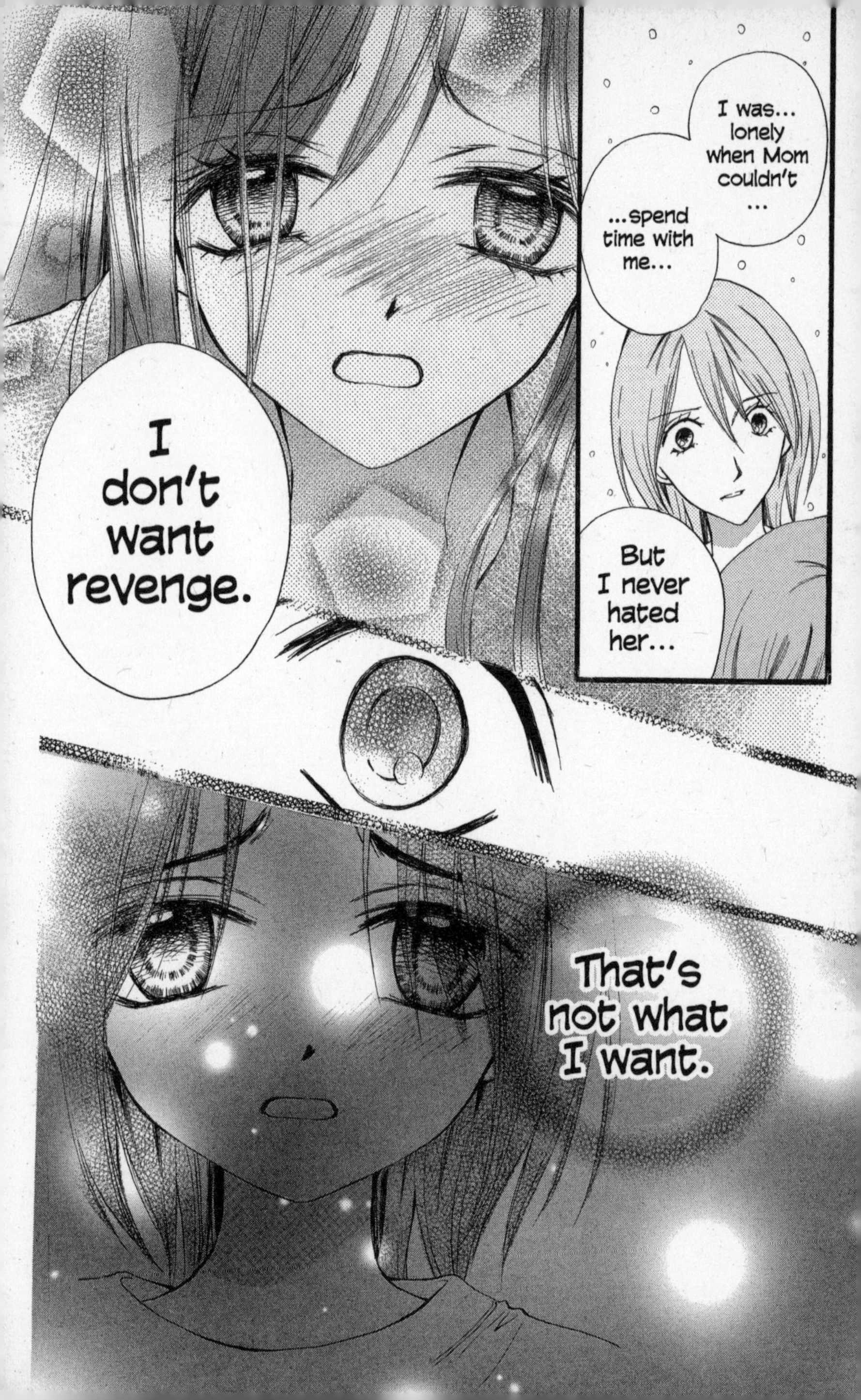
I was... lonely when Mom couldn't ...
...spend time with me...
But I never hated her...
I don't want revenge.
That's not what I want.

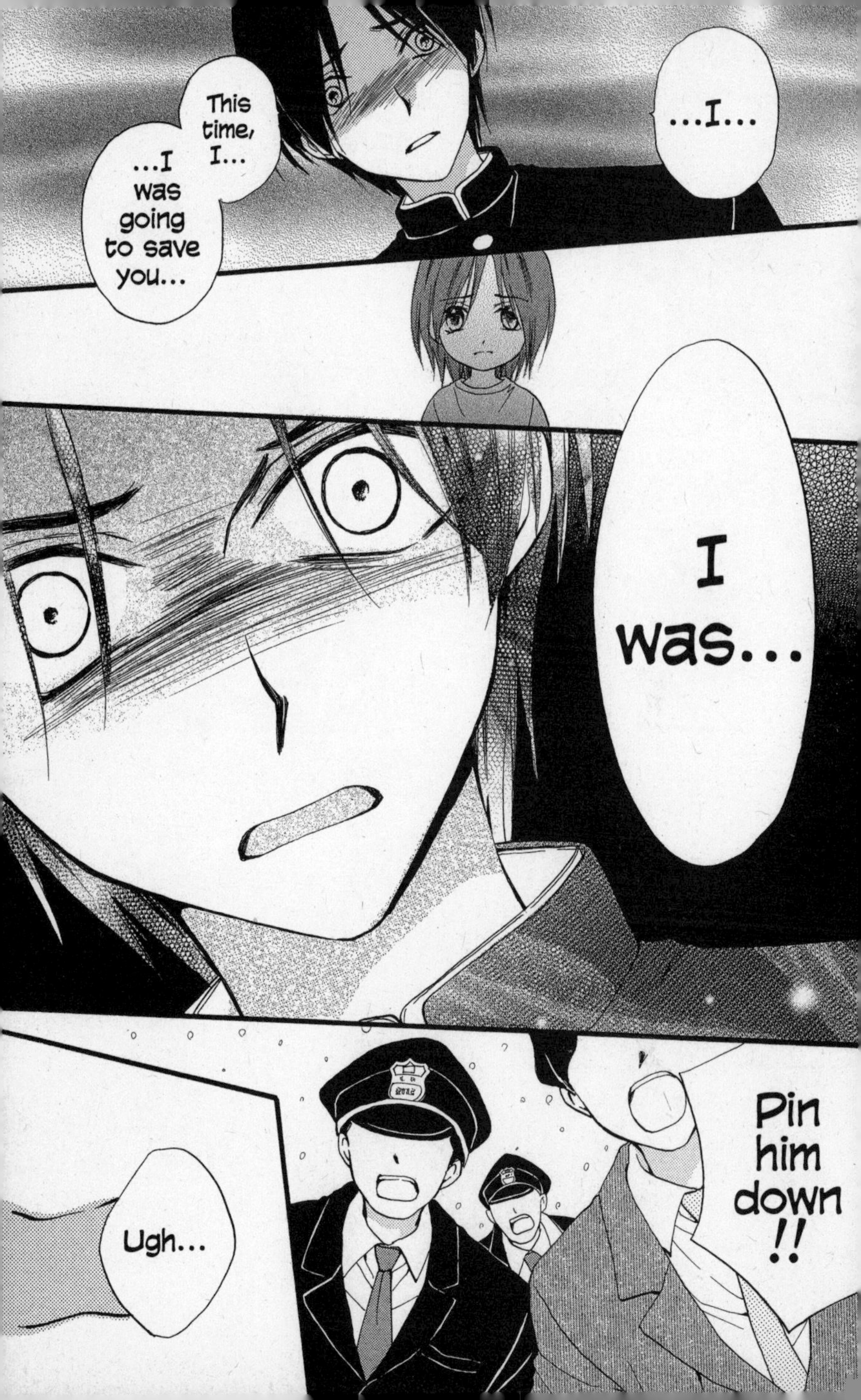
...I...
This time, I...
...I was going to save you...
I was...
Pin him down!!
Ugh...

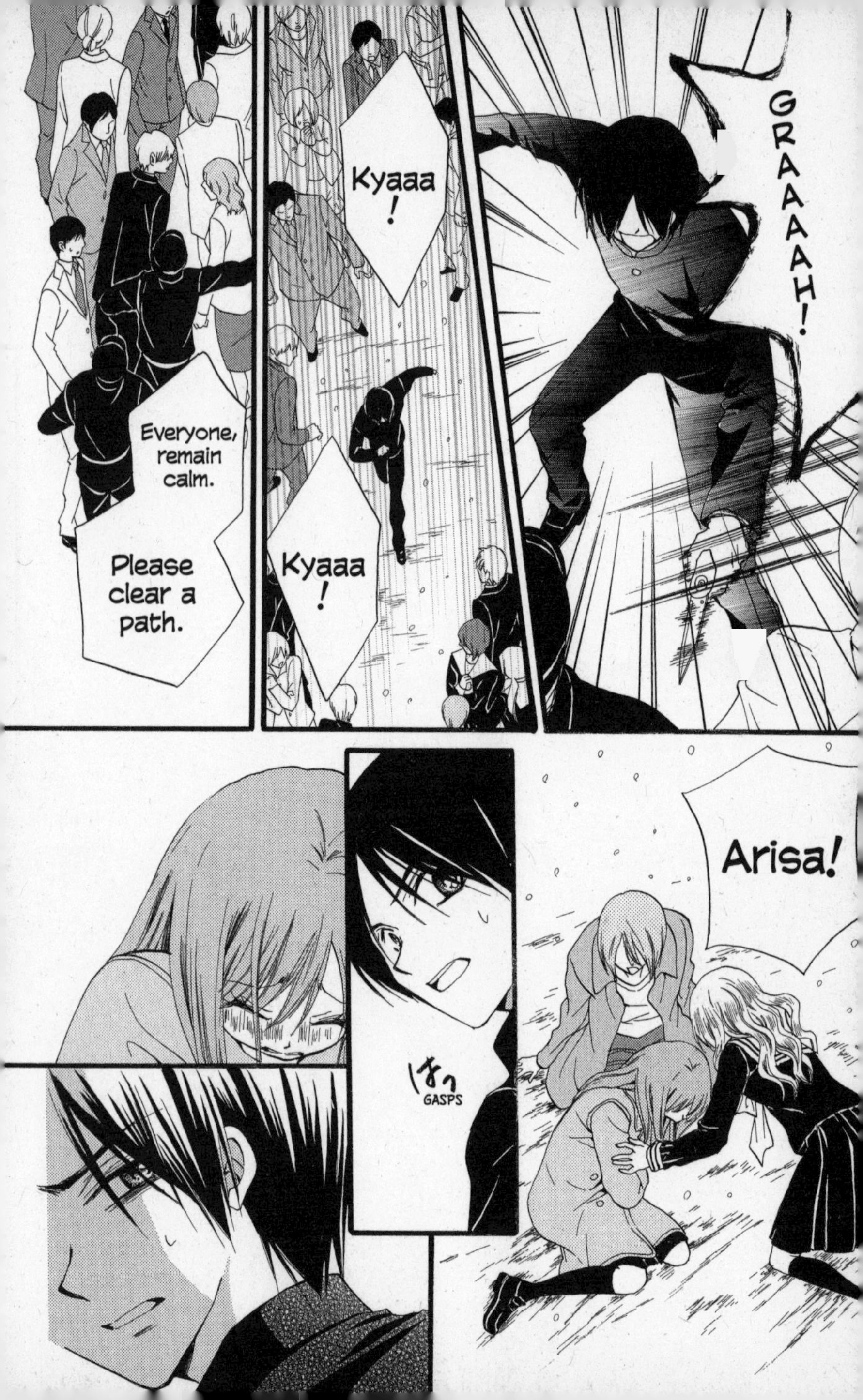
GRAAAAH!
Kyaaa!
Kyaaa!
Everyone, remain calm.
Please clear a path.
Arisa!
はっ
GASPS

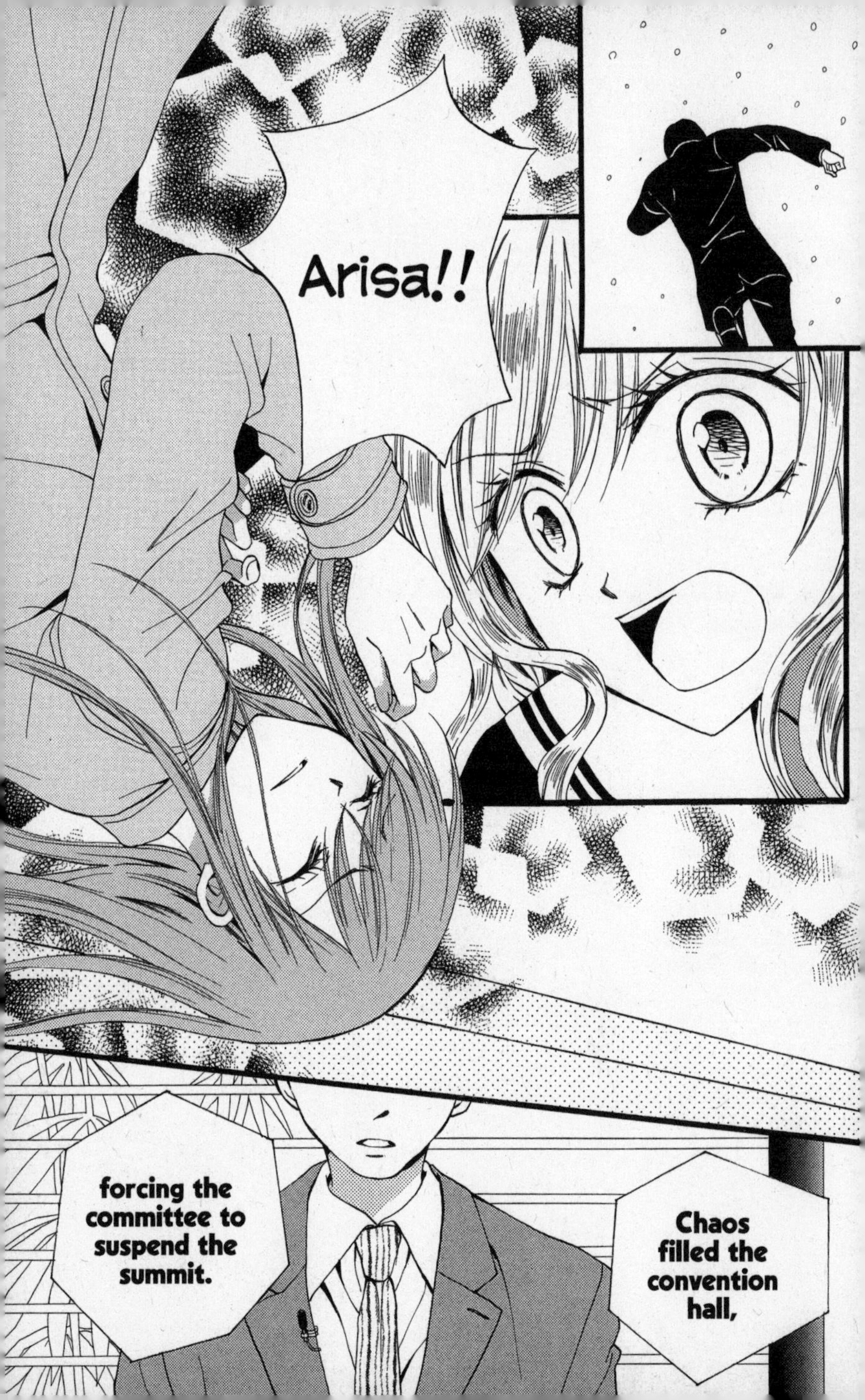
Arisa!!
Chaos filled the convention hall,
forcing the committee to suspend the summit.

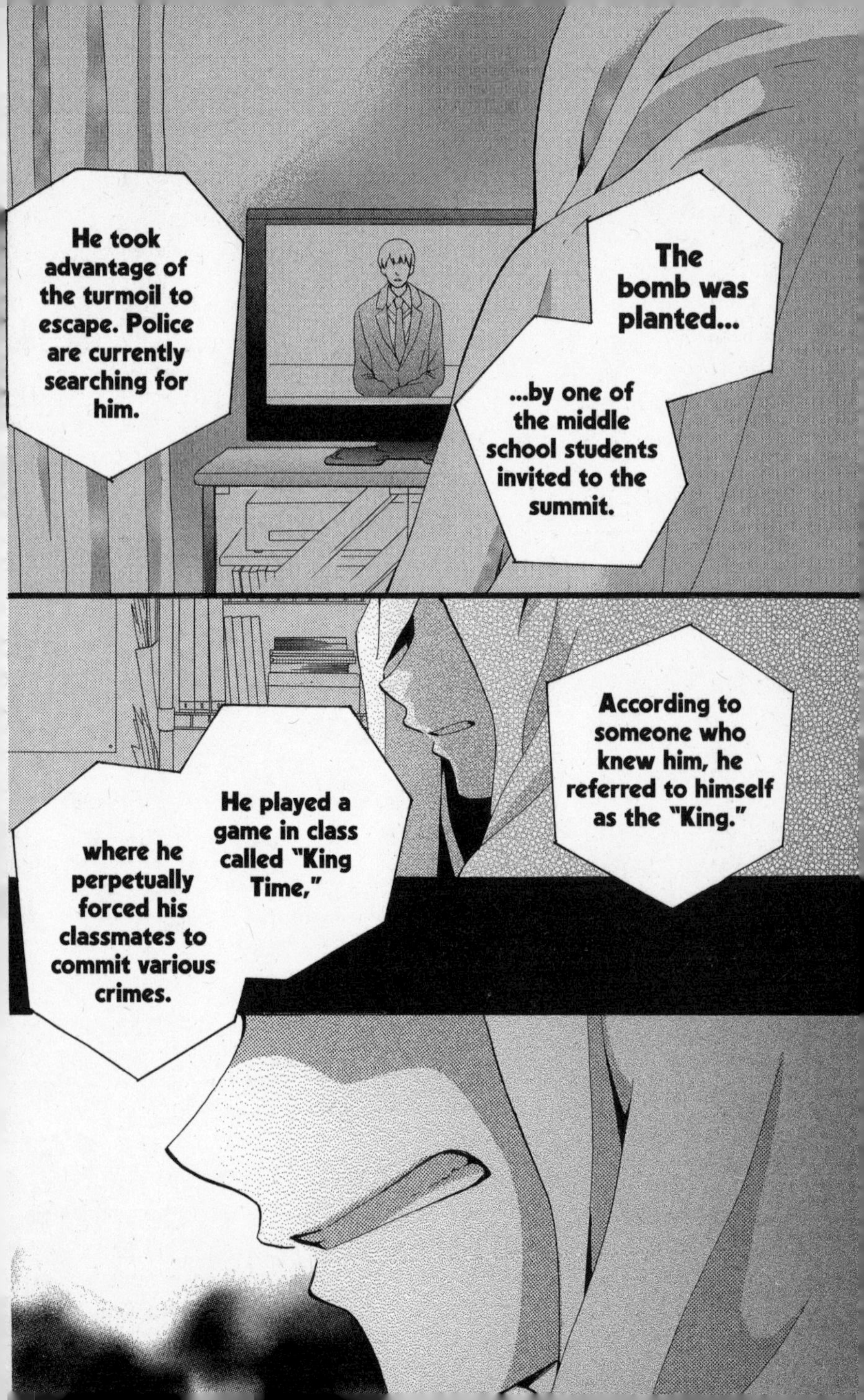
The bomb was planted...
...by one of the middle school students invited to the summit.
He took advantage of the turmoil to escape. Police are currently searching for him.
According to someone who knew him, he referred to himself as the "King."
He played a game in class called "King Time,"
where he perpetually forced his classmates to commit various crimes.

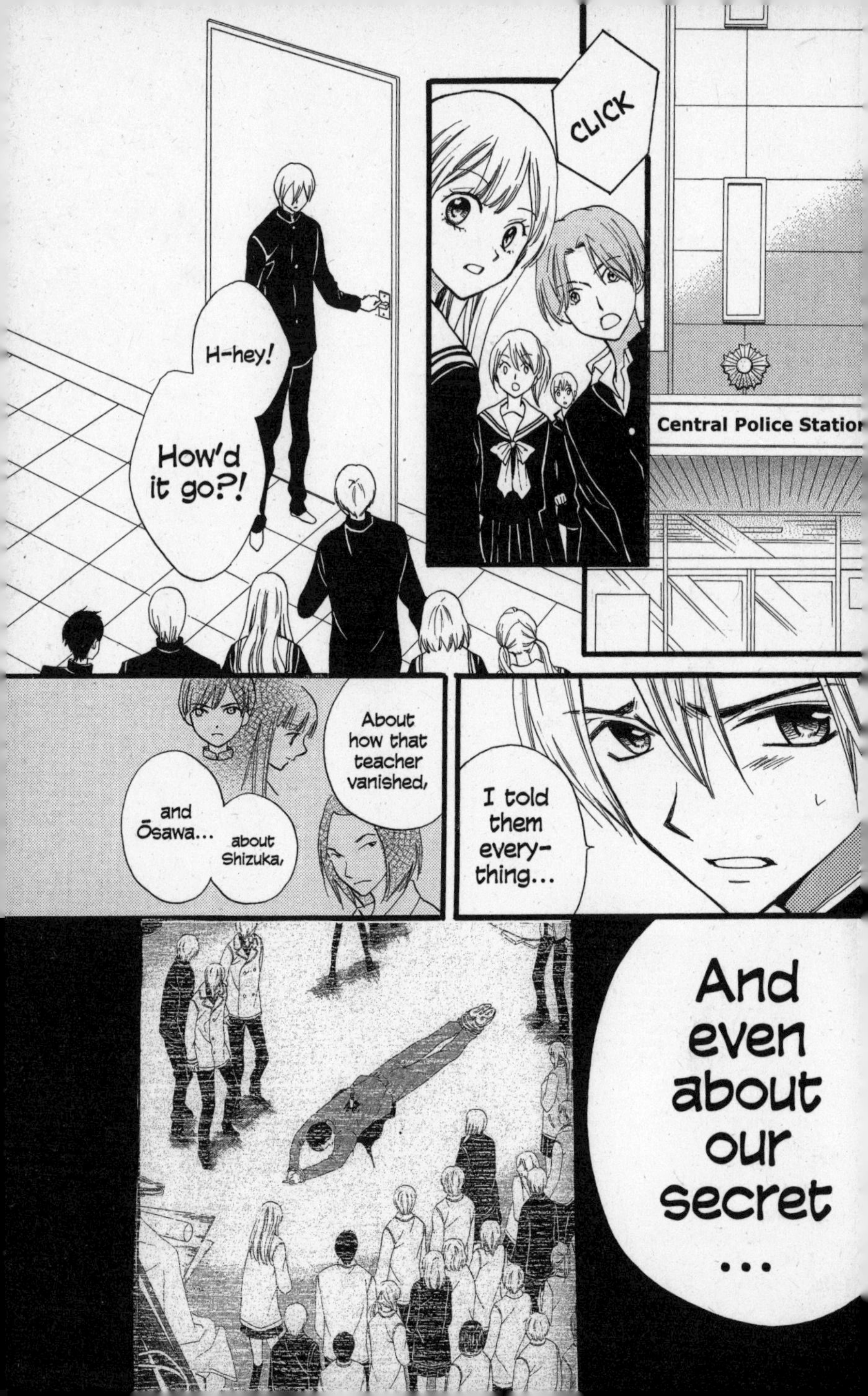
Central Police Station
CLICK
H-hey!
How'd it go?!
I told them every-thing...
About how that teacher vanished,
about Shizuka,
and Ōsawa...
And even about our secret ...

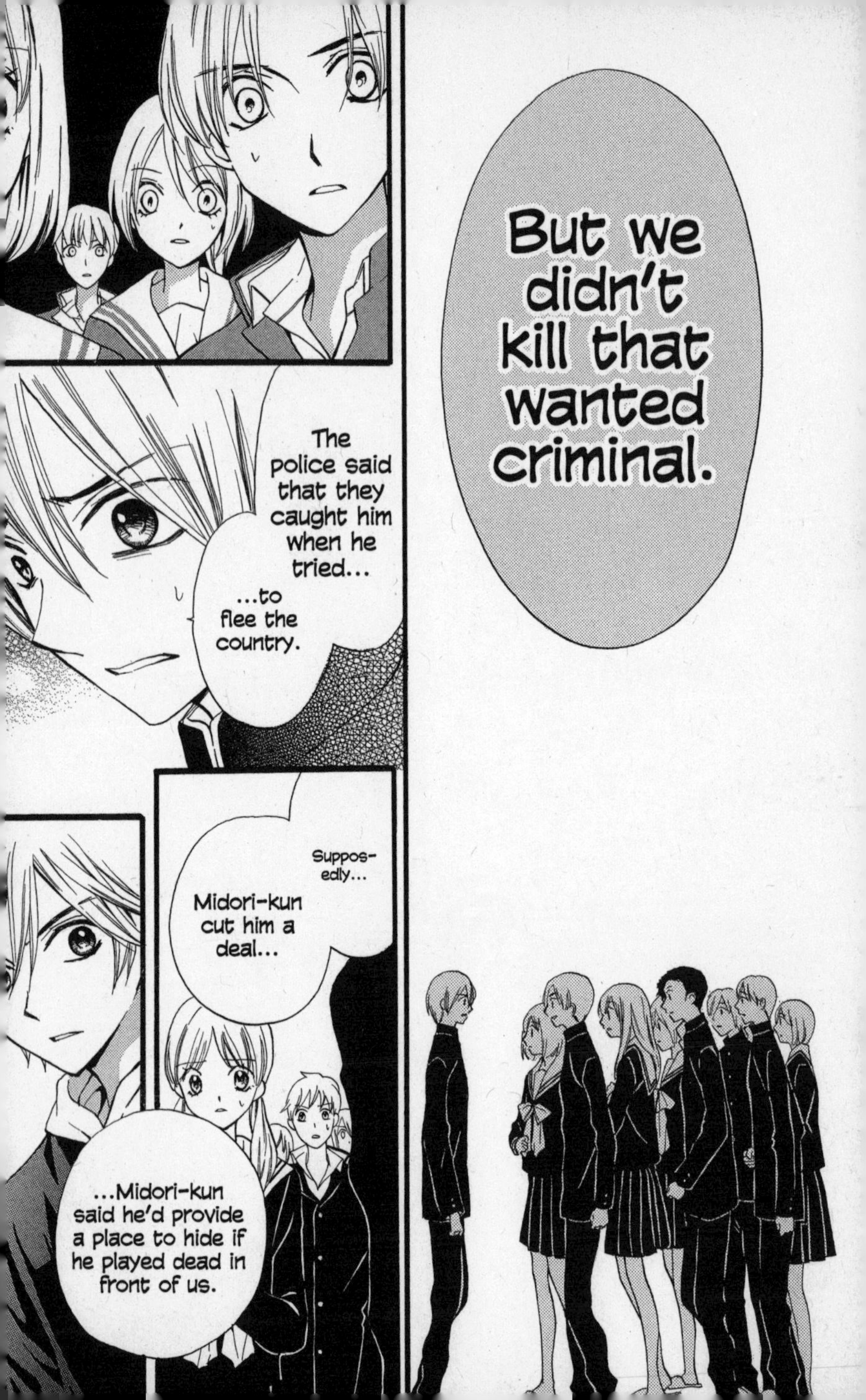
But we didn't kill that wanted criminal.
The police said that they caught him when he tried...
...to flee the country.
Suppos-edly...
Midori-kun cut him a deal...
...Midori-kun said he'd provide a place to hide if he played dead in front of us.

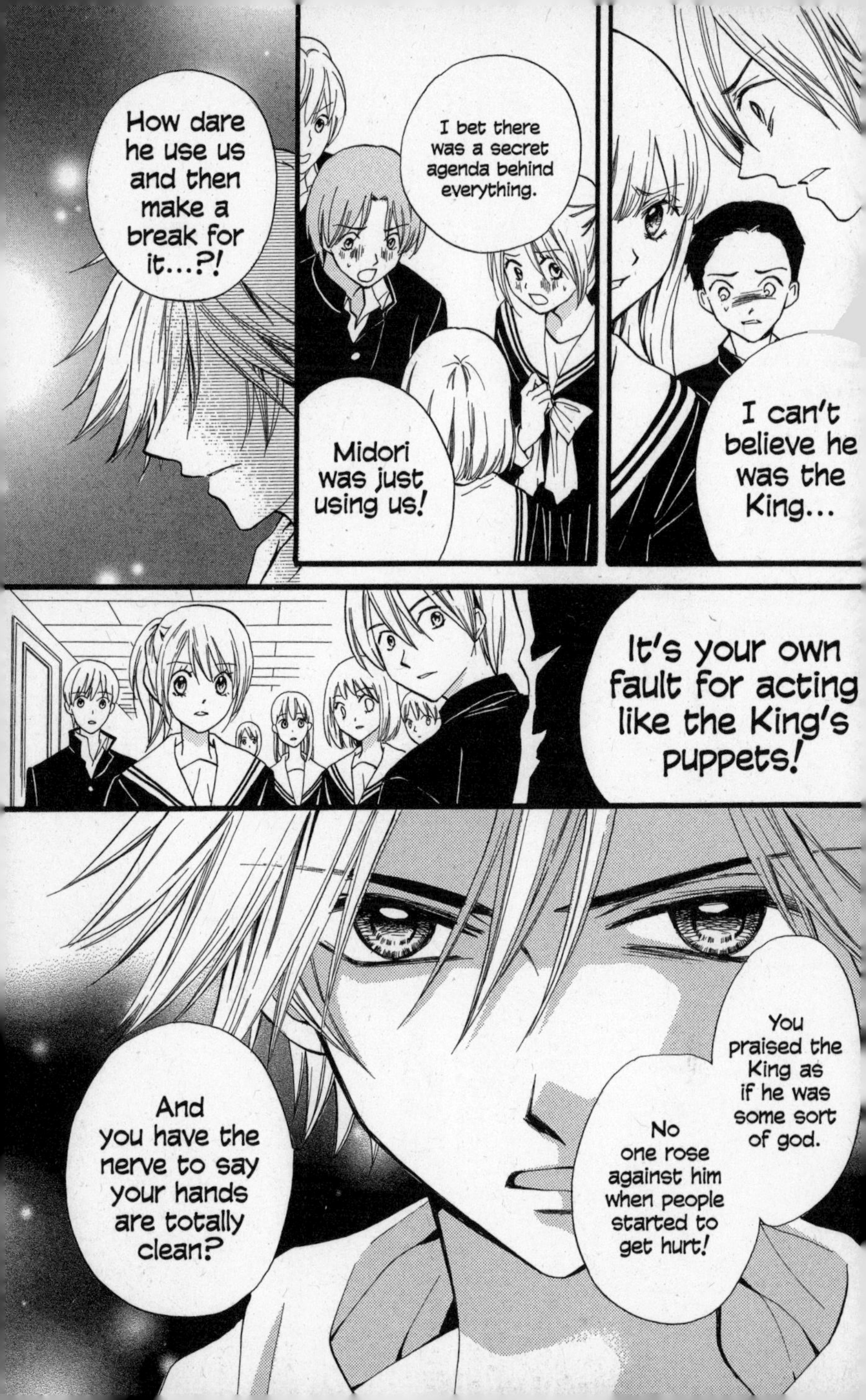
I can't believe he was the King...
I bet there was a secret agenda behind everything.
Midori was just using us!
How dare he use us and then make a break for it...?!
It's your own fault for acting like the King's puppets!
You praised the King as if he was some sort of god.
No one rose against him when people started to get hurt!
And you have the nerve to say your hands are totally clean?

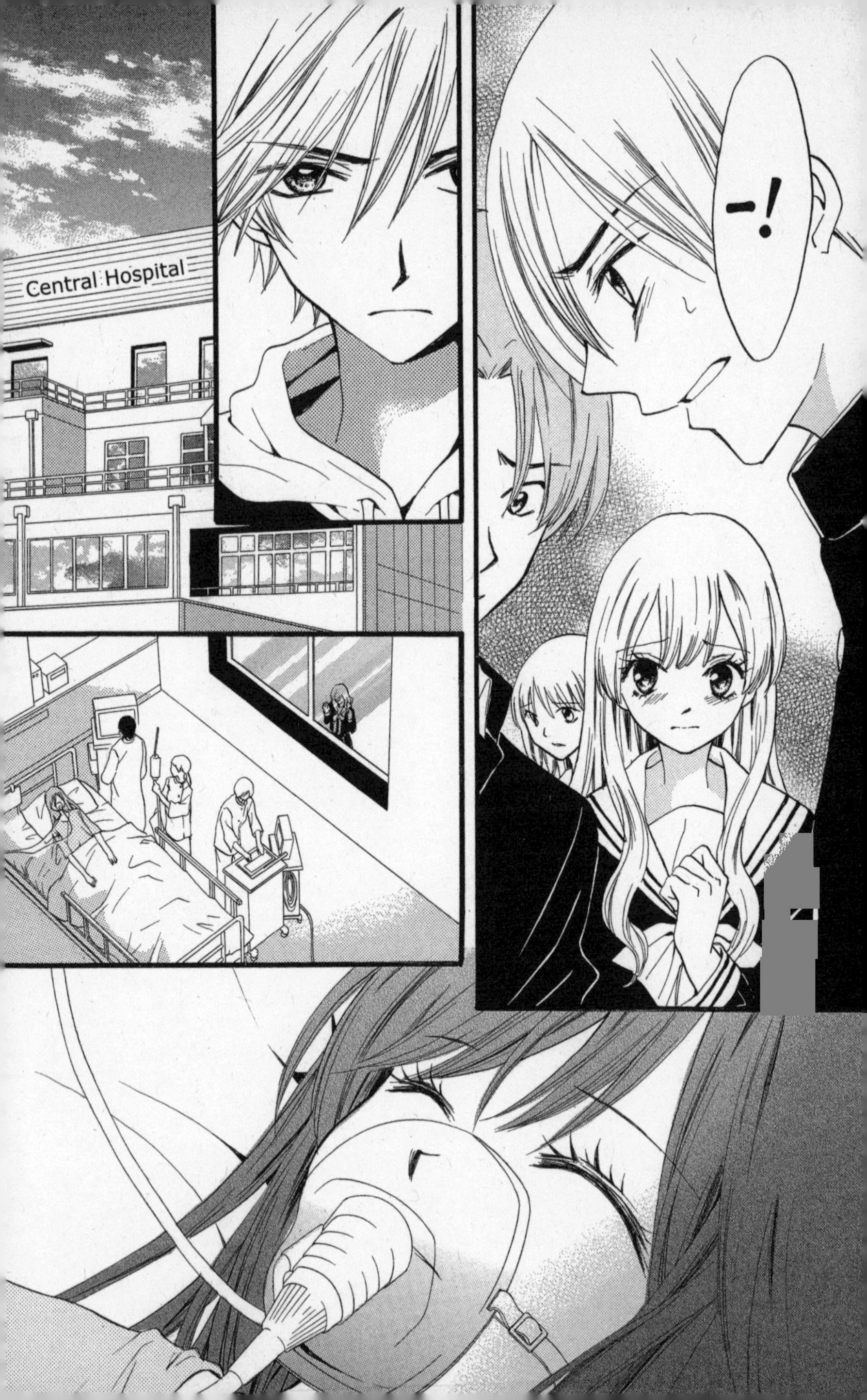
–!
Central Hospital

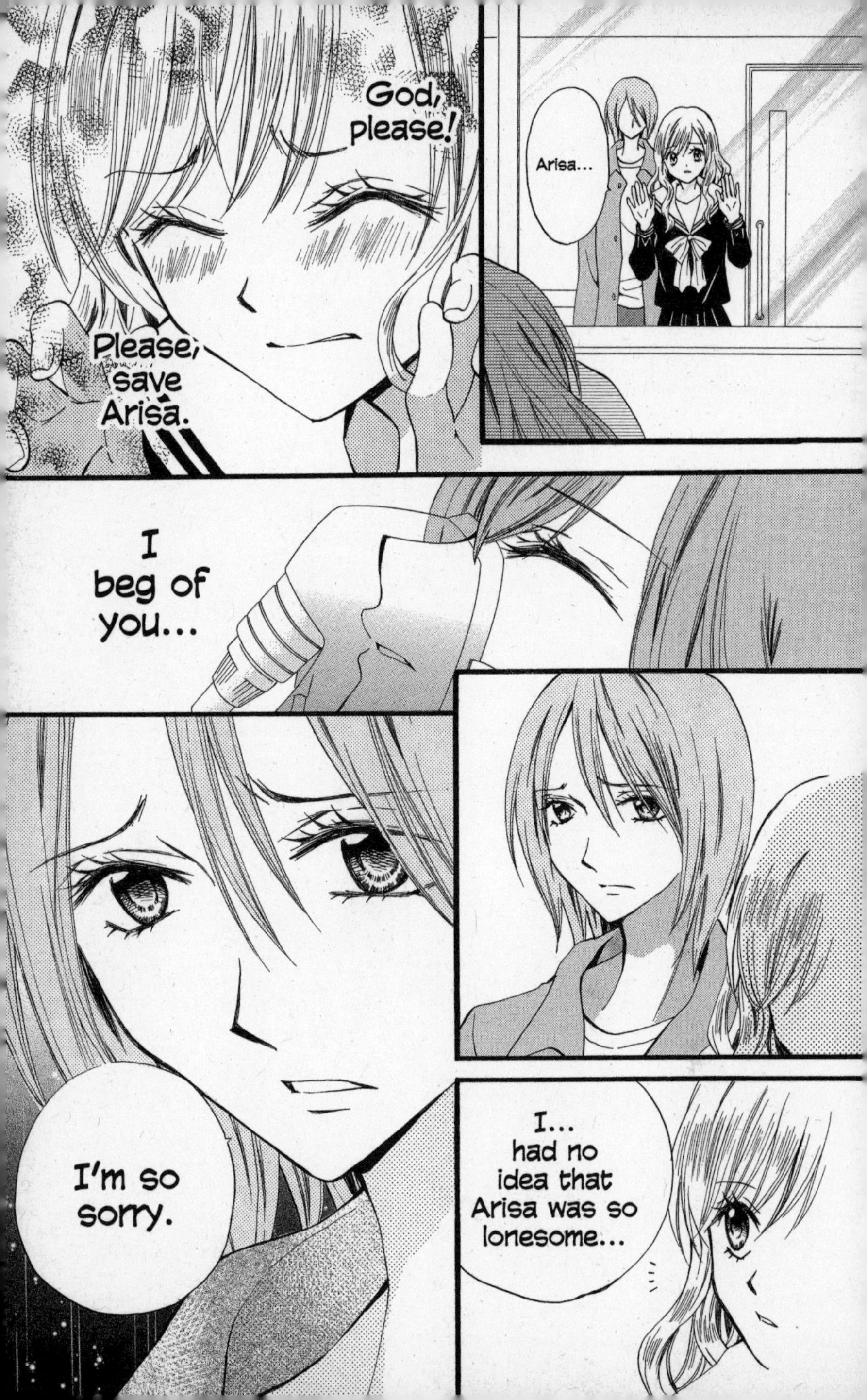
Arisa...
God, please!
Please, save Arisa.
I beg of you...
I... had no idea that Arisa was so lonesome...
I'm so sorry.

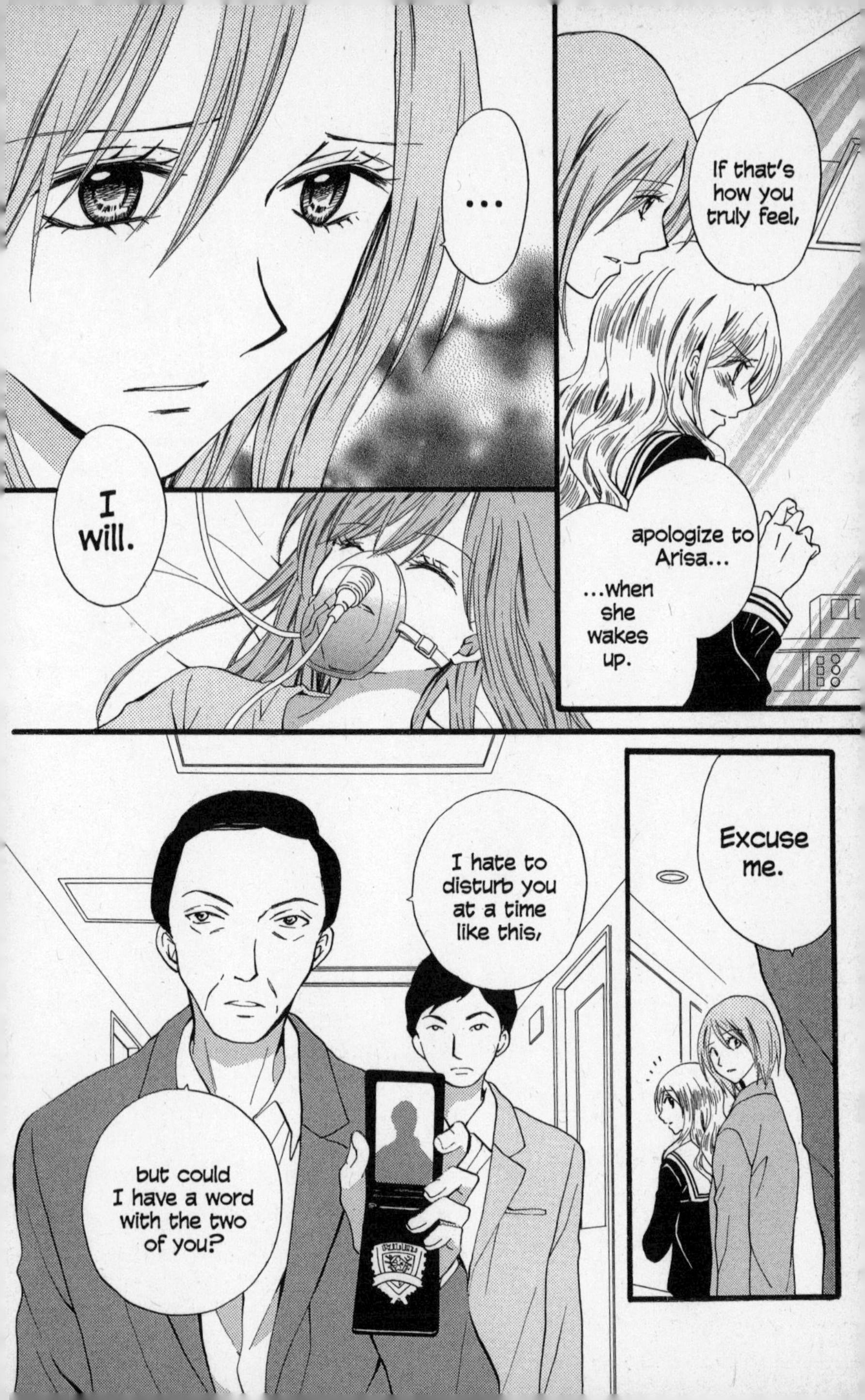

If that's how you truly feel,
apologize to Arisa...
...when she wakes up.
...
I will.
Excuse me.
I hate to disturb you at a time like this,
but could I have a word with the two of you?

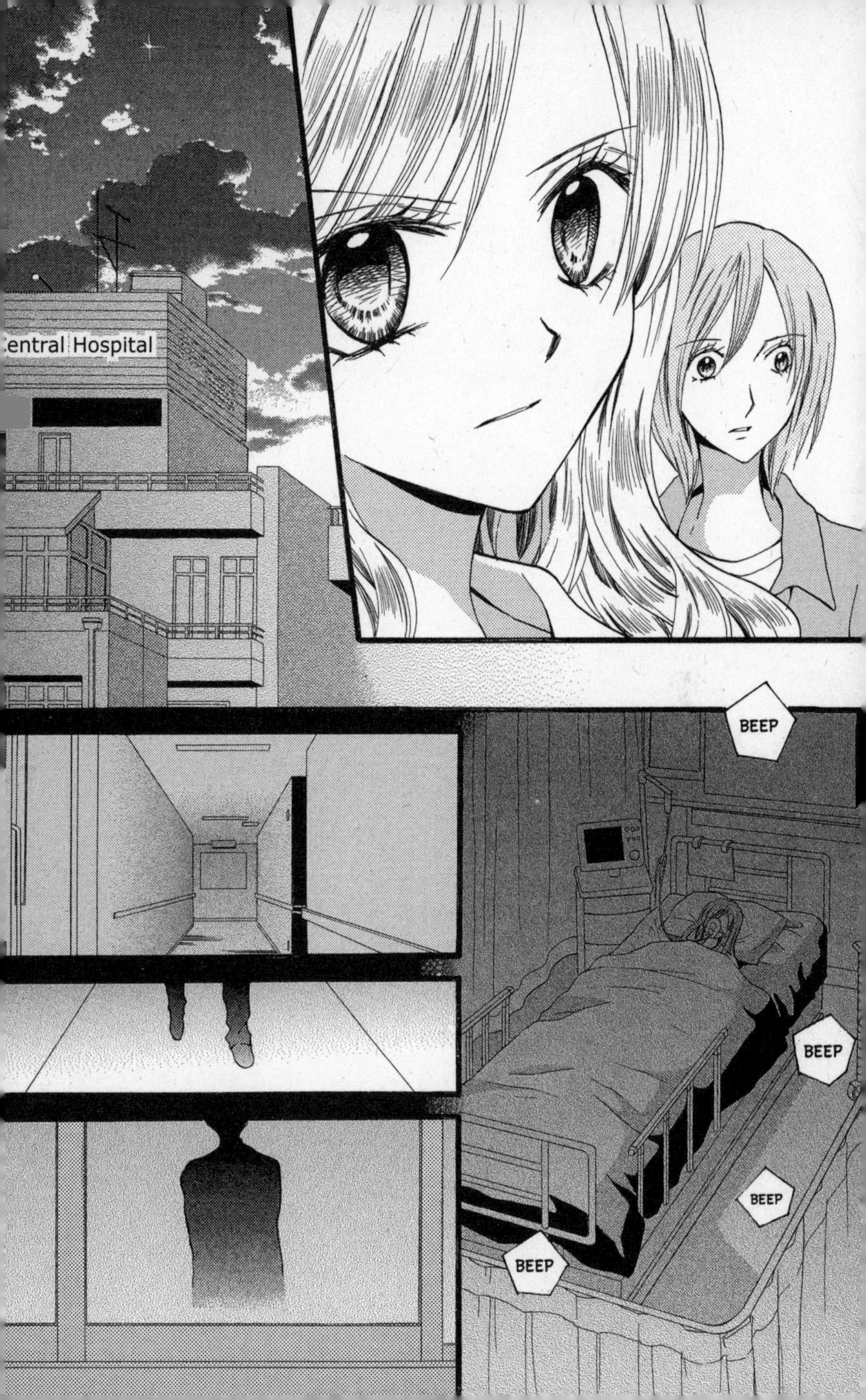
Central Hospital
BEEP
BEEP
BEEP
BEEP

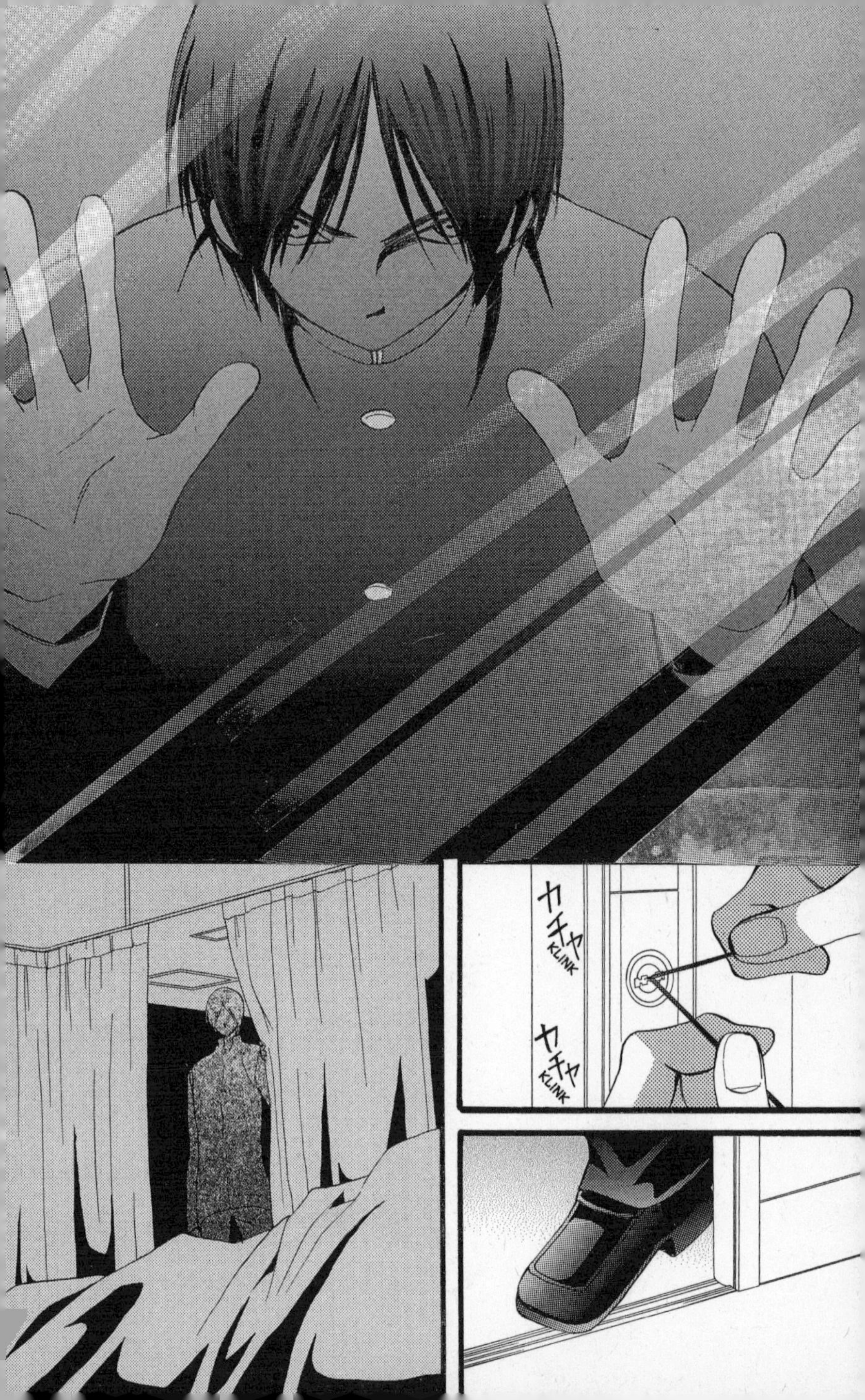
カチャ KLINK
カチャ KLINK

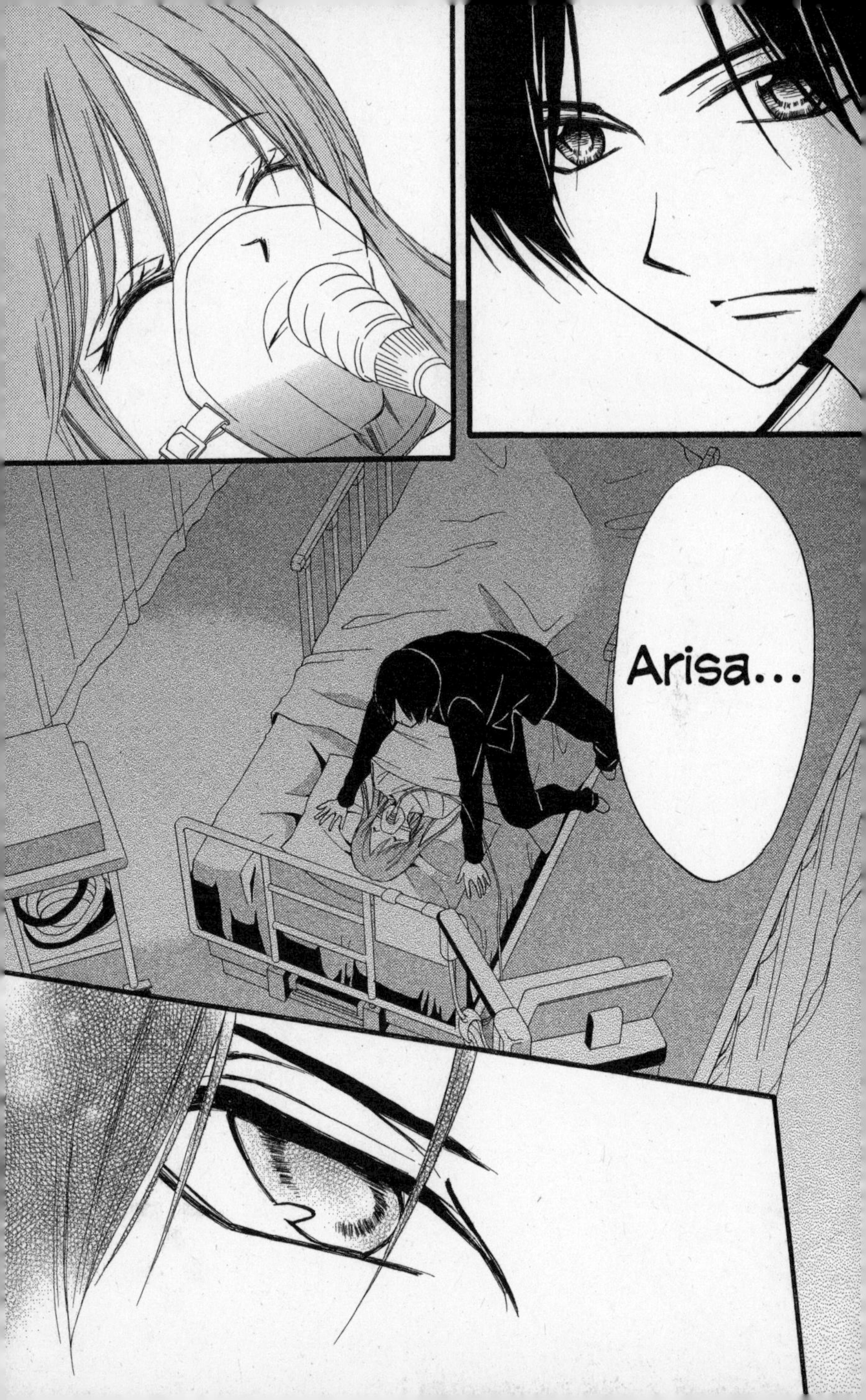
Arisa...

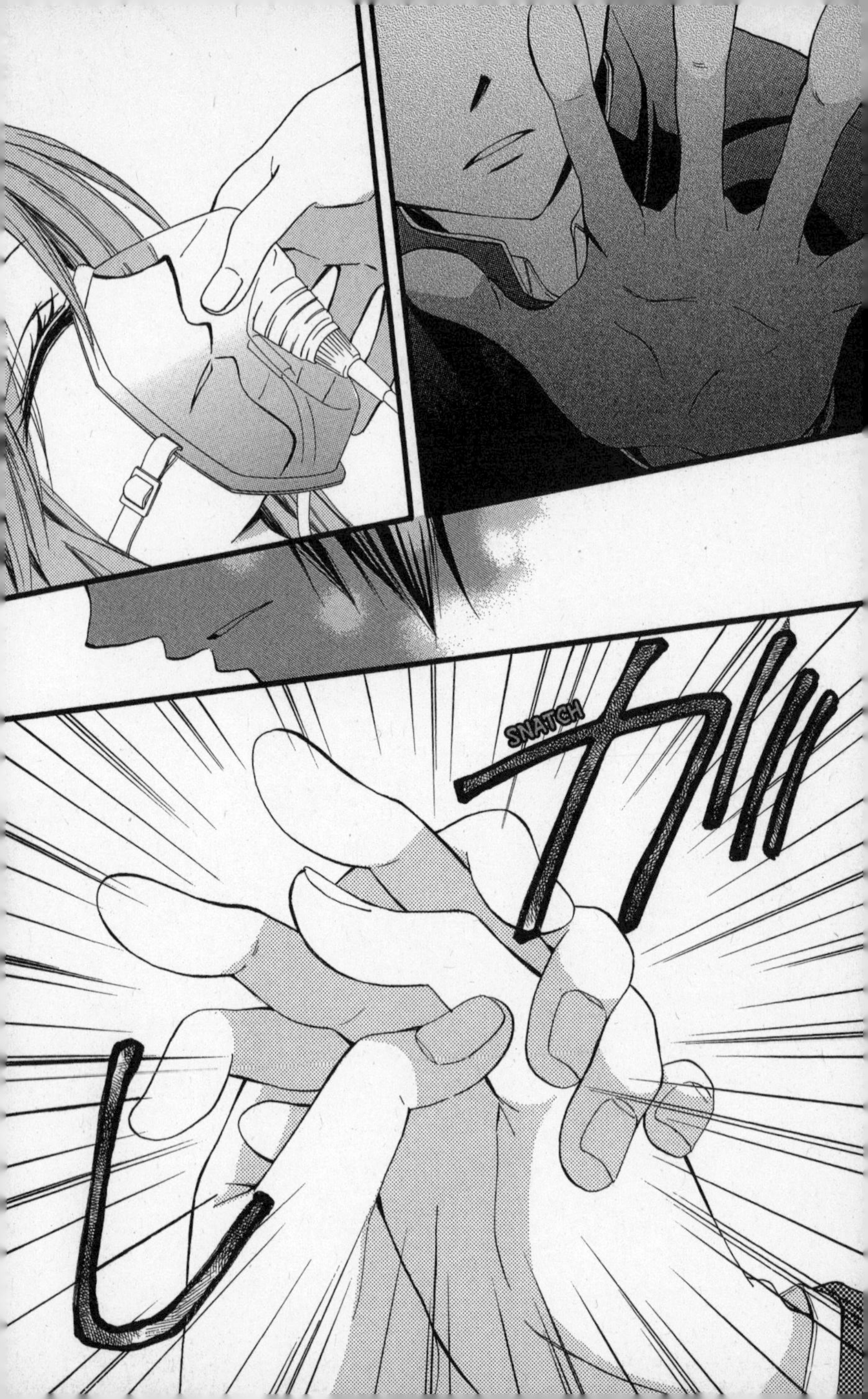
SNATCH

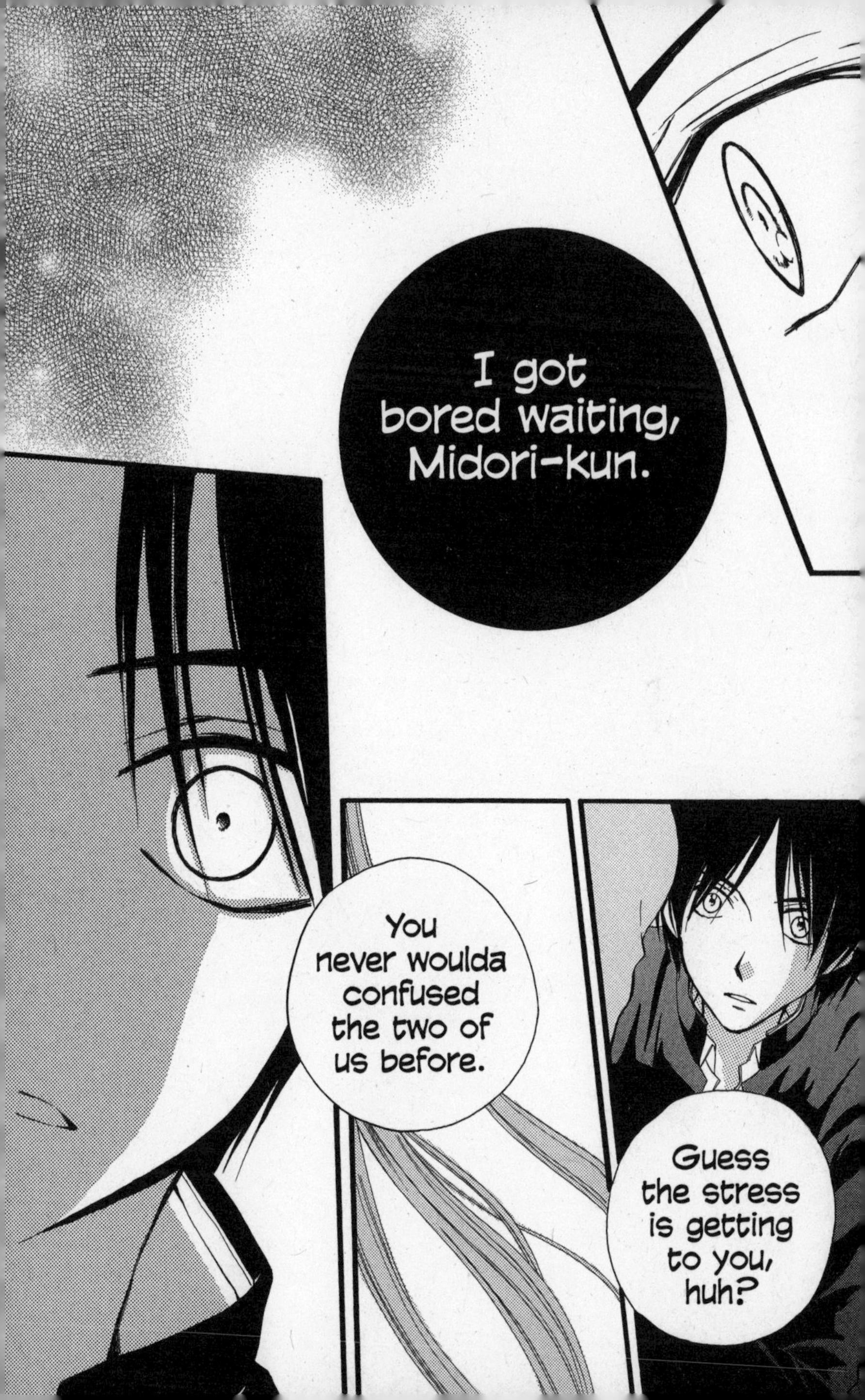
I got bored waiting, Midori-kun.
You never woulda confused the two of us before.
Guess the stress is getting to you, huh?

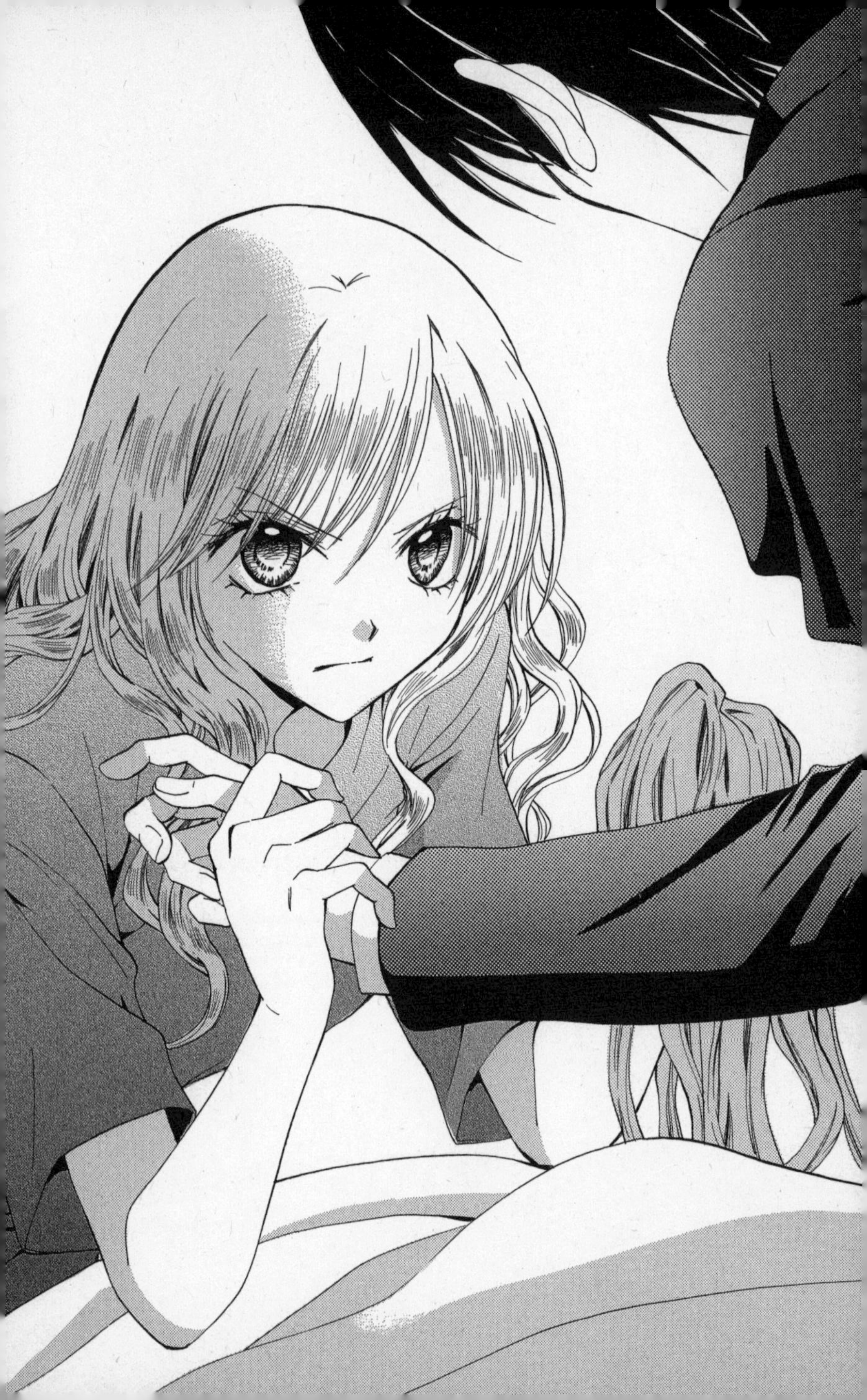

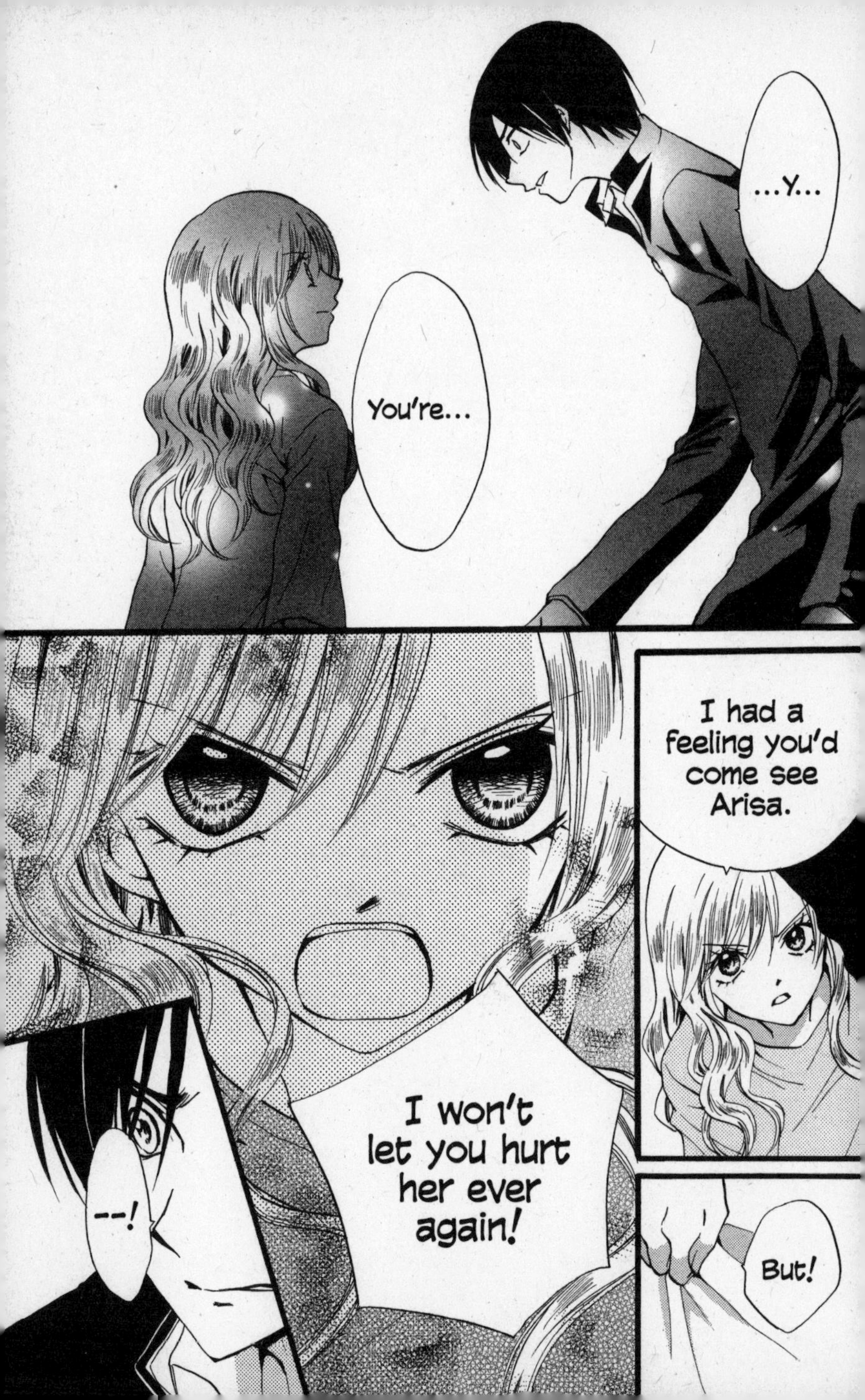
...Y...
You're...
I had a feeling you'd come see Arisa.
But!
I won't let you hurt her ever again!
--!

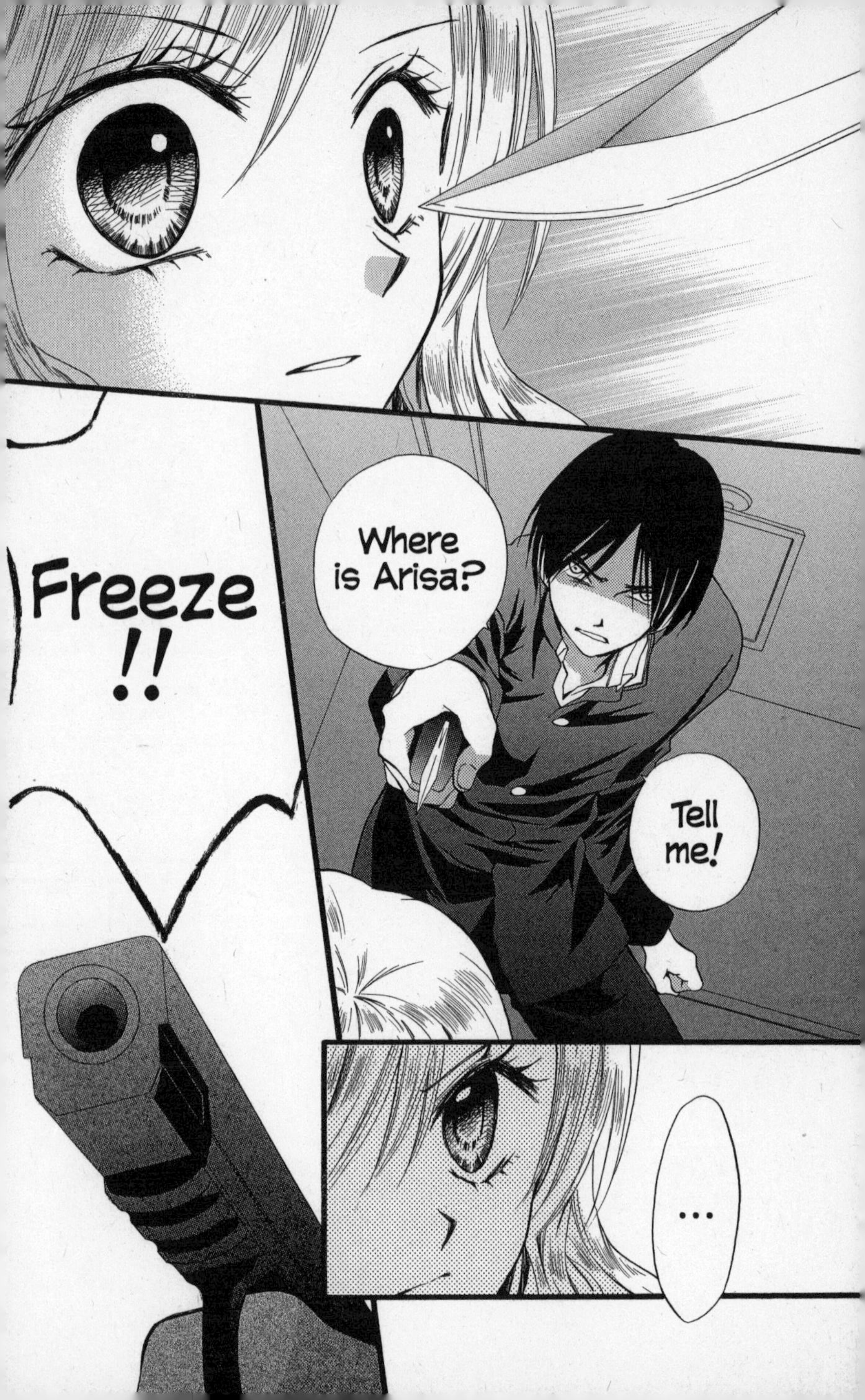
Where is Arisa?
Tell me!
...
Freeze!!

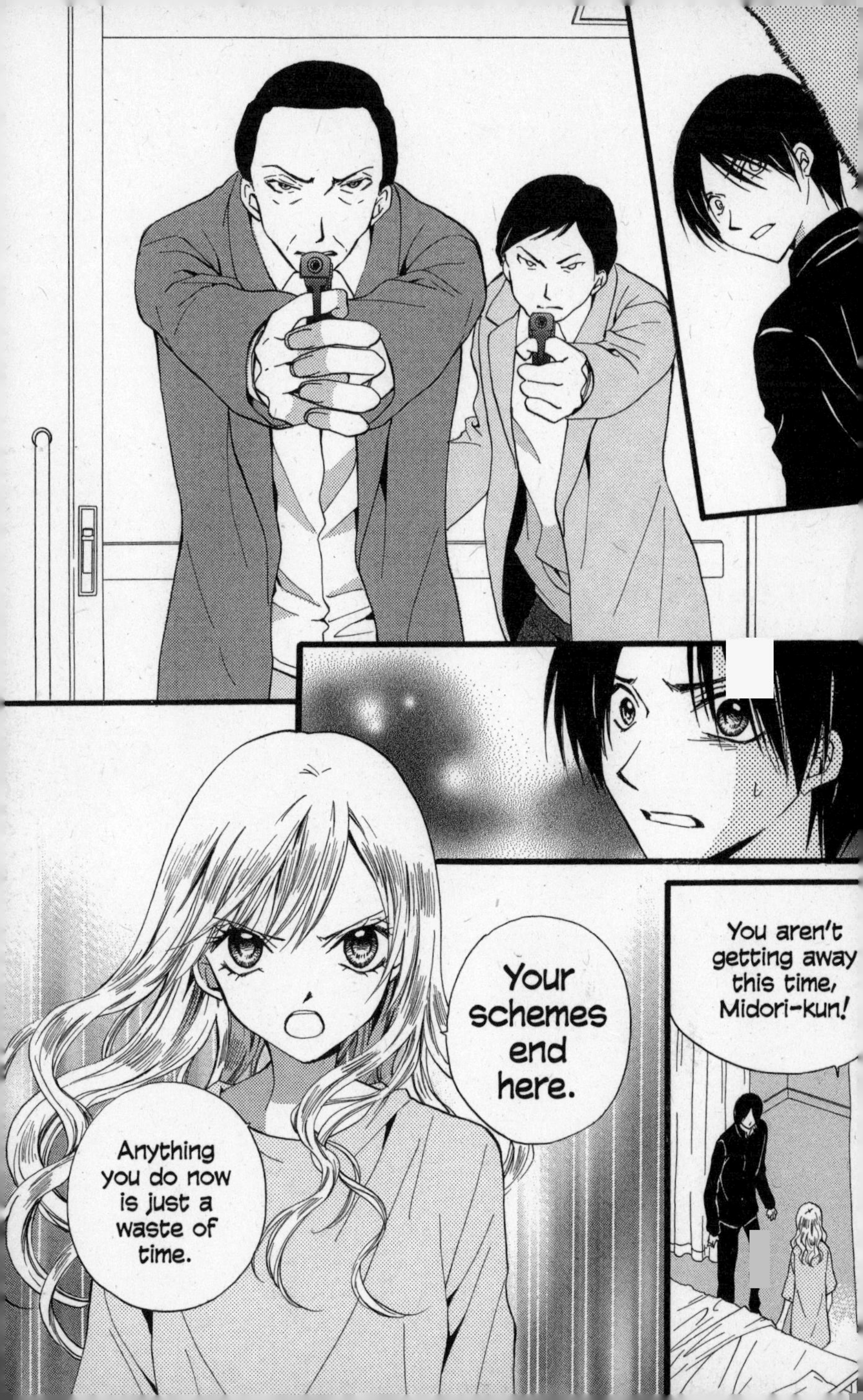
You aren't getting away this time, Midori-kun!
Your schemes end here.
Anything you do now is just a waste of time.

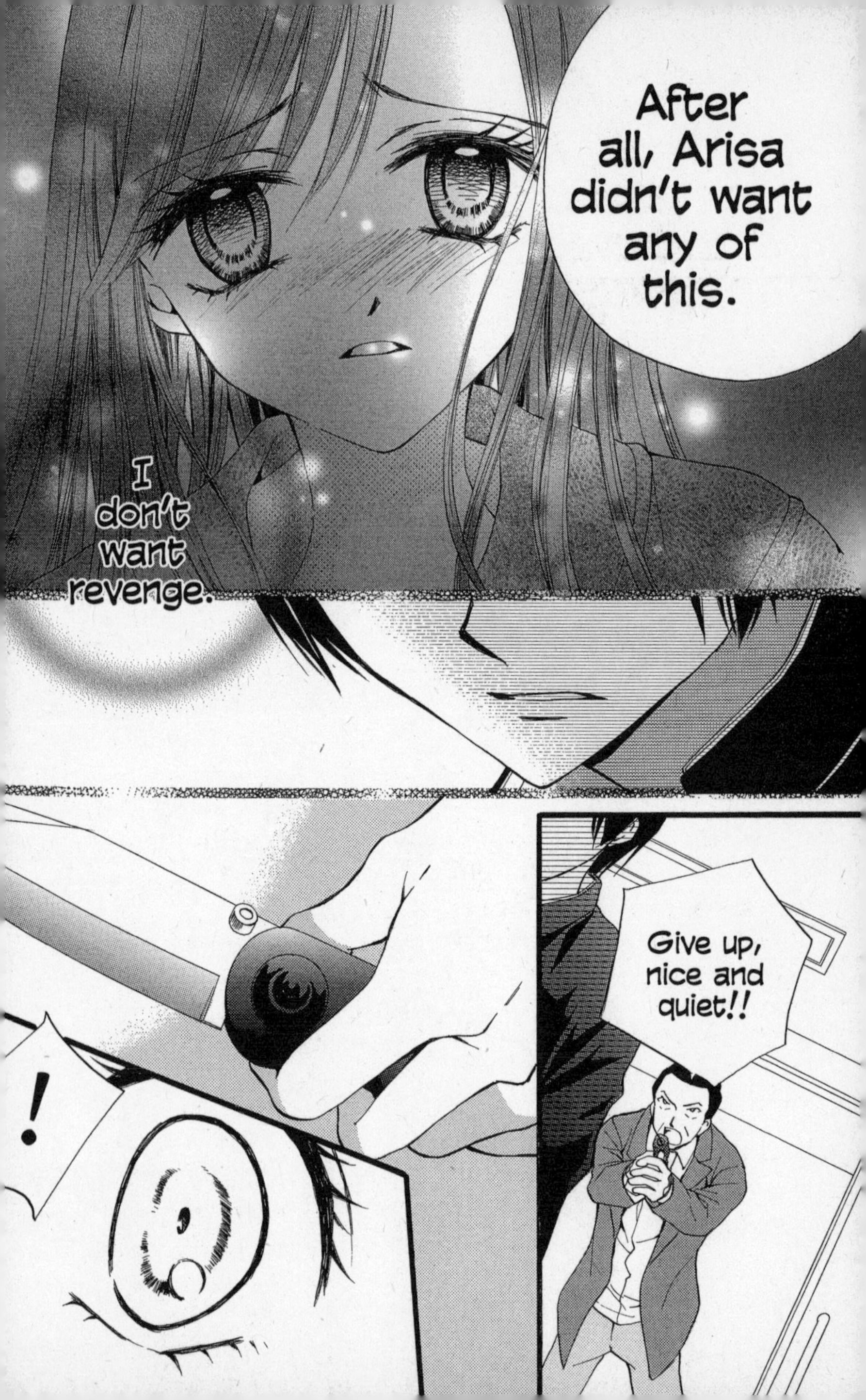
After all, Arisa didn't want any of this.
I don't want revenge.
Give up, nice and quiet!!
!

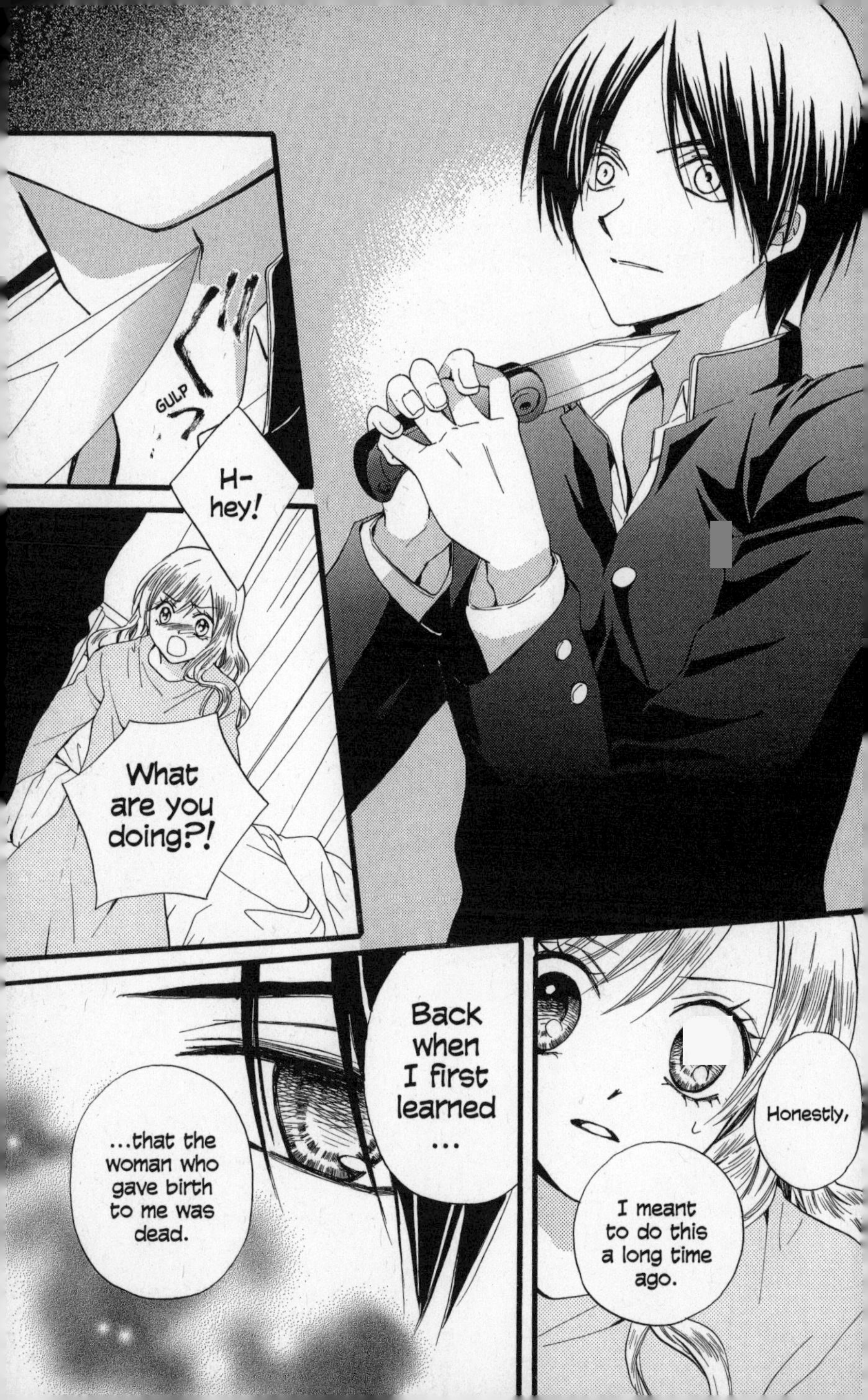
GULP
H-hey!
What are you doing?!
Honestly,
I meant to do this a long time ago.
Back when I first learned...
...that the woman who gave birth to me was dead.

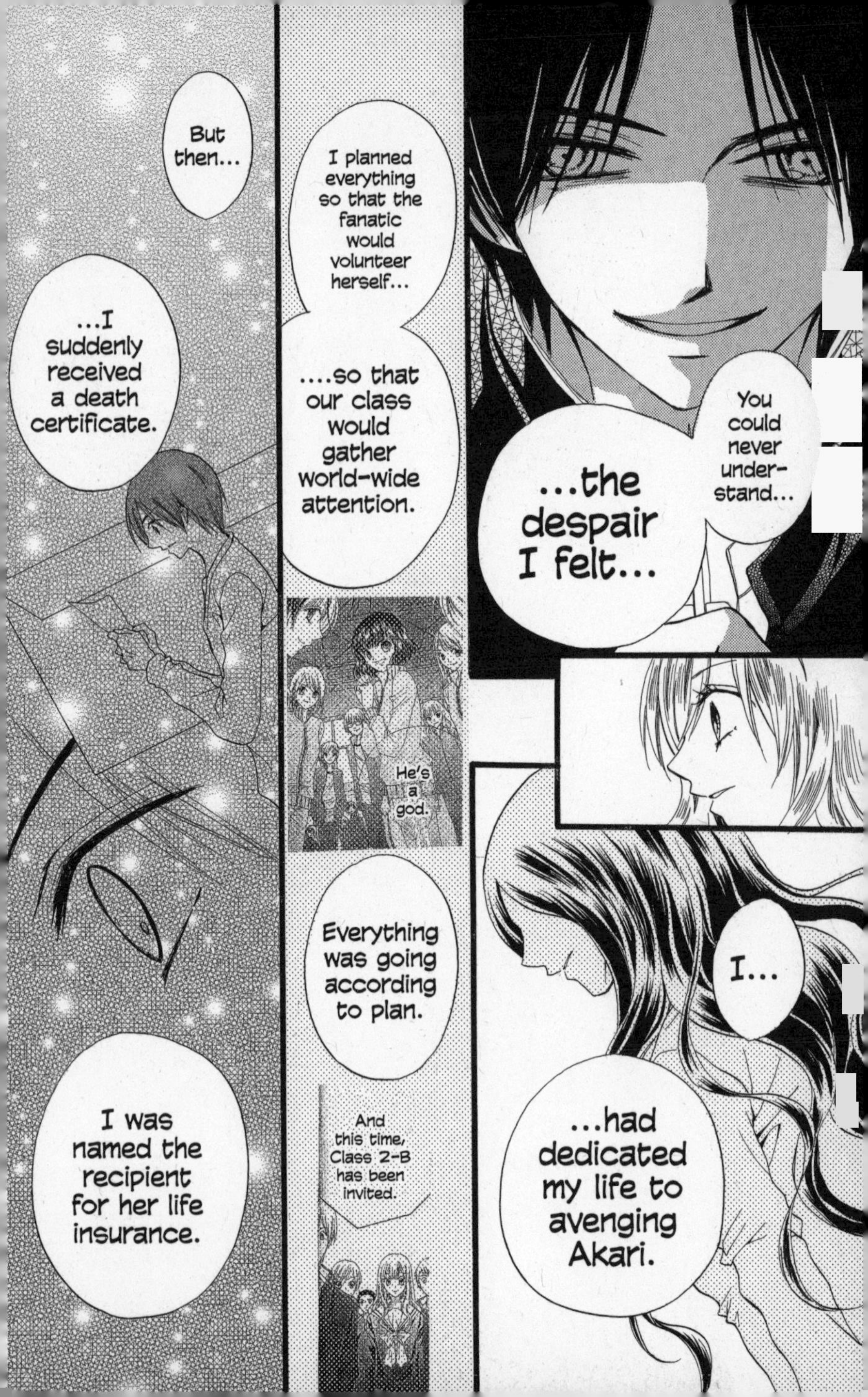
You could never under-stand...
...the despair I felt...
I...
...had dedicated my life to avenging Akari.
I planned everything so that the fanatic would volunteer herself...
....so that our class would gather world-wide attention.
He's a god.
Everything was going according to plan.
And this time, Class 2-B has been invited.
But then...
...I suddenly received a death certificate.
I was named the recipient for her life insurance.

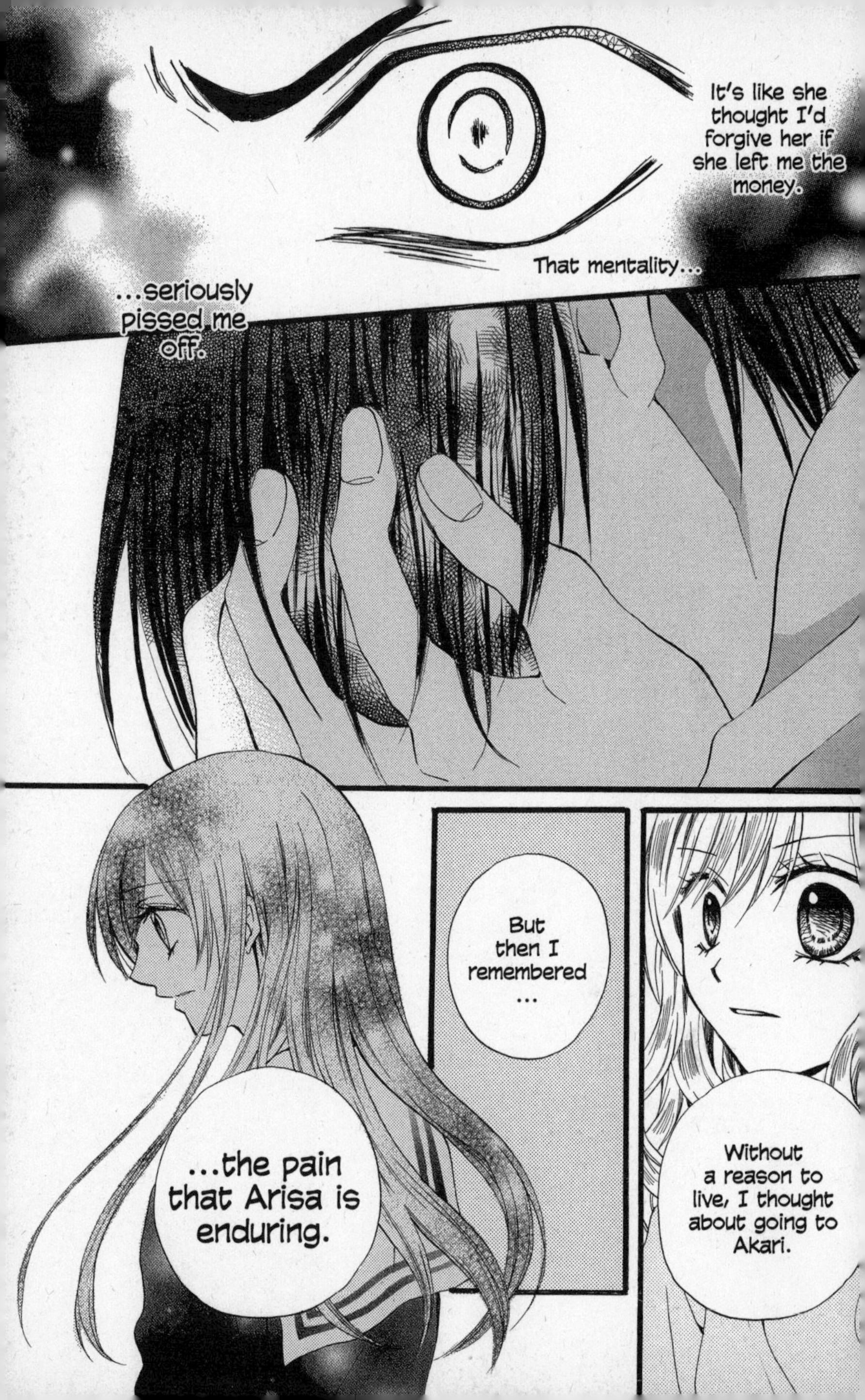
It's like she thought I'd forgive her if she left me the money.
That mentality...
...seriously pissed me off.
Without a reason to live, I thought about going to Akari.
But then I remembered ...
...the pain that Arisa is enduring.

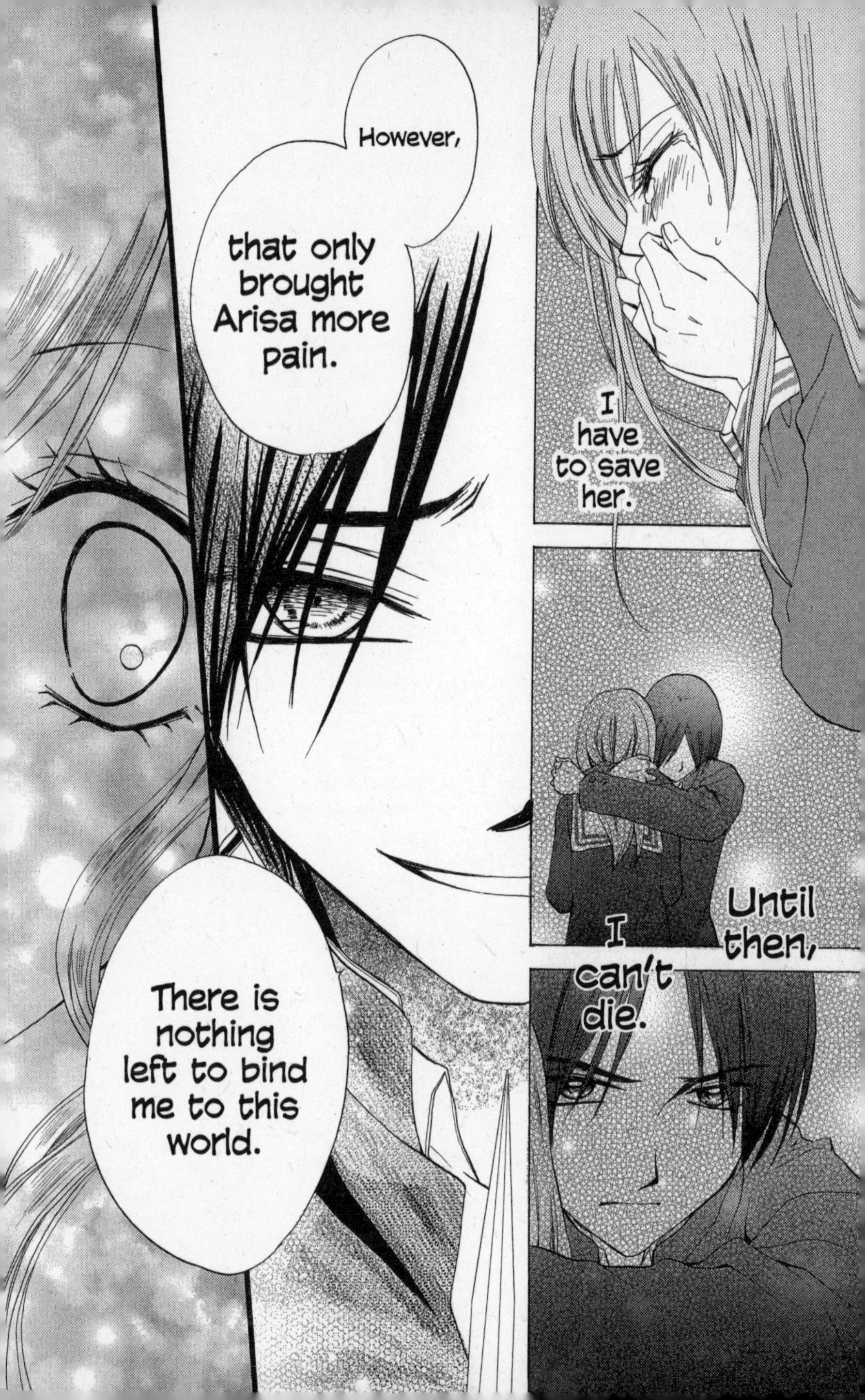
I have to save her.
Until then,
I can't die.
However,
that only brought Arisa more pain.
There is nothing left to bind me to this world.

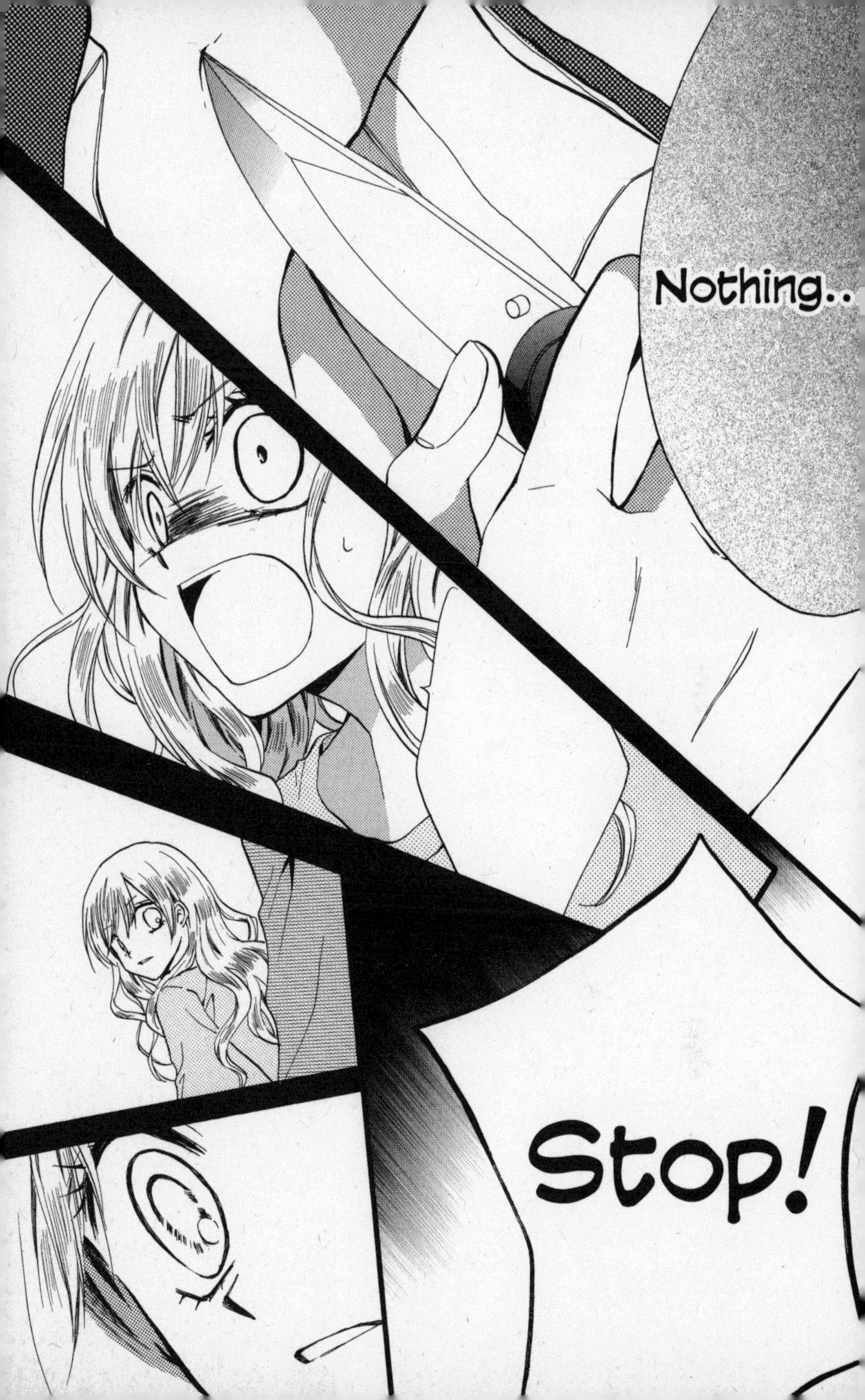
Nothing..
Stop!

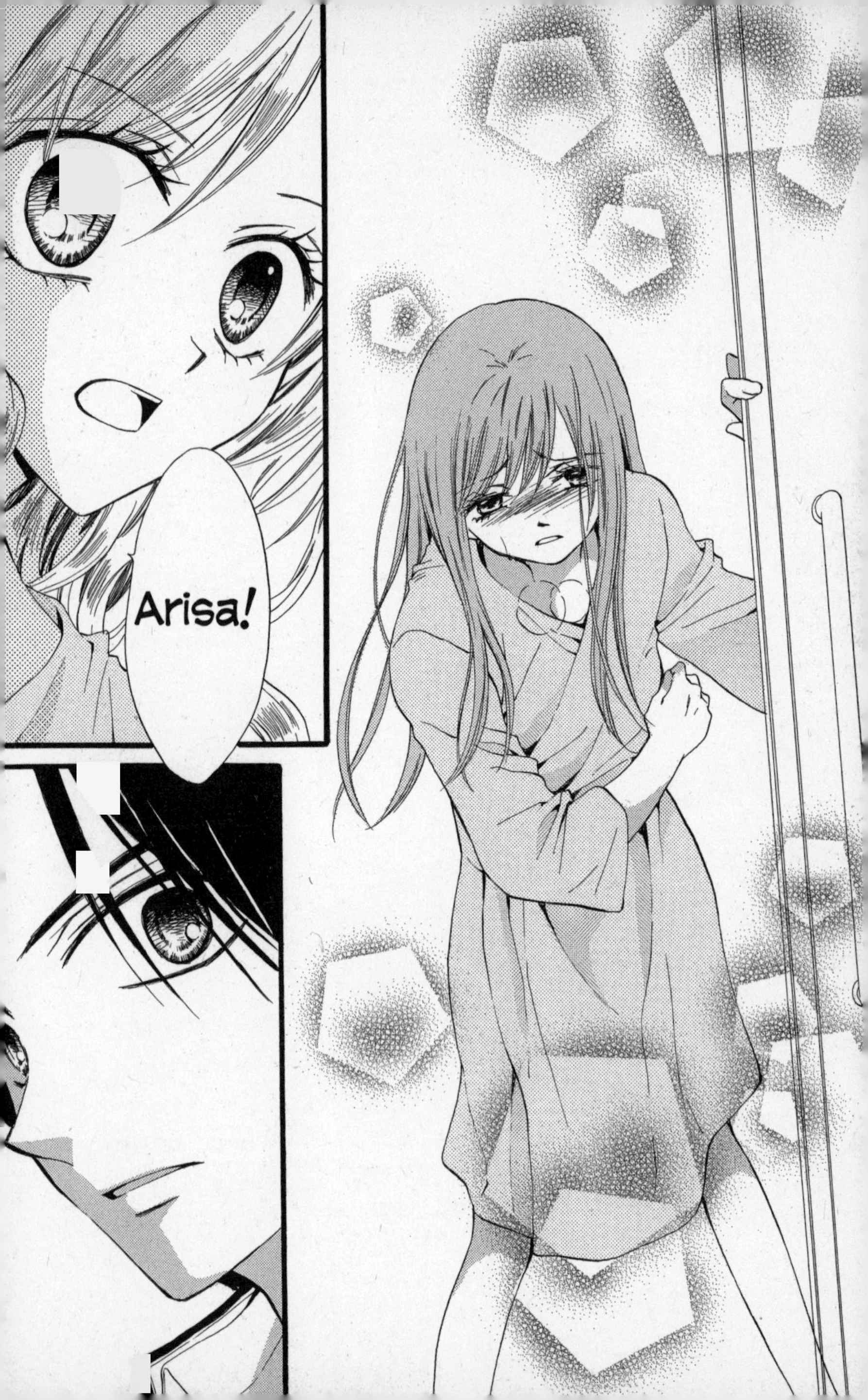
Arisa!

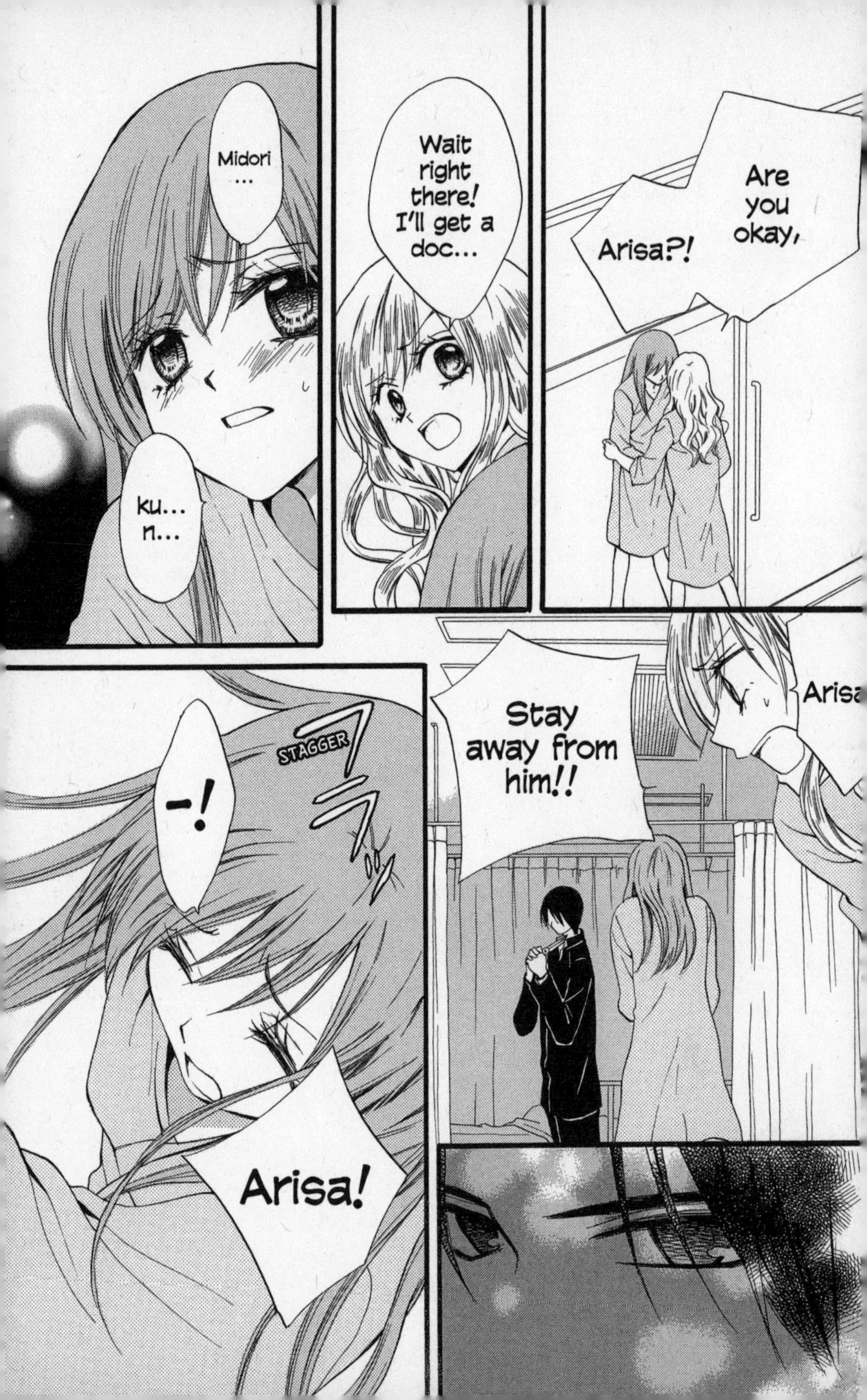
Are you okay, Arisa?!
Wait right there! I'll get a doc...
Midori...
ku...n...
Arisa
Stay away from him!!
STAGGER
–!
Arisa!

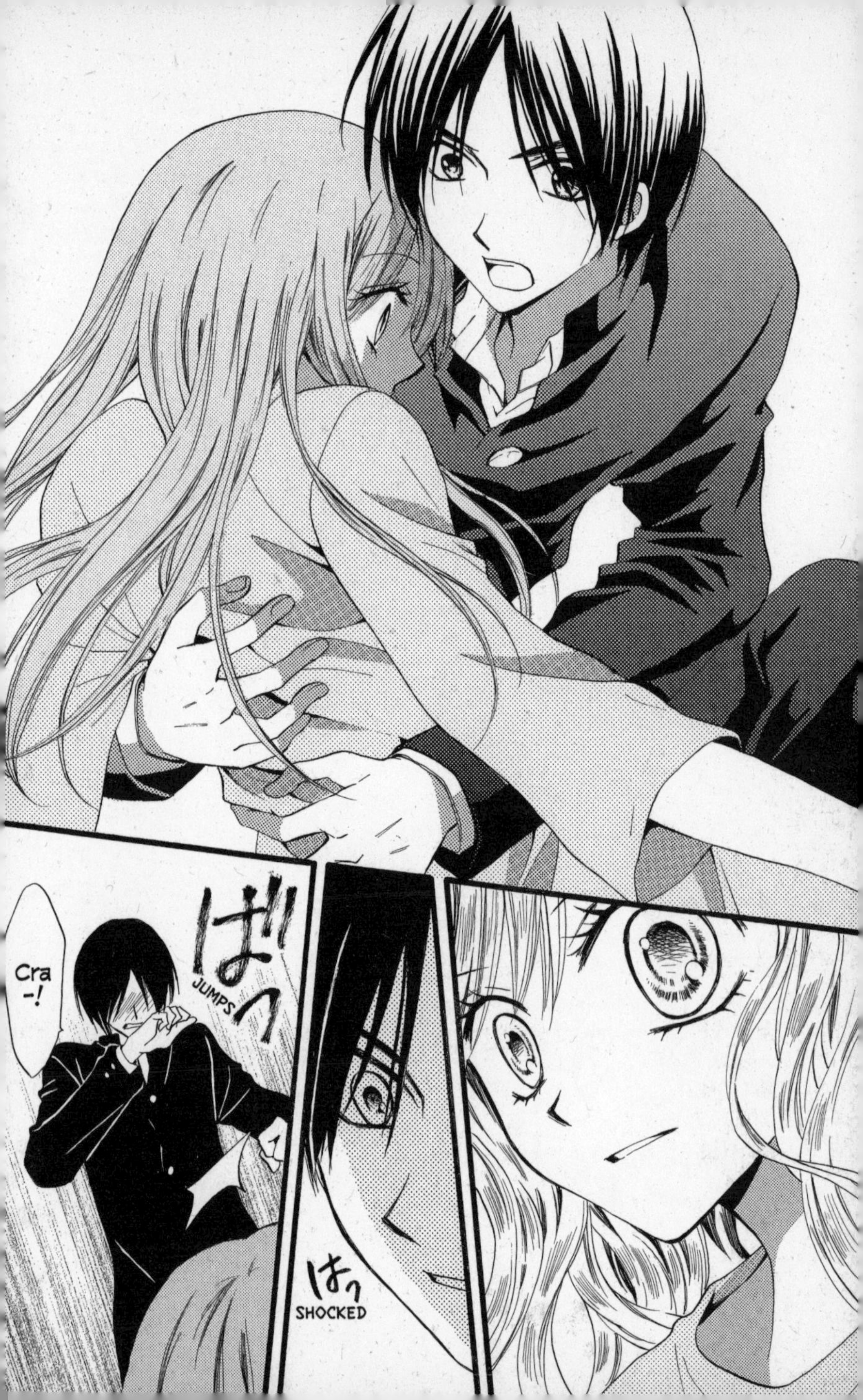
はっ
SHOCKED
ばっ
JUMPS
Cra -!

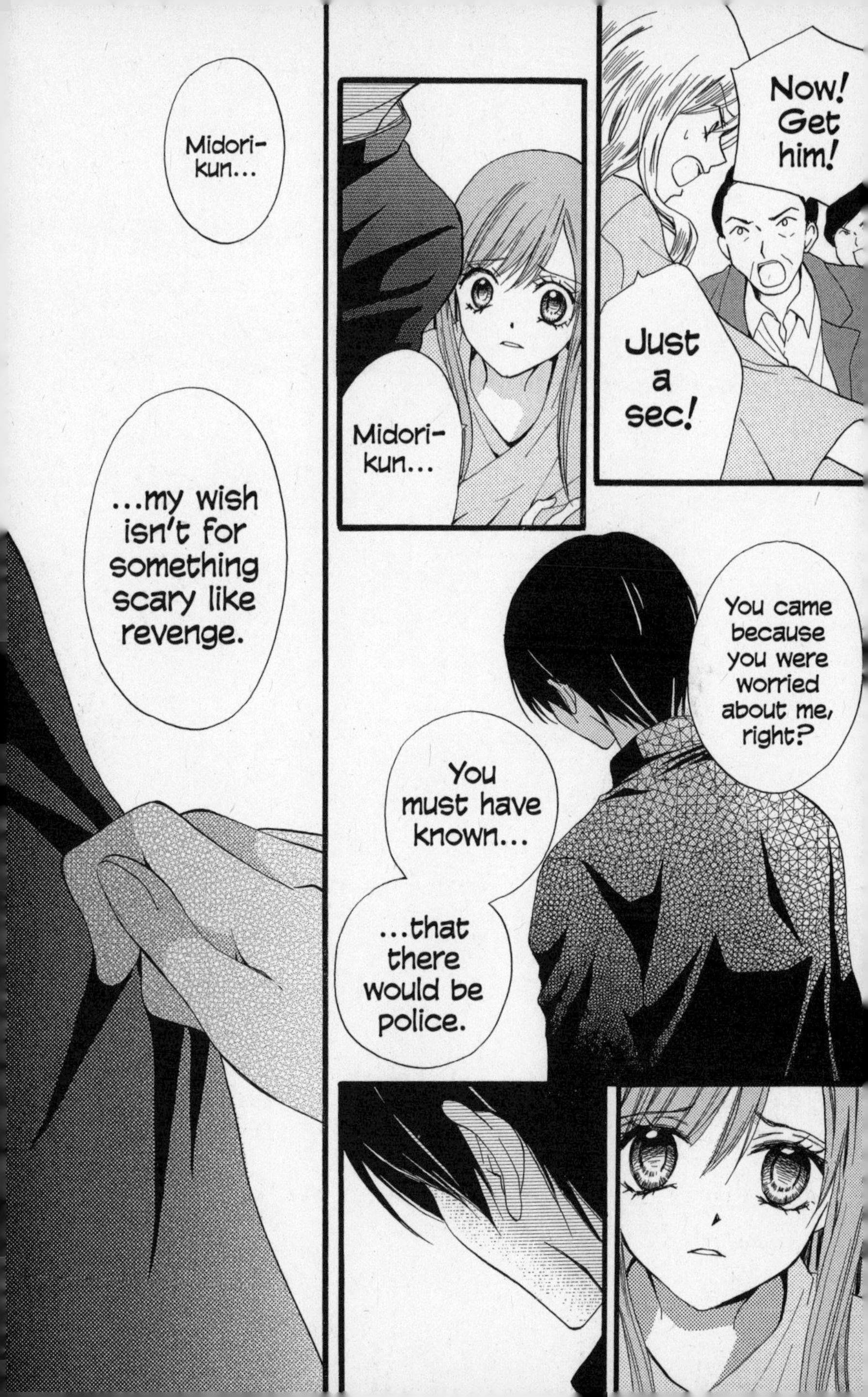
Now! Get him!
Just a sec!
Midori-kun...
You came because you were worried about me, right?
You must have known...
...that there would be police.
Midori-kun...
...my wish isn't for something scary like revenge.

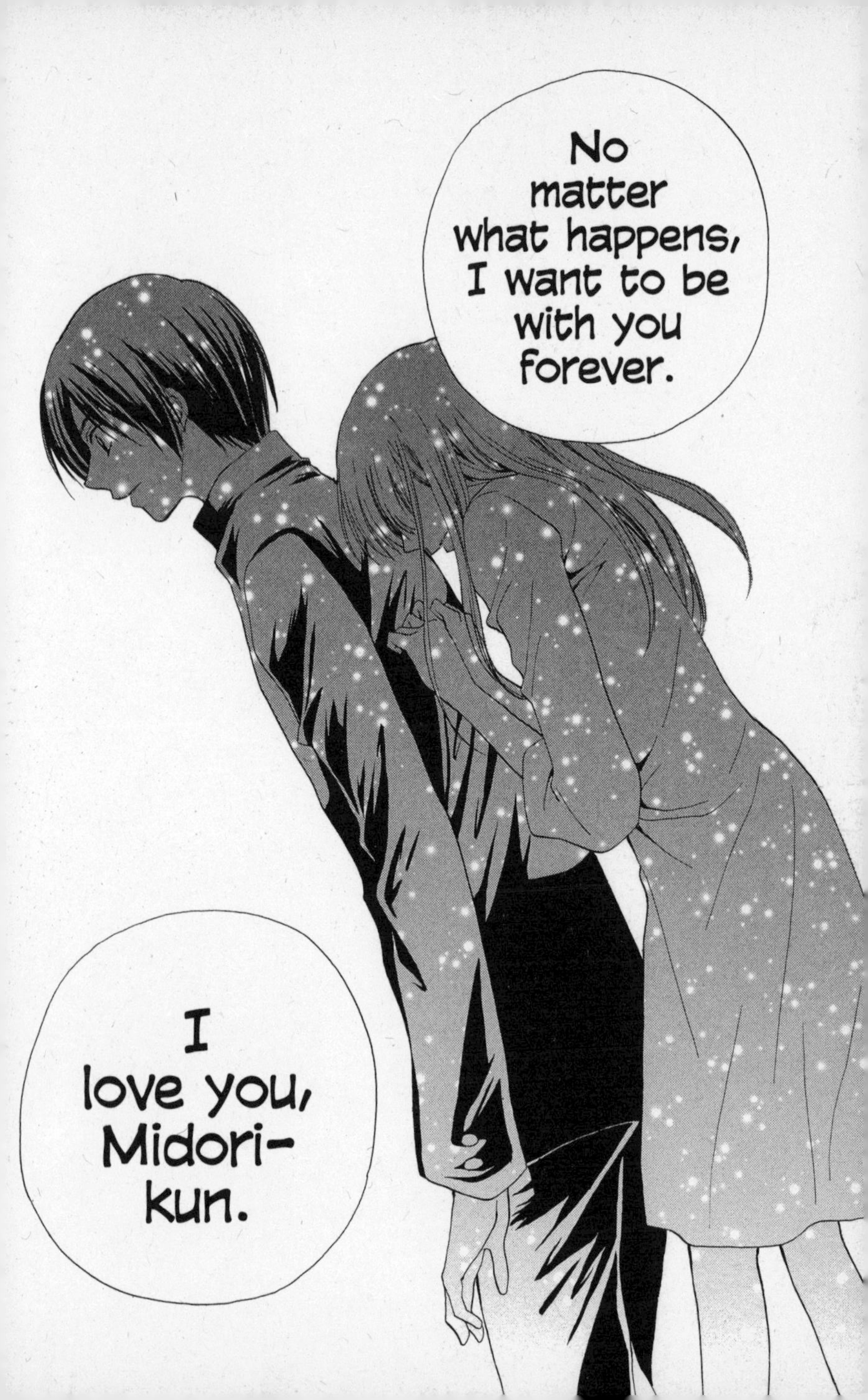
No matter what happens, I want to be with you forever.
I love you, Midori-kun.

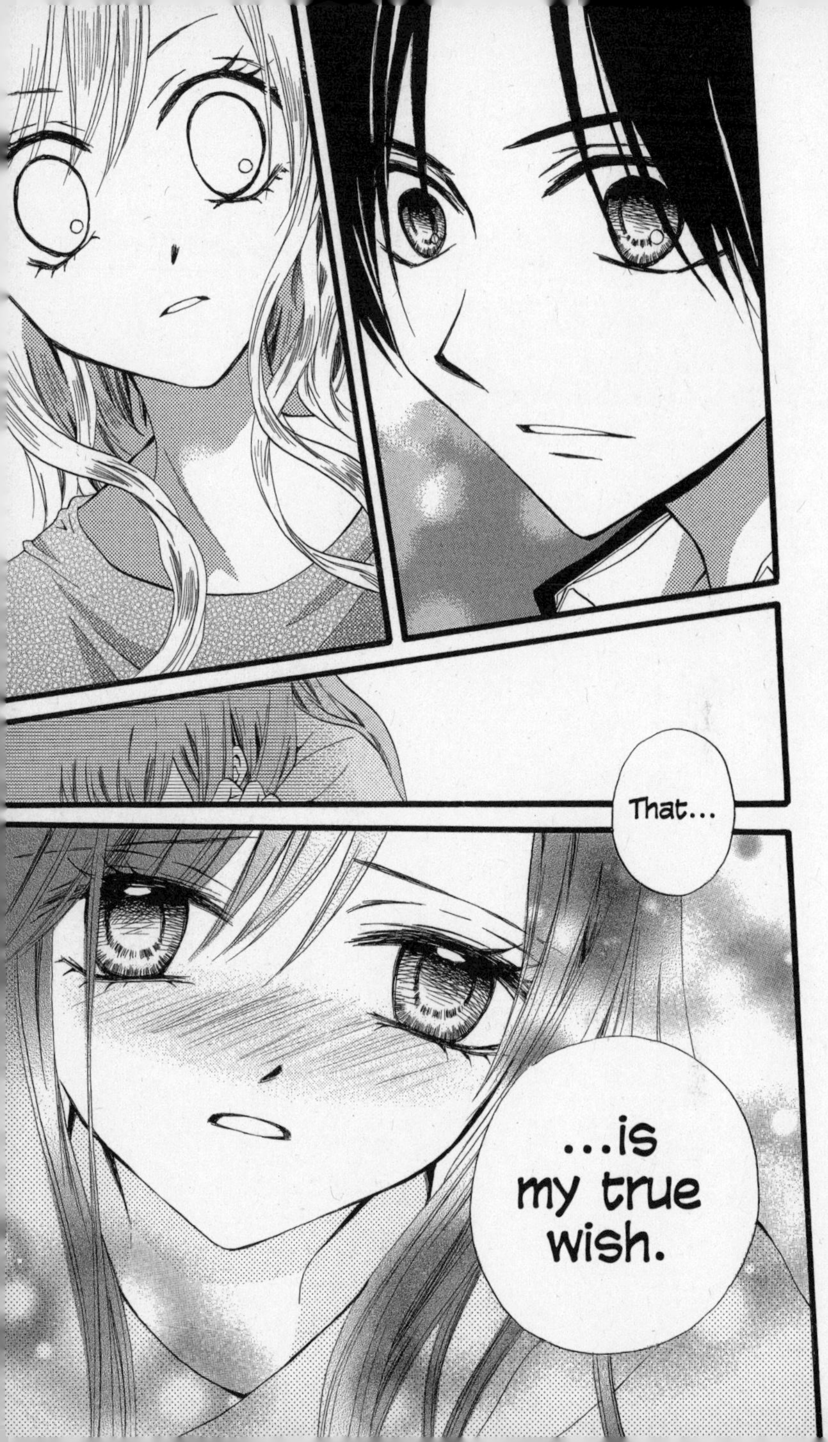
That...
...is my true wish.

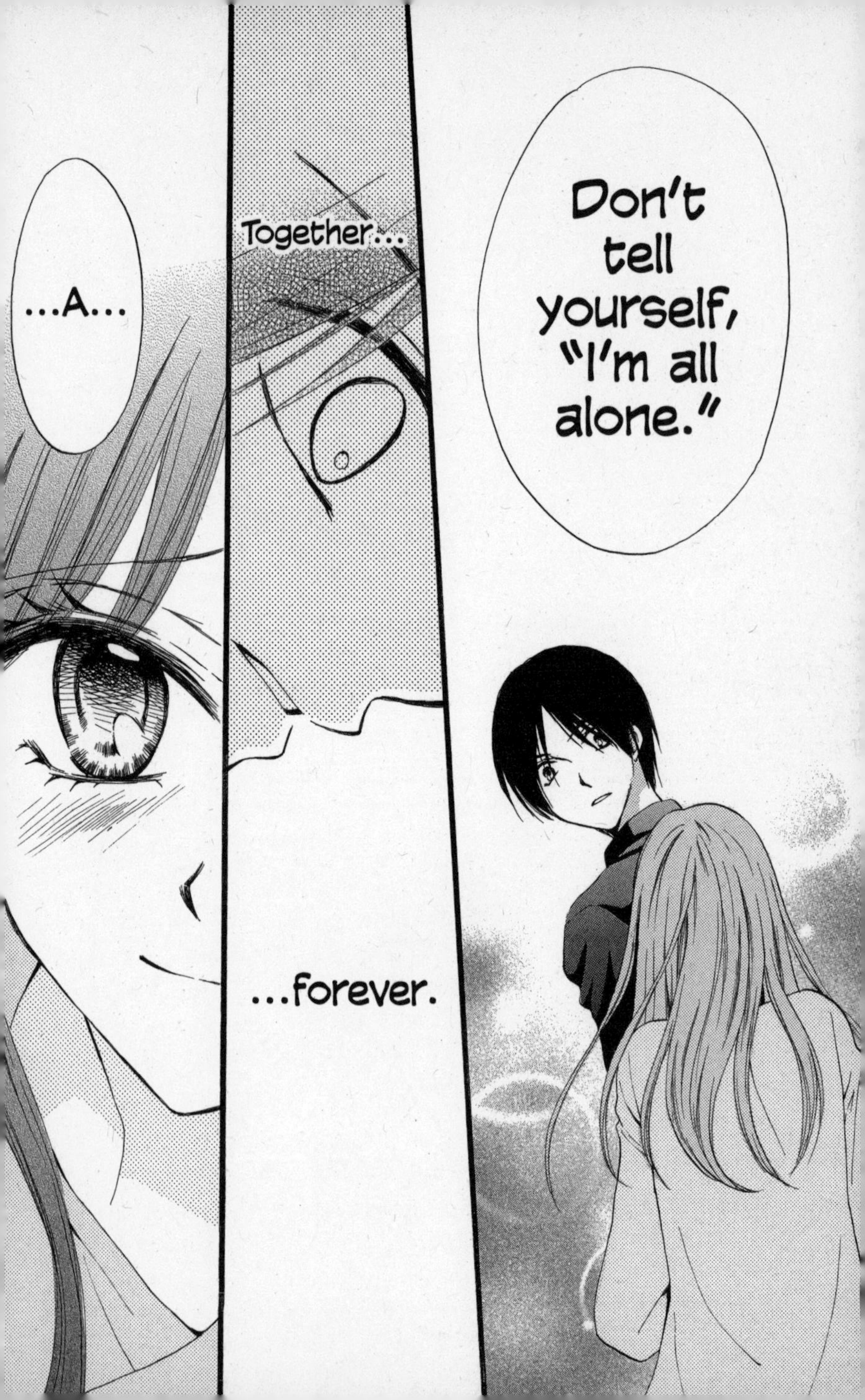
Don't tell yourself, "I'm all alone."
Together...
...forever.
...A...

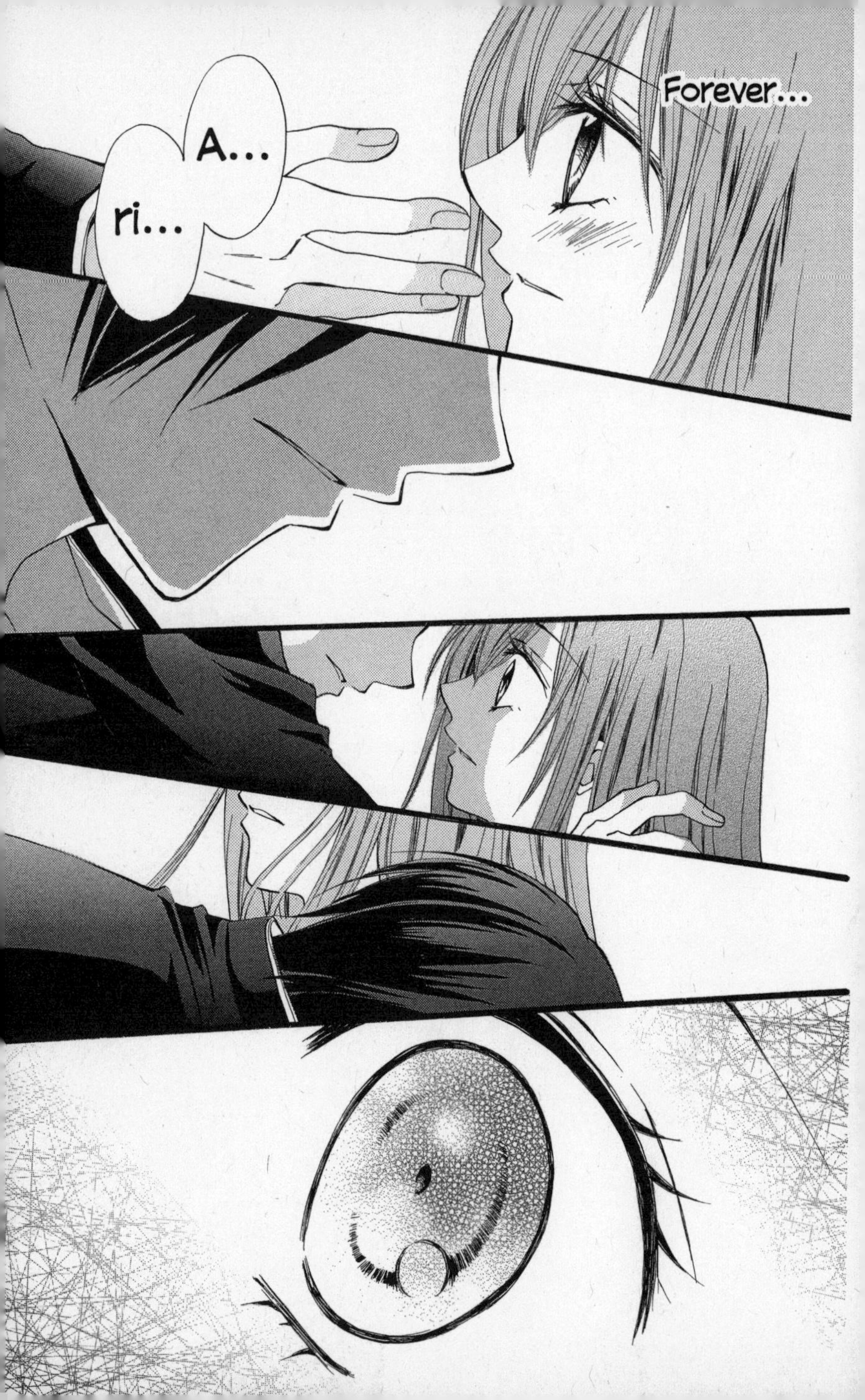
Forever...
A...
ri...

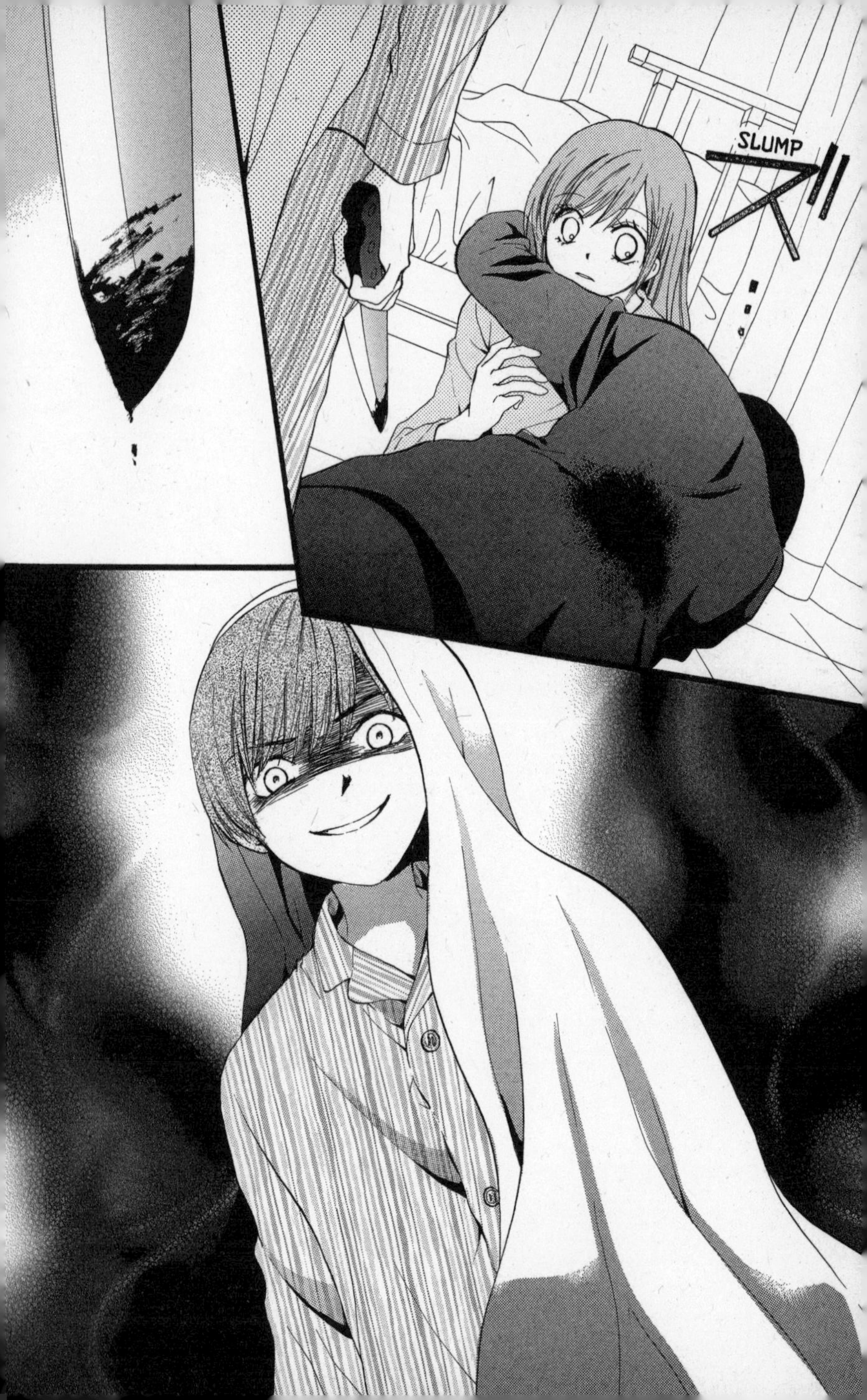
SLUMP

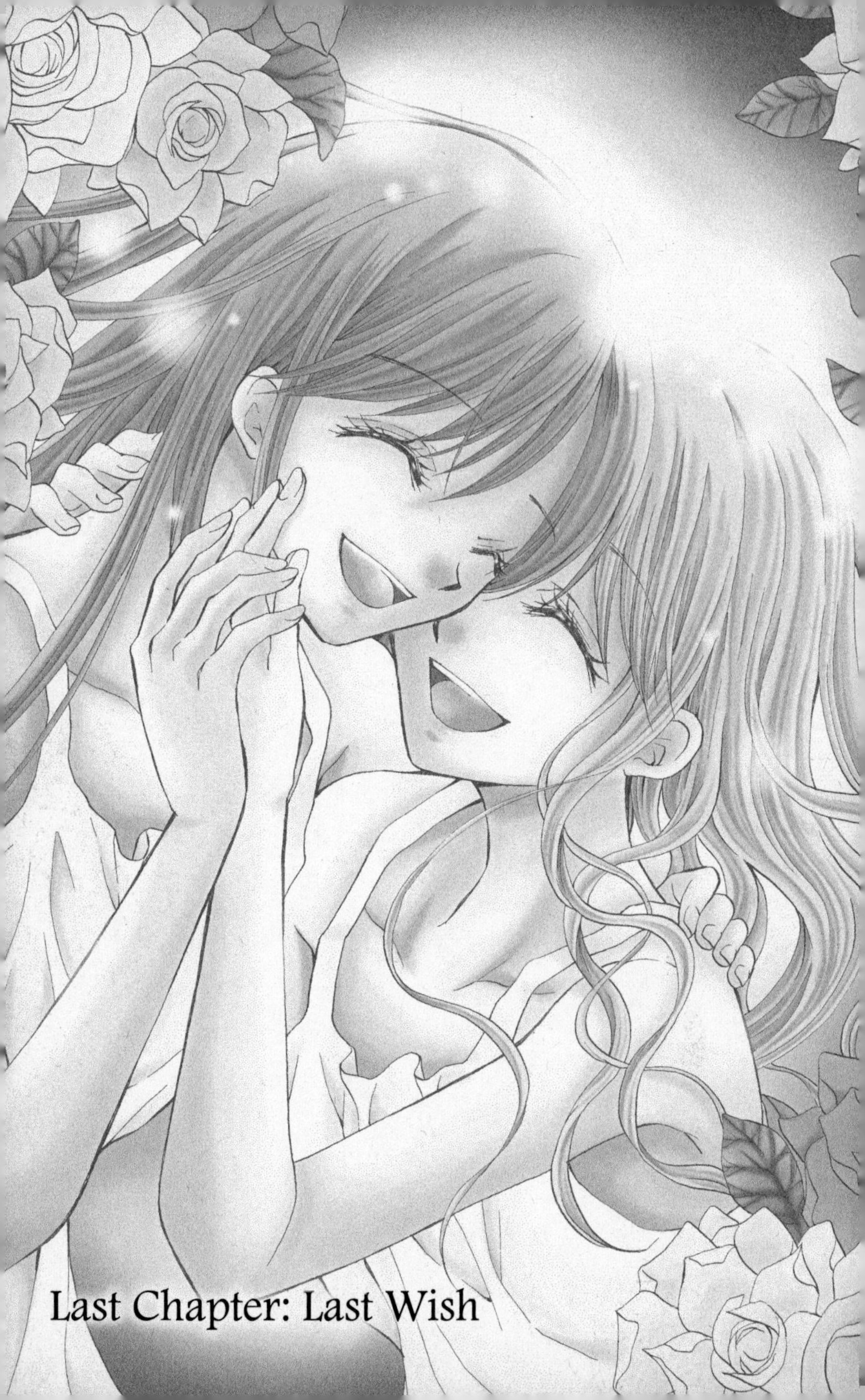

Last Chapter: Last Wish

ARISA

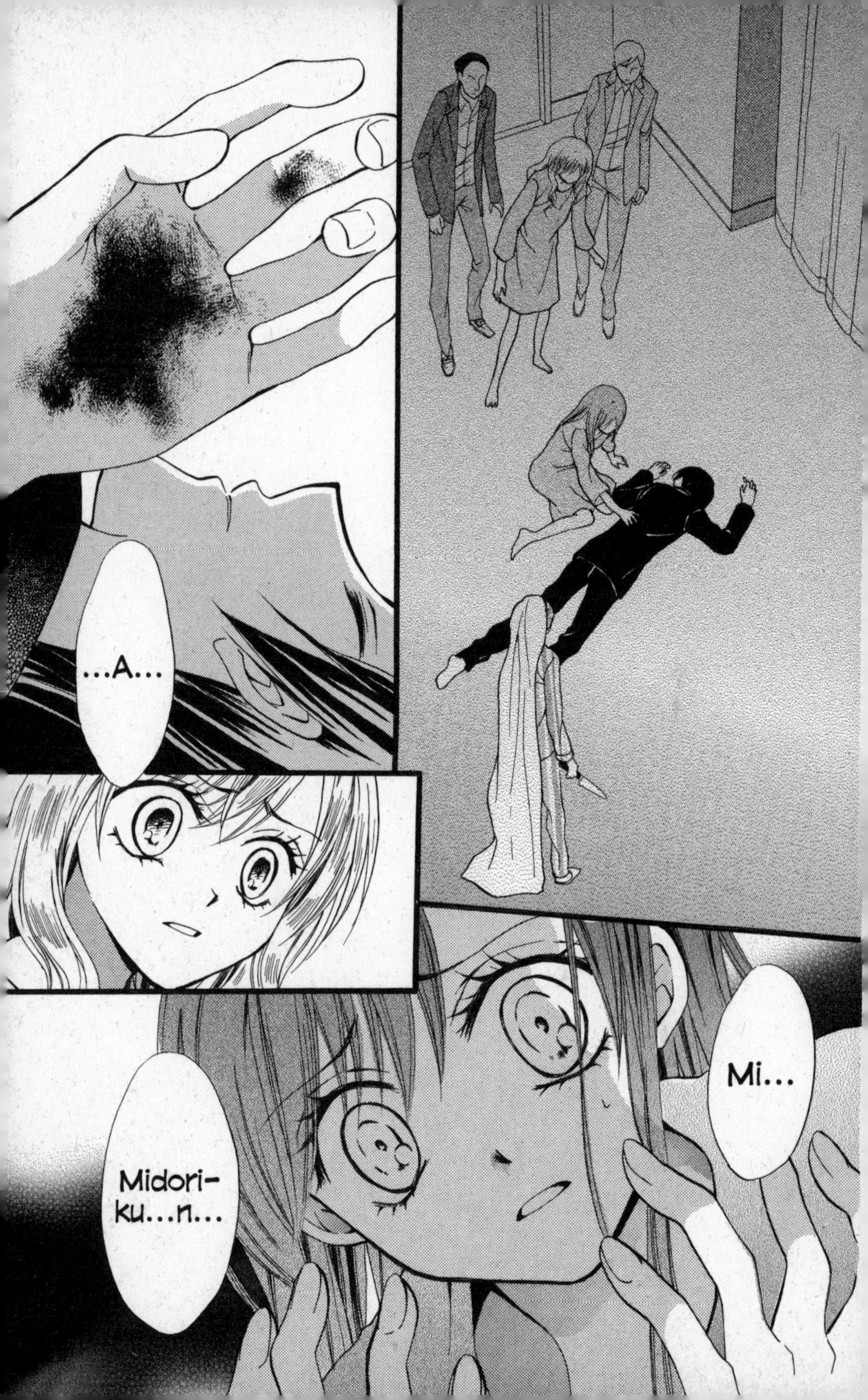
...A...
Mi...
Midori-ku...n...

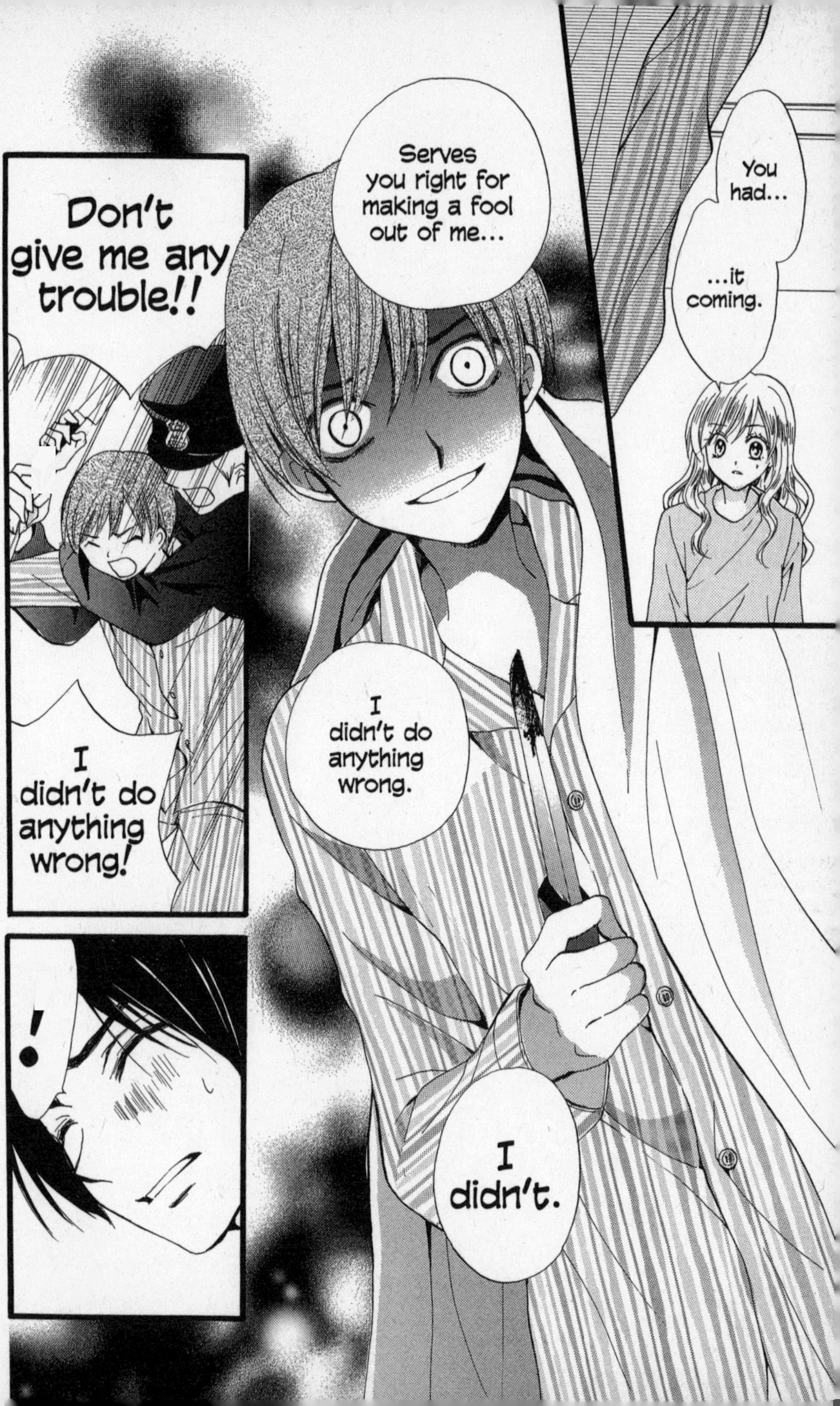
You had...
...it coming.
Serves you right for making a fool out of me...
I didn't do anything wrong.
I didn't.
Don't give me any trouble!!
I didn't do anything wrong!
!

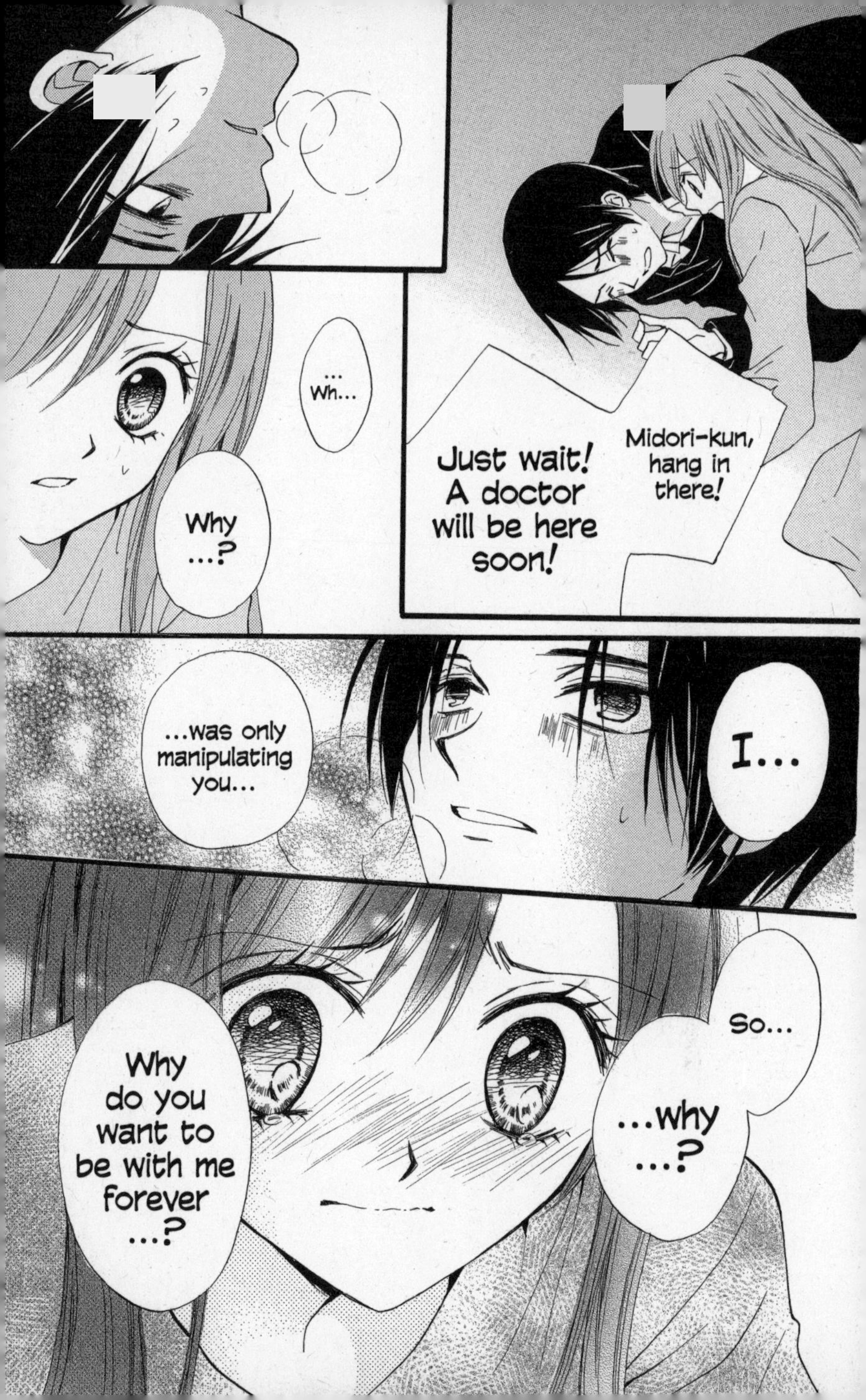
Midori-kun, hang in there!
Just wait! A doctor will be here soon!
... Wh...
Why ...?
I...
...was only manipulating you...
So...
...why ...?
Why do you want to be with me forever ...?

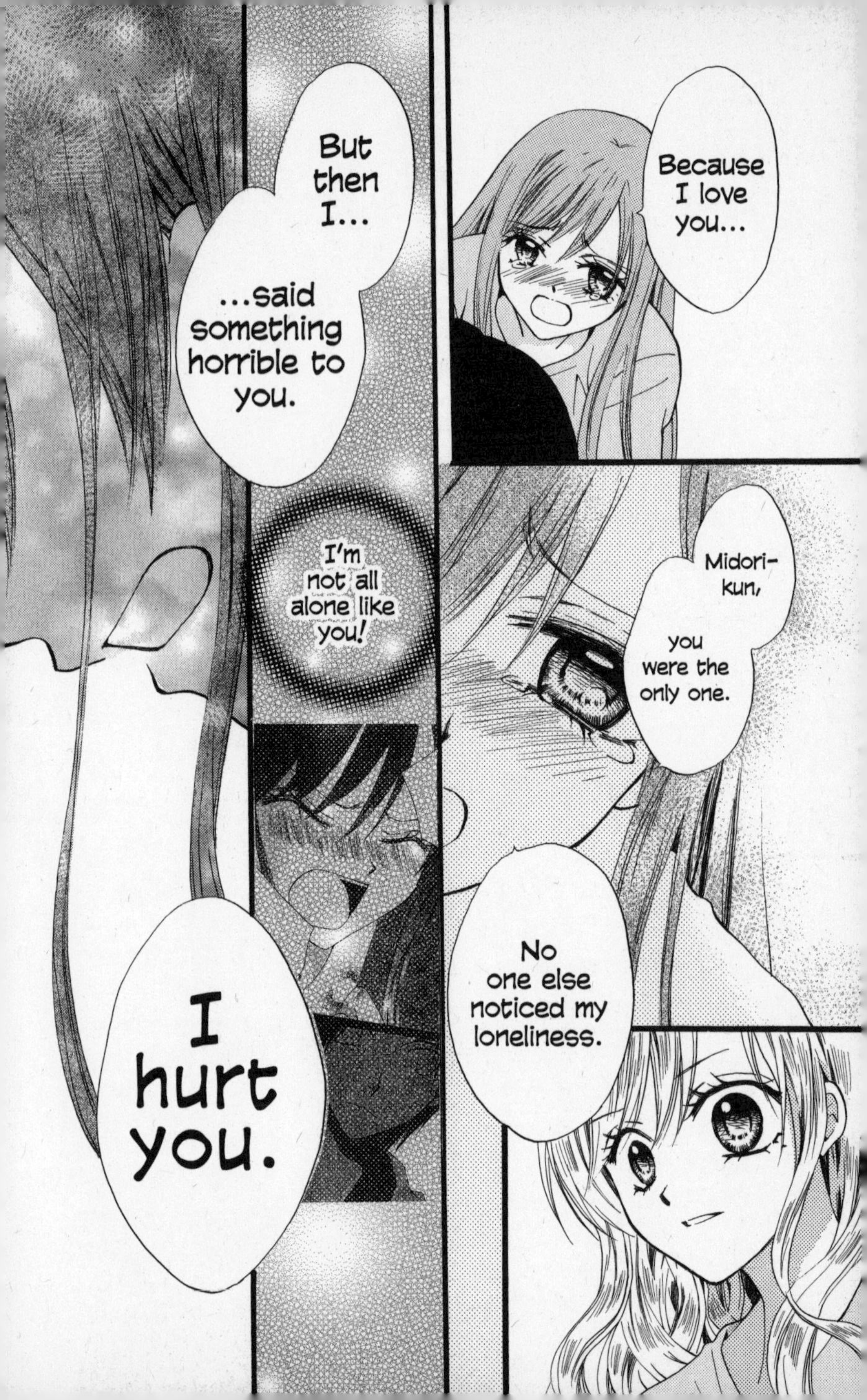
Because I love you...
Midori-kun,
you were the only one.
No one else noticed my loneliness.
But then I...
...said something horrible to you.
I'm not all alone like you!
I hurt you.

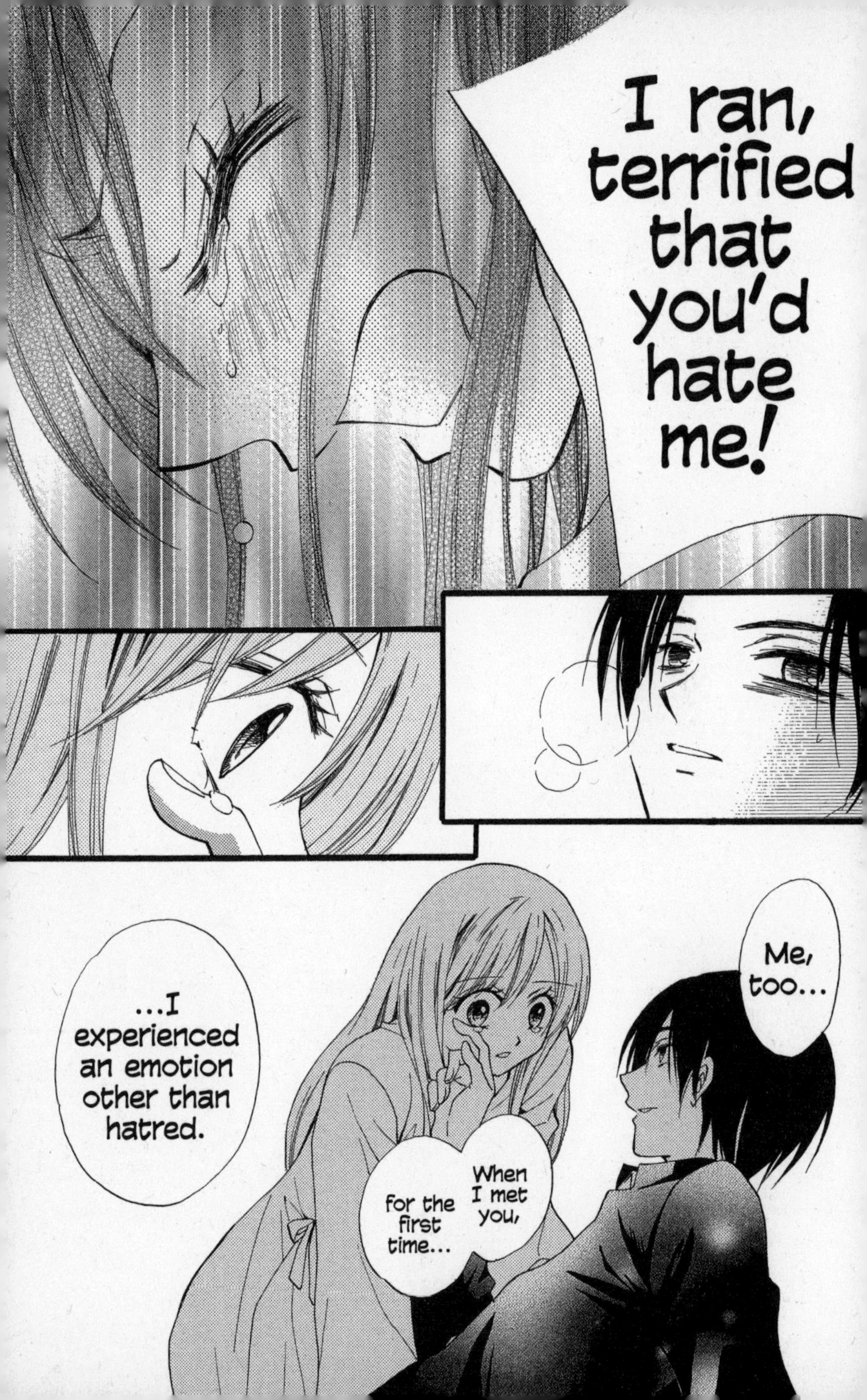
I ran, terrified that you'd hate me!
Me, too...
When I met you,
for the first time...
...I experienced an emotion other than hatred.

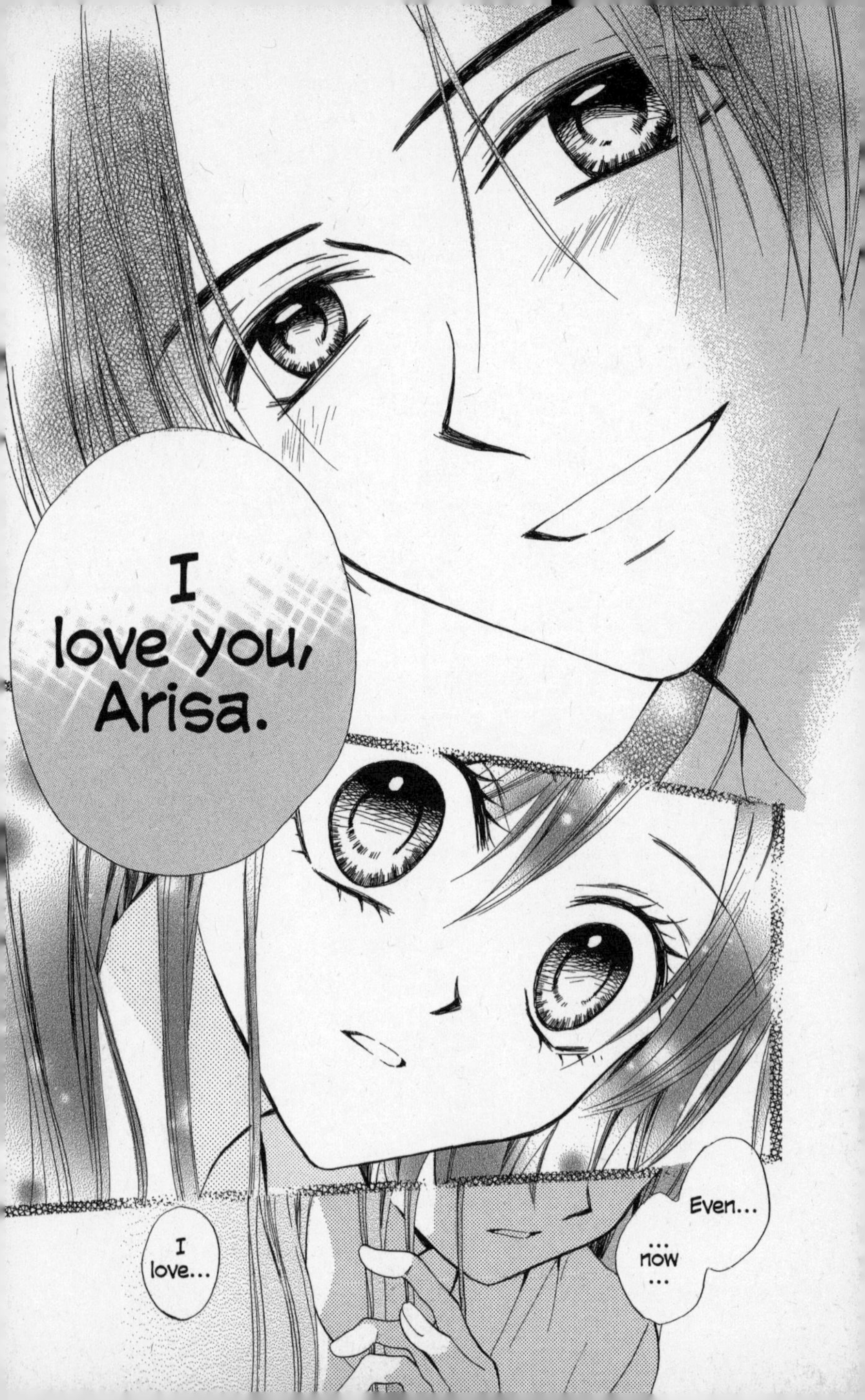
I love you, Arisa.
Even... ...now...
I love...

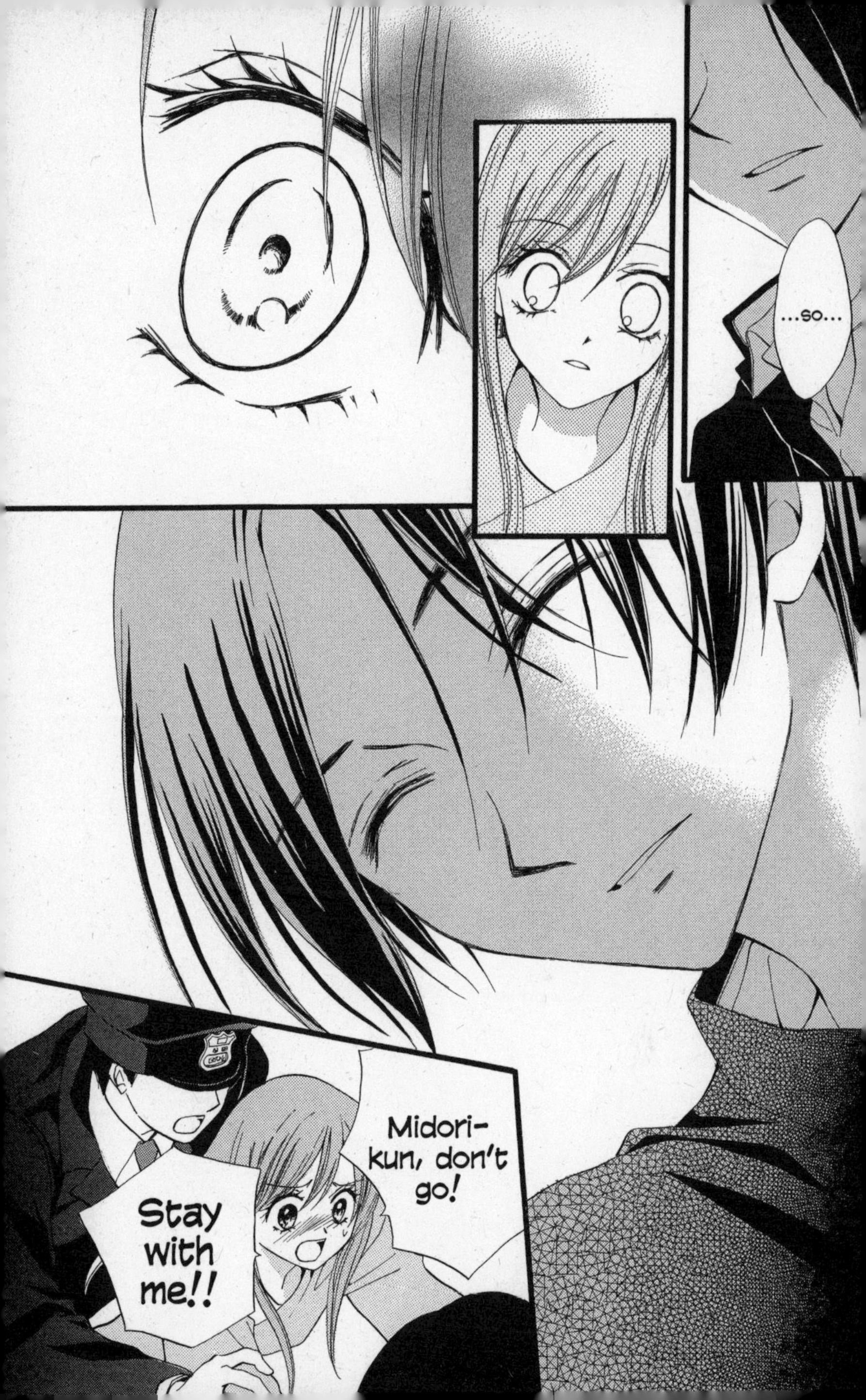
...so...
Midori-kun, don't go!
Stay with me!!

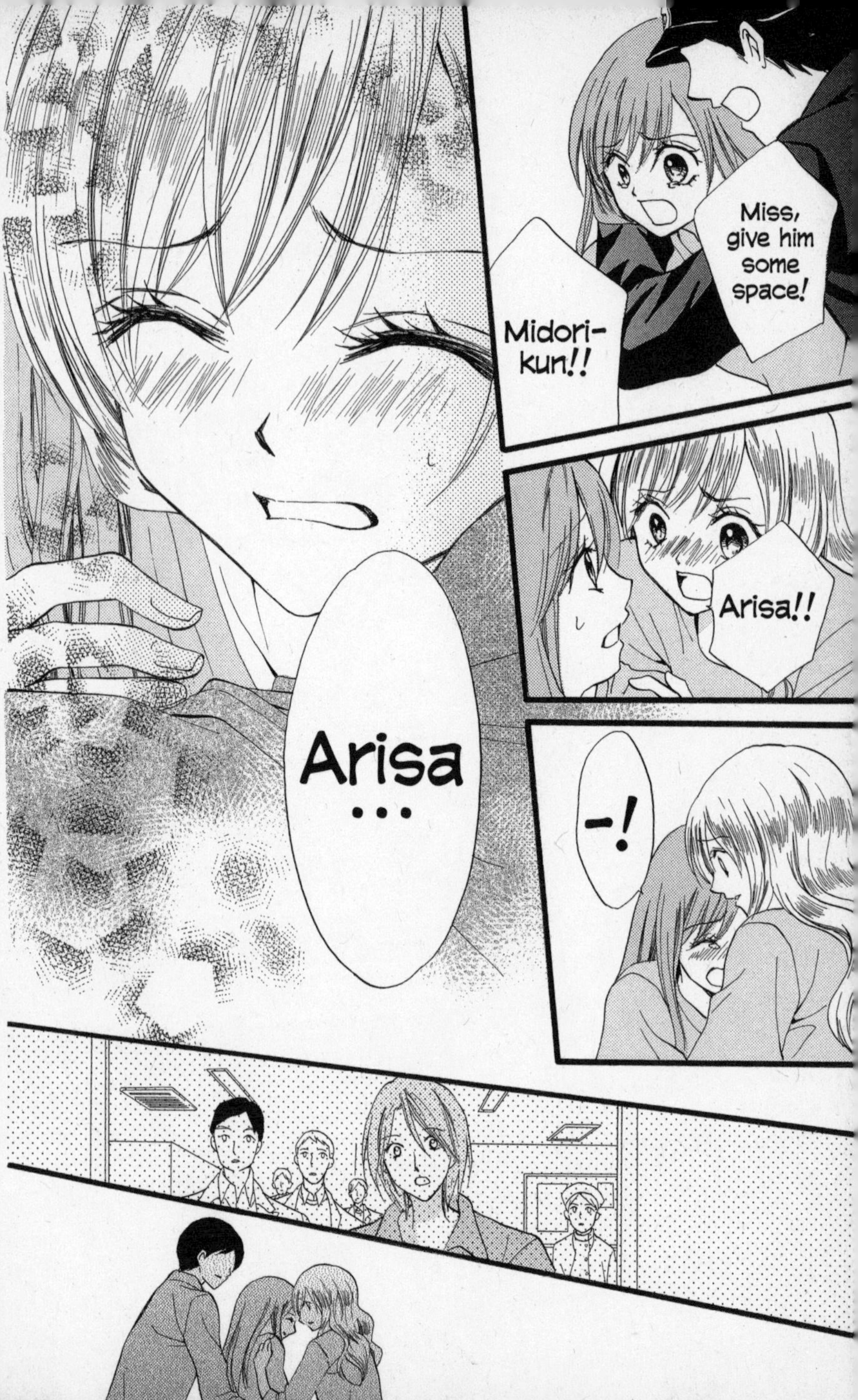
Miss, give him some space!
Midori-kun!!
Arisa!!
-!
Arisa ...

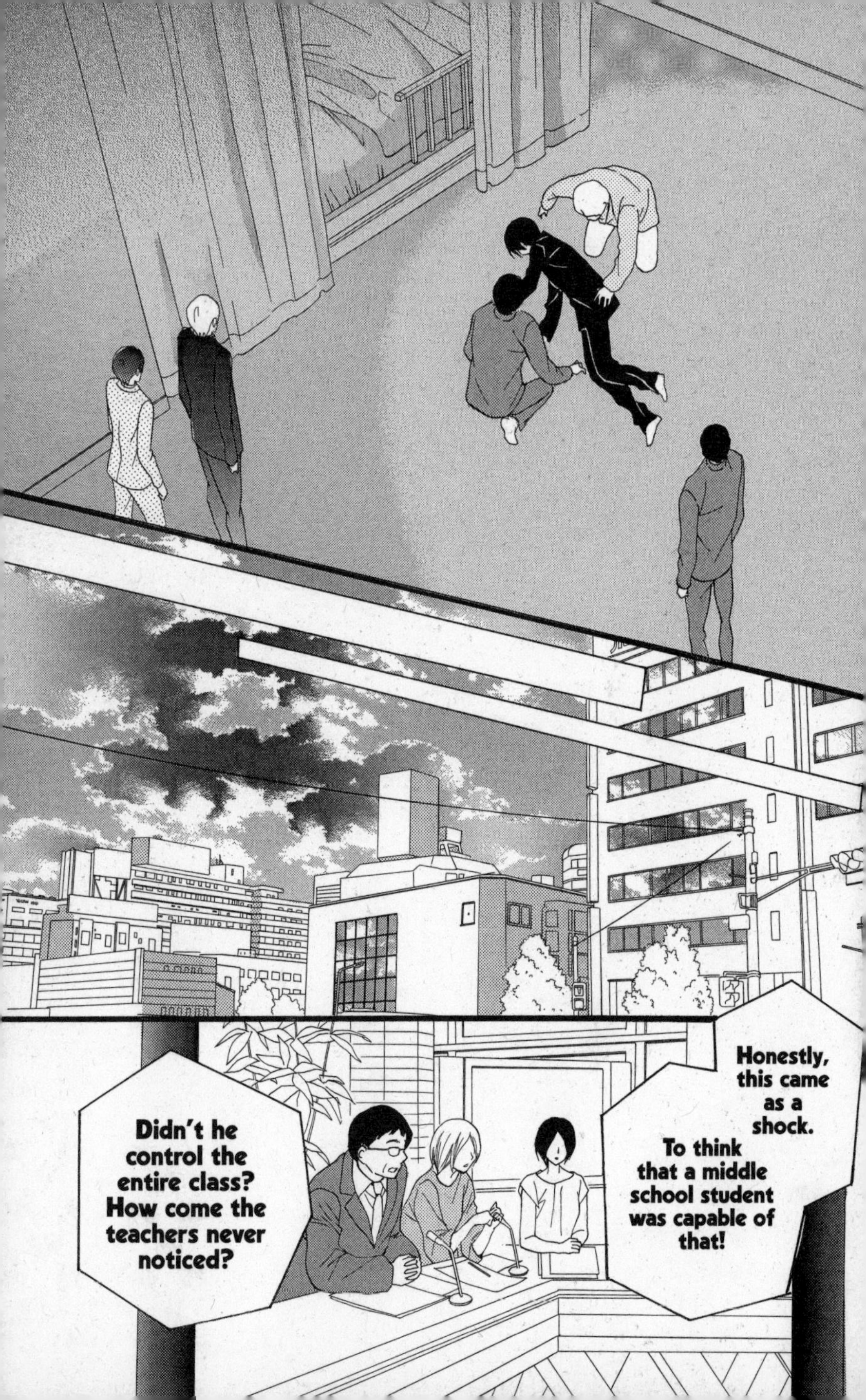
Honestly, this came as a shock.
To think that a middle school student was capable of that!
Didn't he control the entire class? How come the teachers never noticed?

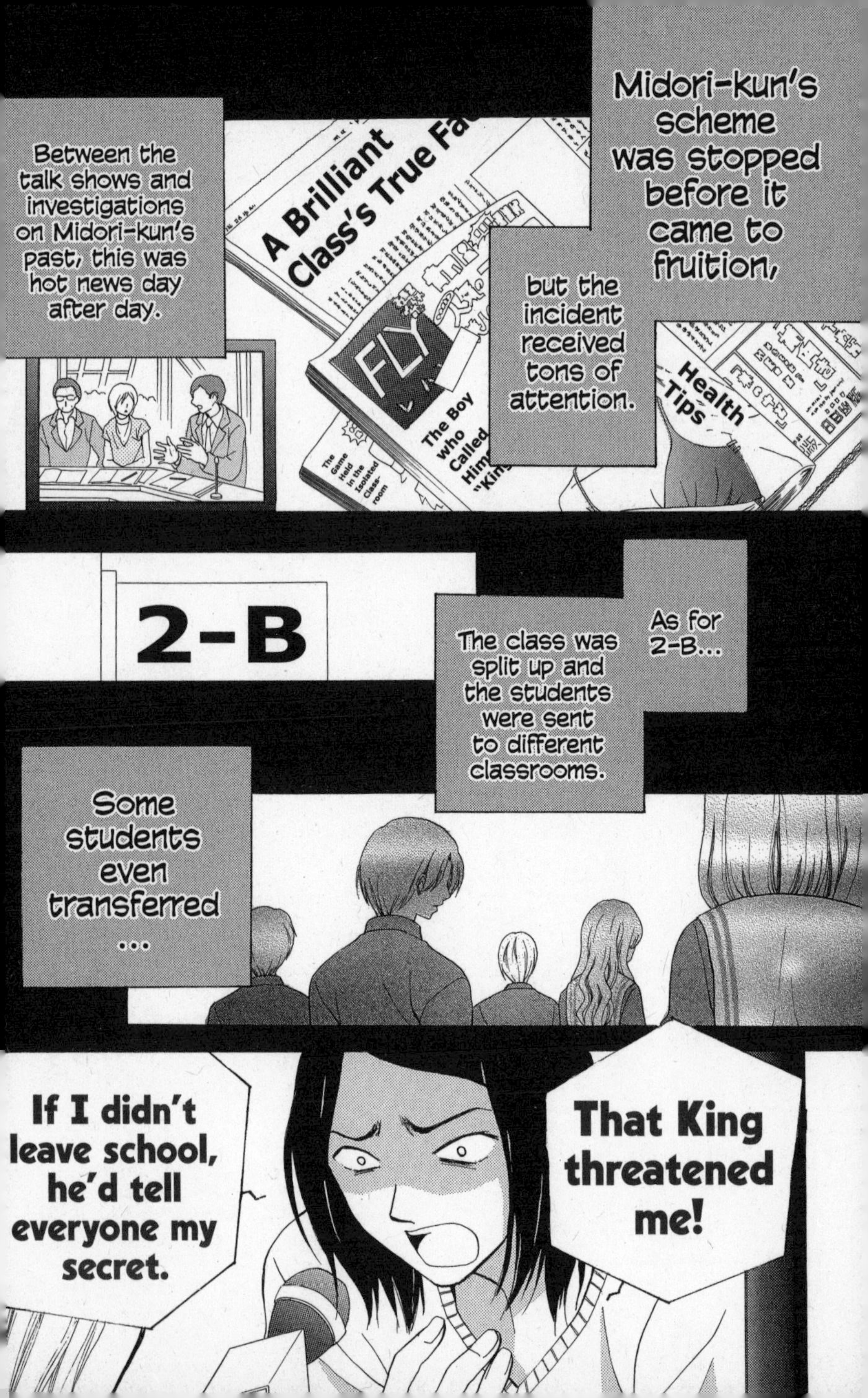

Midori-kun's scheme was stopped before it came to fruition,
but the incident received tons of attention.
Health Tips
FLY
The Game Held in the Isolated Class-room
Between the talk shows and investigations on Midori-kun's past, this was hot news day after day.
As for 2-B...
The class was split up and the students were sent to different classrooms.
2-B
Some students even transferred...
That King threatened me!
If I didn't leave school, he'd tell everyone my secret.

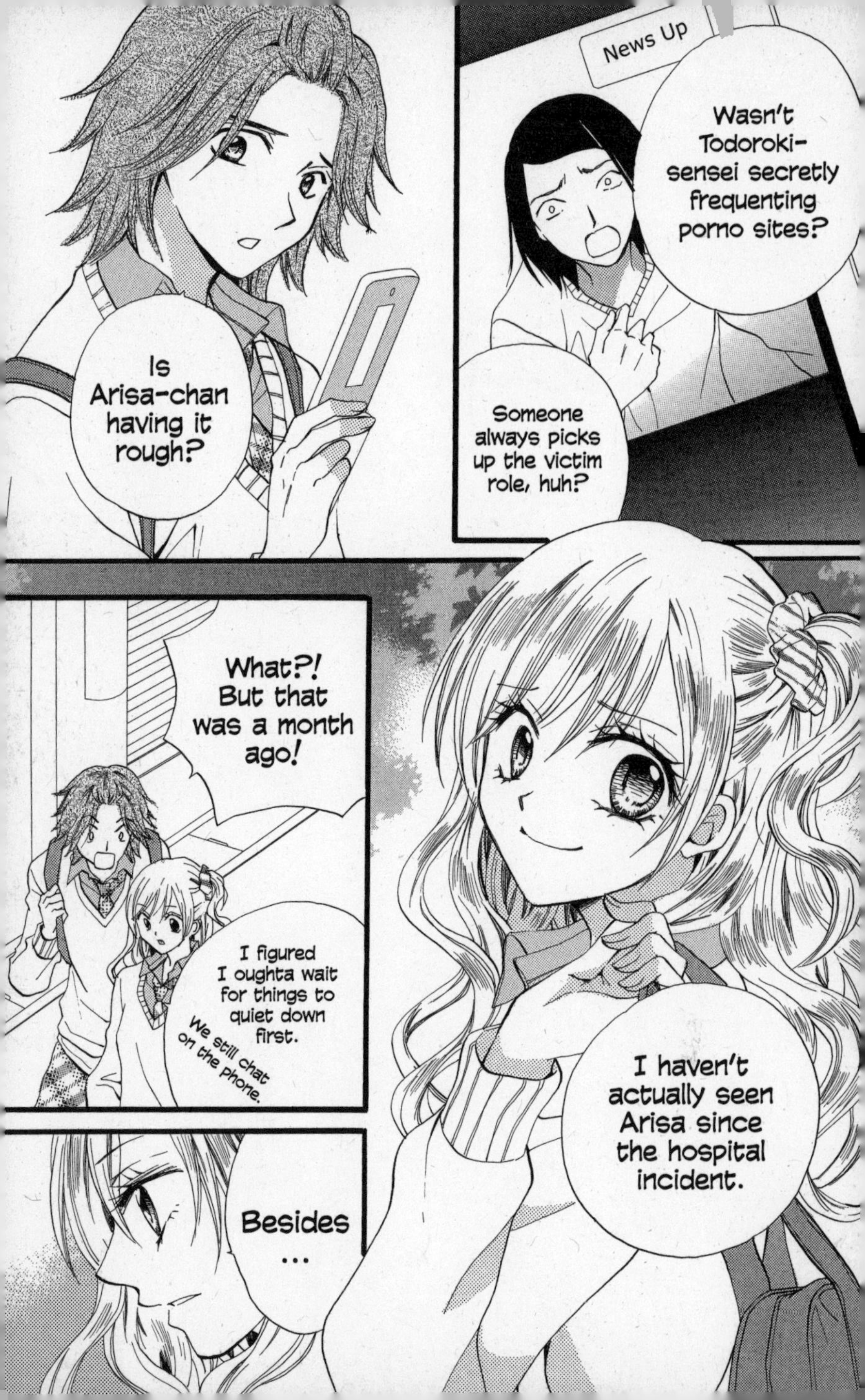
News Up
Wasn't Todoroki-sensei secretly frequenting porno sites?
Someone always picks up the victim role, huh?
Is Arisa-chan having it rough?
I haven't actually seen Arisa since the hospital incident.
What?! But that was a month ago!
I figured I oughta wait for things to quiet down first.
We still chat on the phone.
Besides ...

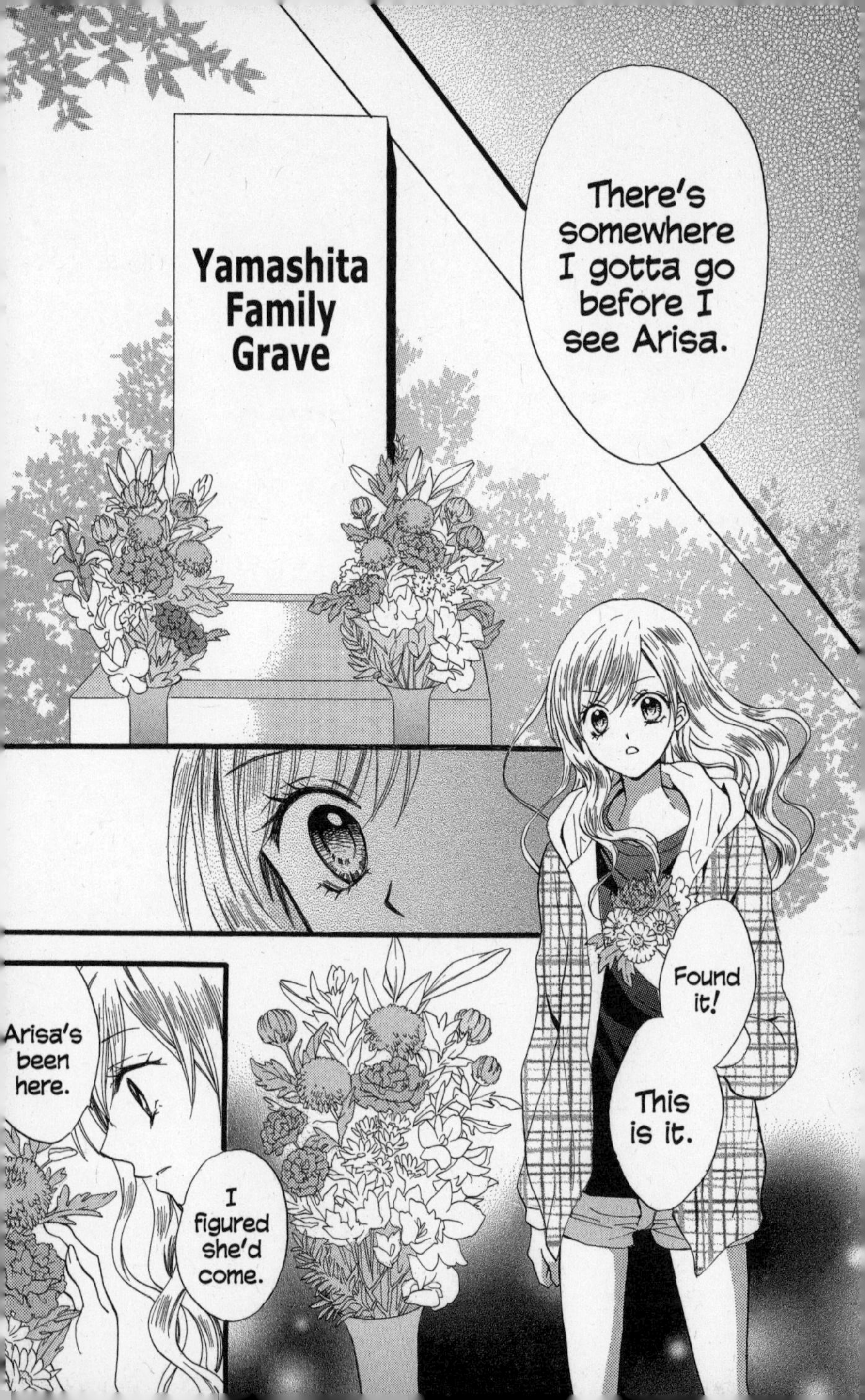
There's somewhere I gotta go before I see Arisa.
Yamashita Family Grave
Found it!
This is it.
Arisa's been here.
I figured she'd come.

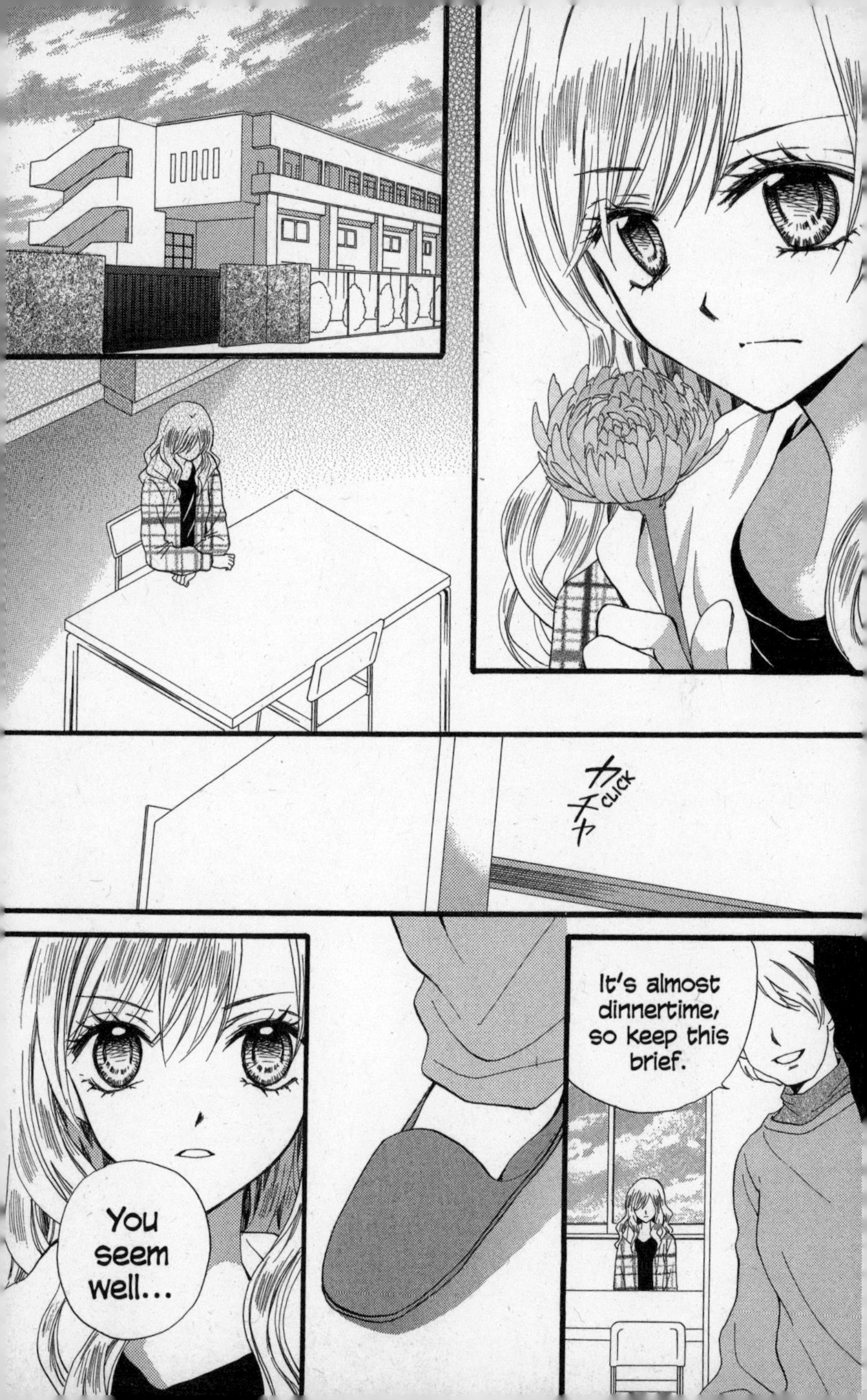
カチャ
CLICK
It's almost dinnertime, so keep this brief.
You seem well...

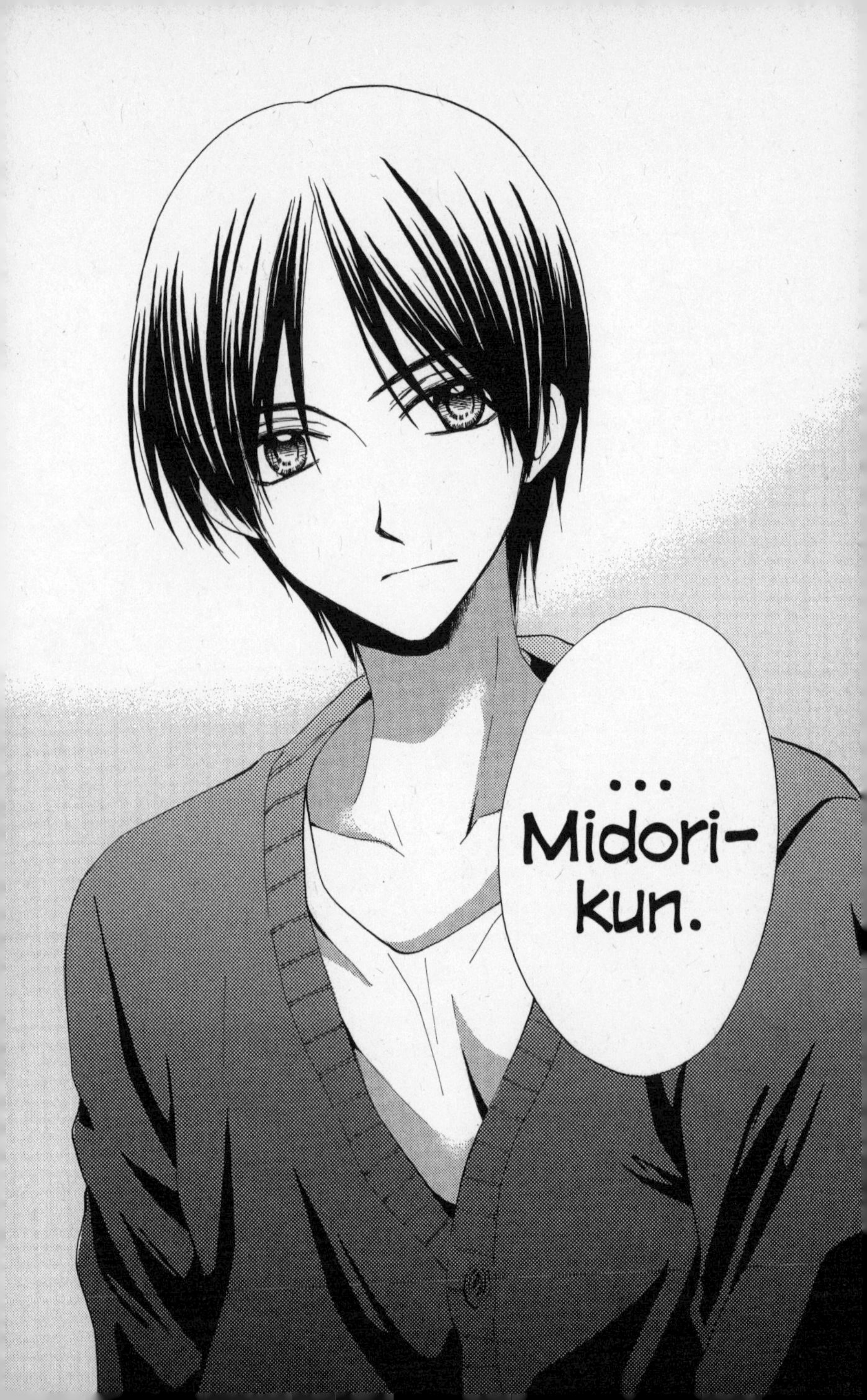
...Midori-kun.

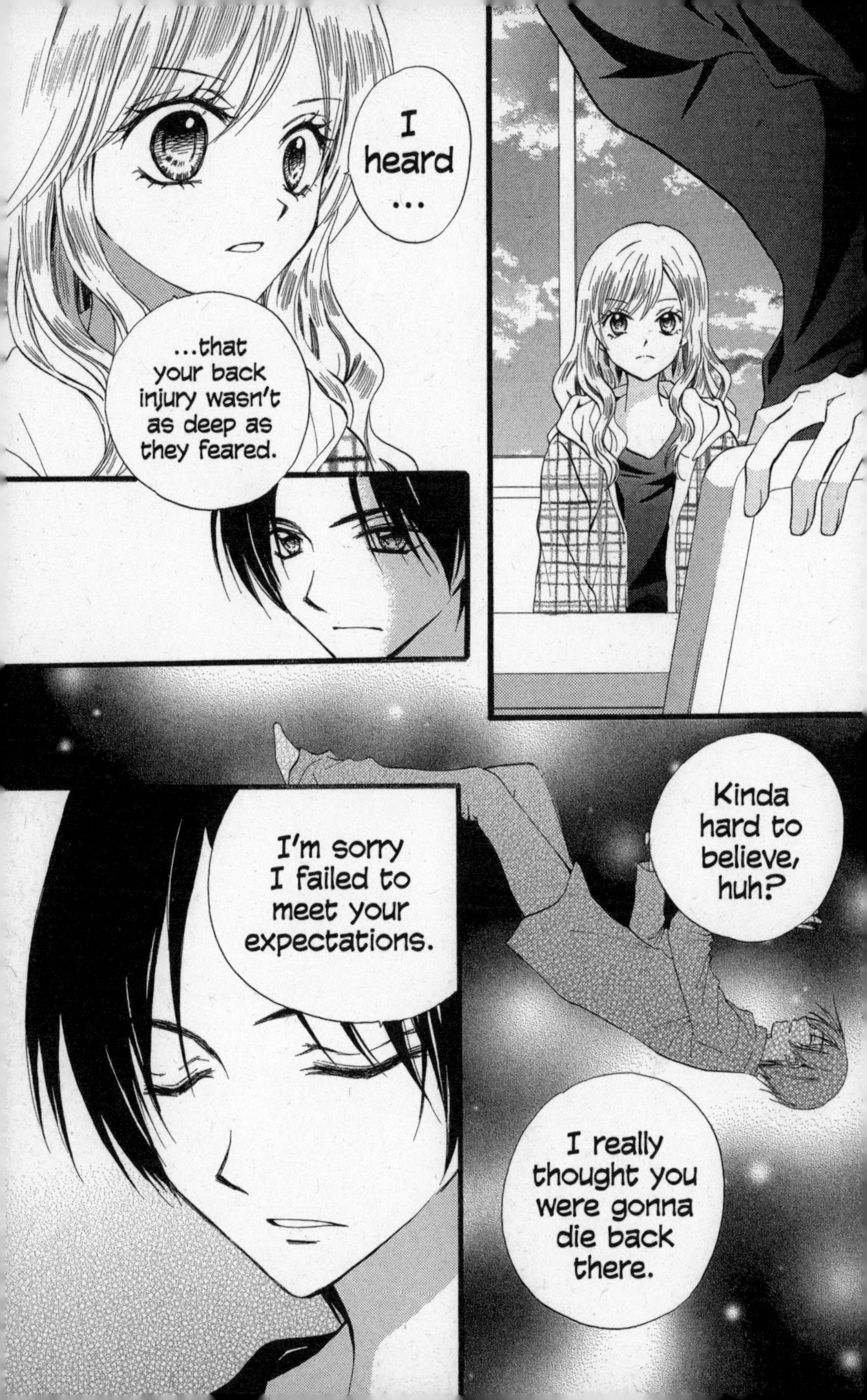
I heard...
...that your back injury wasn't as deep as they feared.
Kinda hard to believe, huh?
I really thought you were gonna die back there.
I'm sorry I failed to meet your expectations.

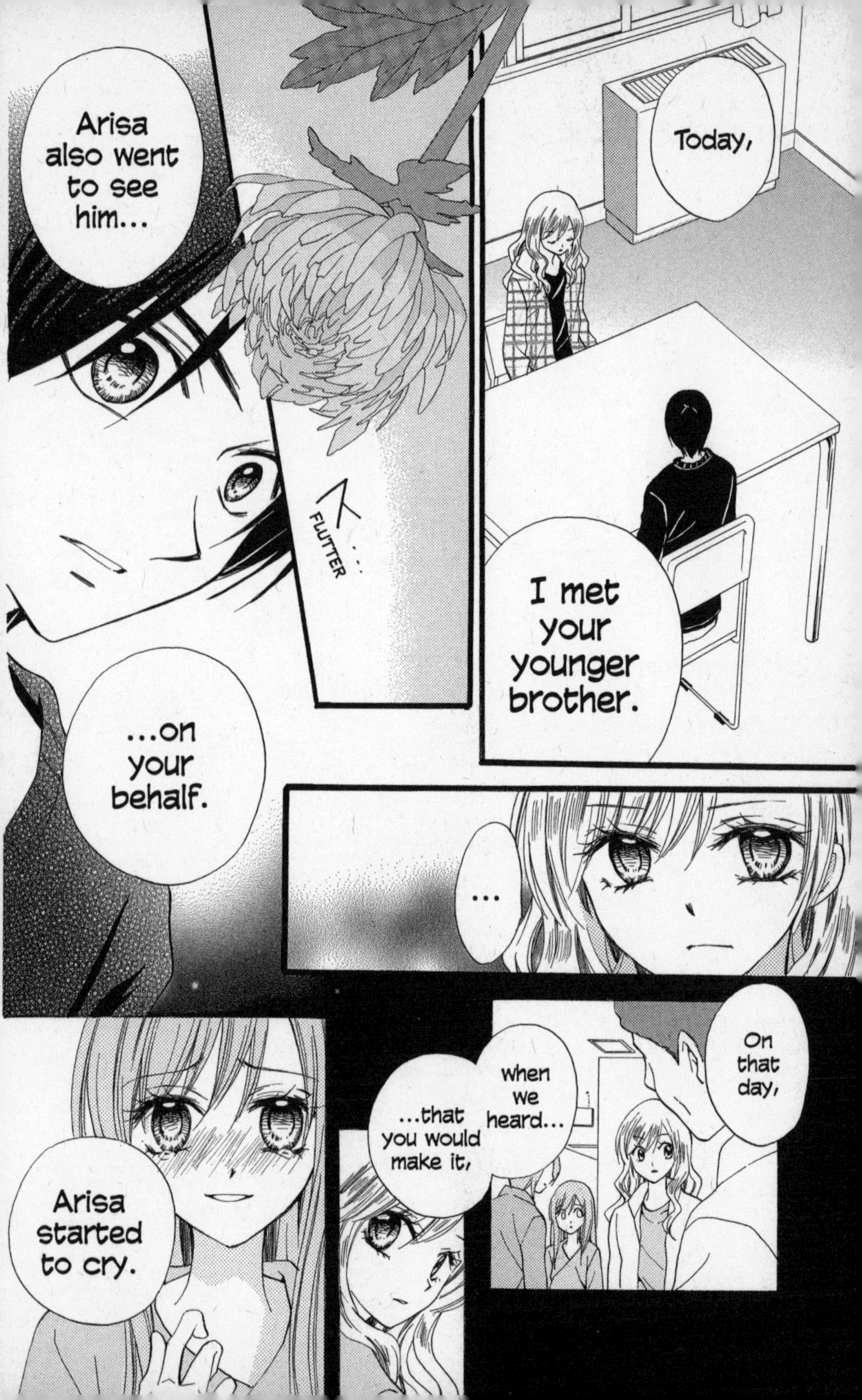
Today,
I met your younger brother.
Arisa also went to see him...
FLUTTER
...on your behalf.
...
On that day,
when we heard...
...that you would make it,
Arisa started to cry.

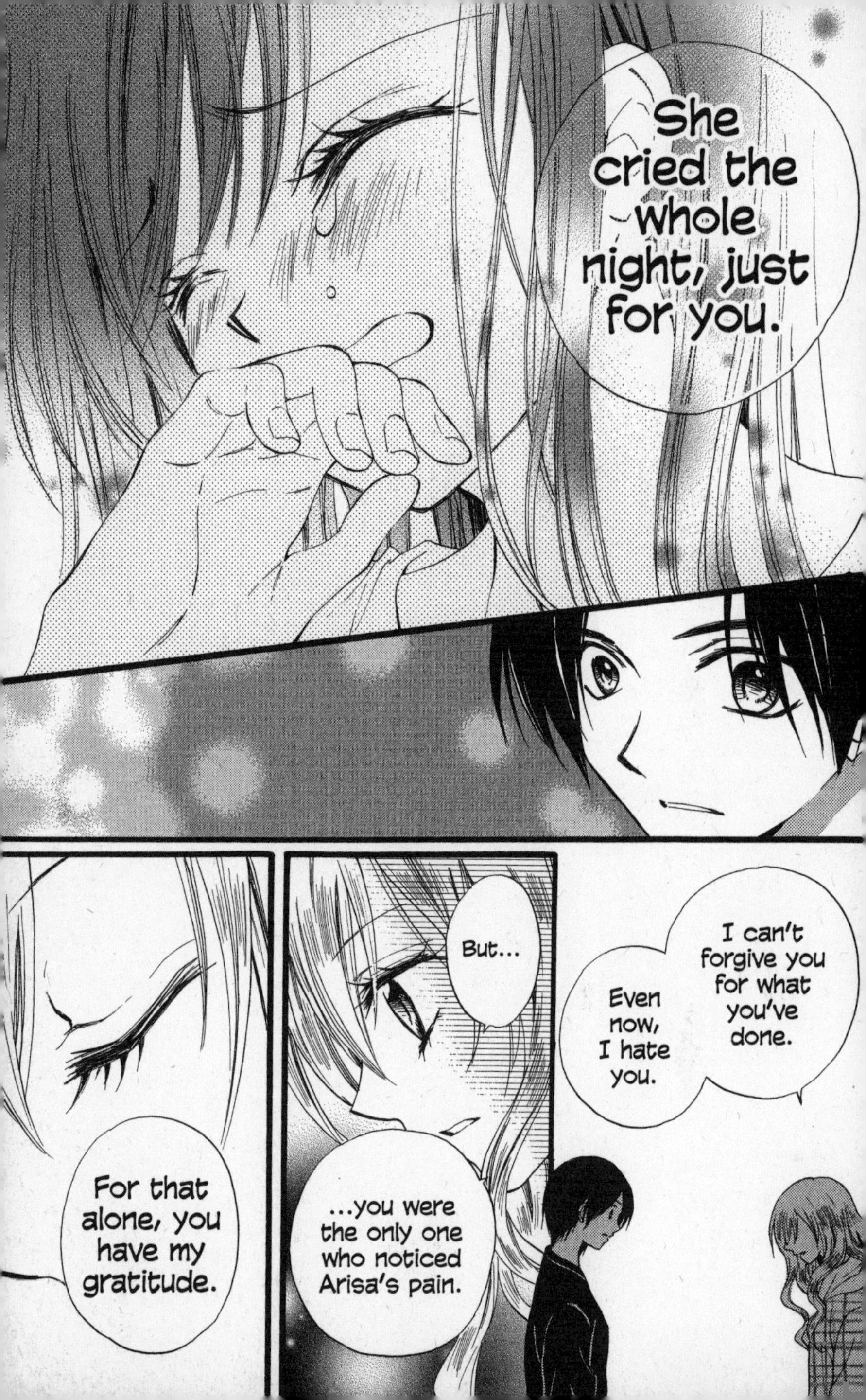
She cried the whole night, just for you.
I can't forgive you for what you've done.
Even now, I hate you.
But...
...you were the only one who noticed Arisa's pain.
For that alone, you have my gratitude.

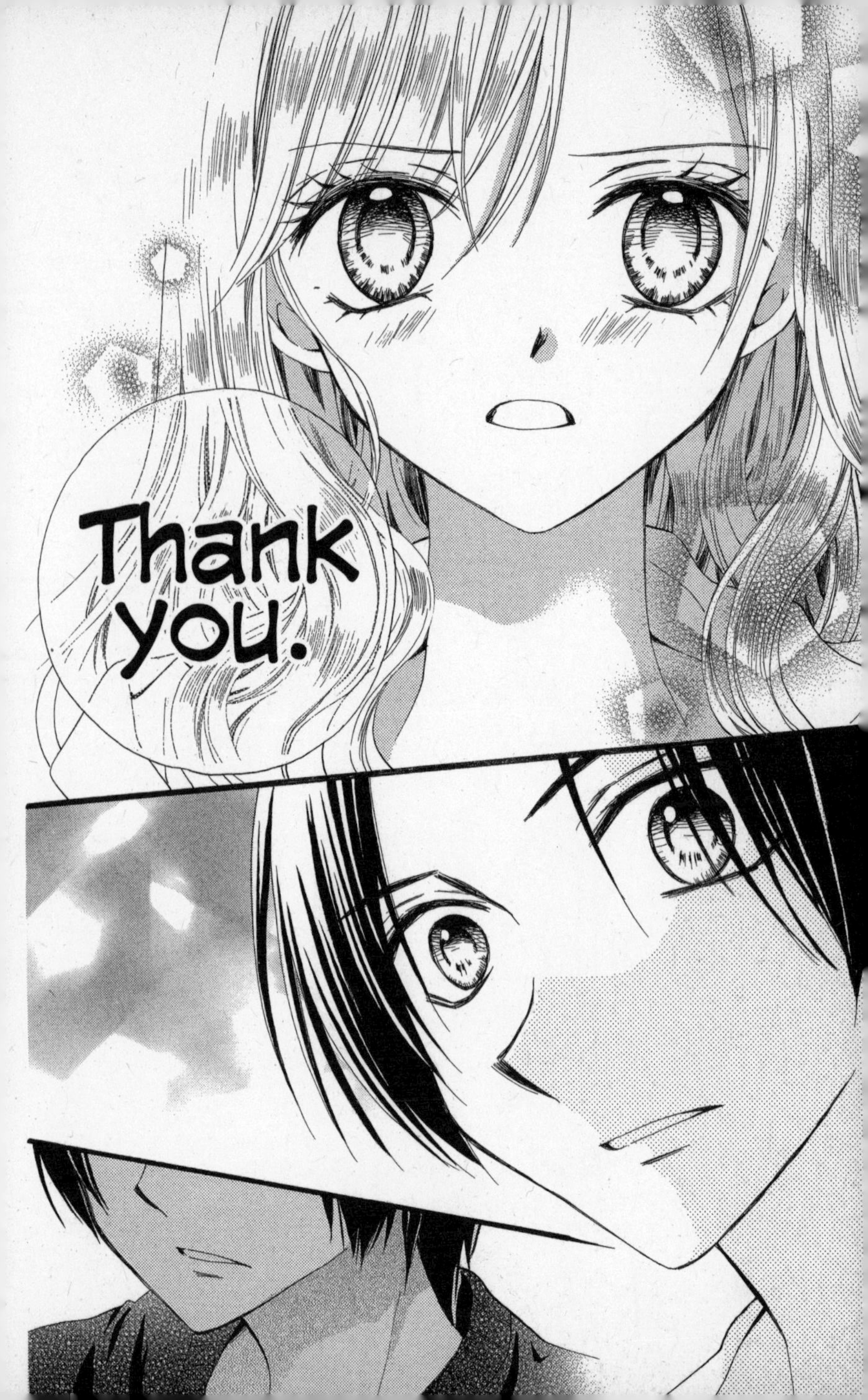
Thank you.

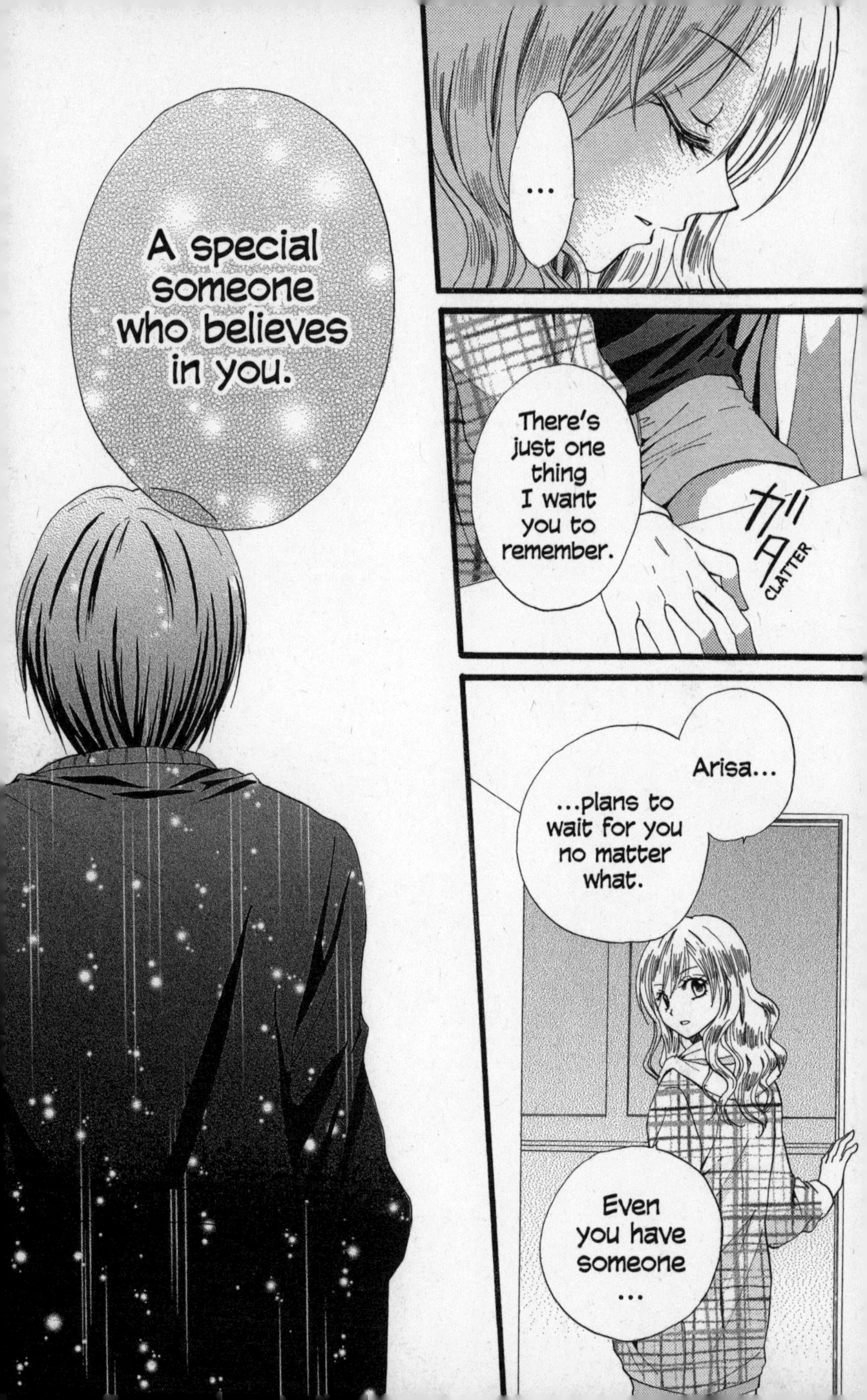
...
There's just one thing I want you to remember.
ガタ
CLATTER
Arisa...
...plans to wait for you no matter what.
Even you have someone ...
A special someone who believes in you.

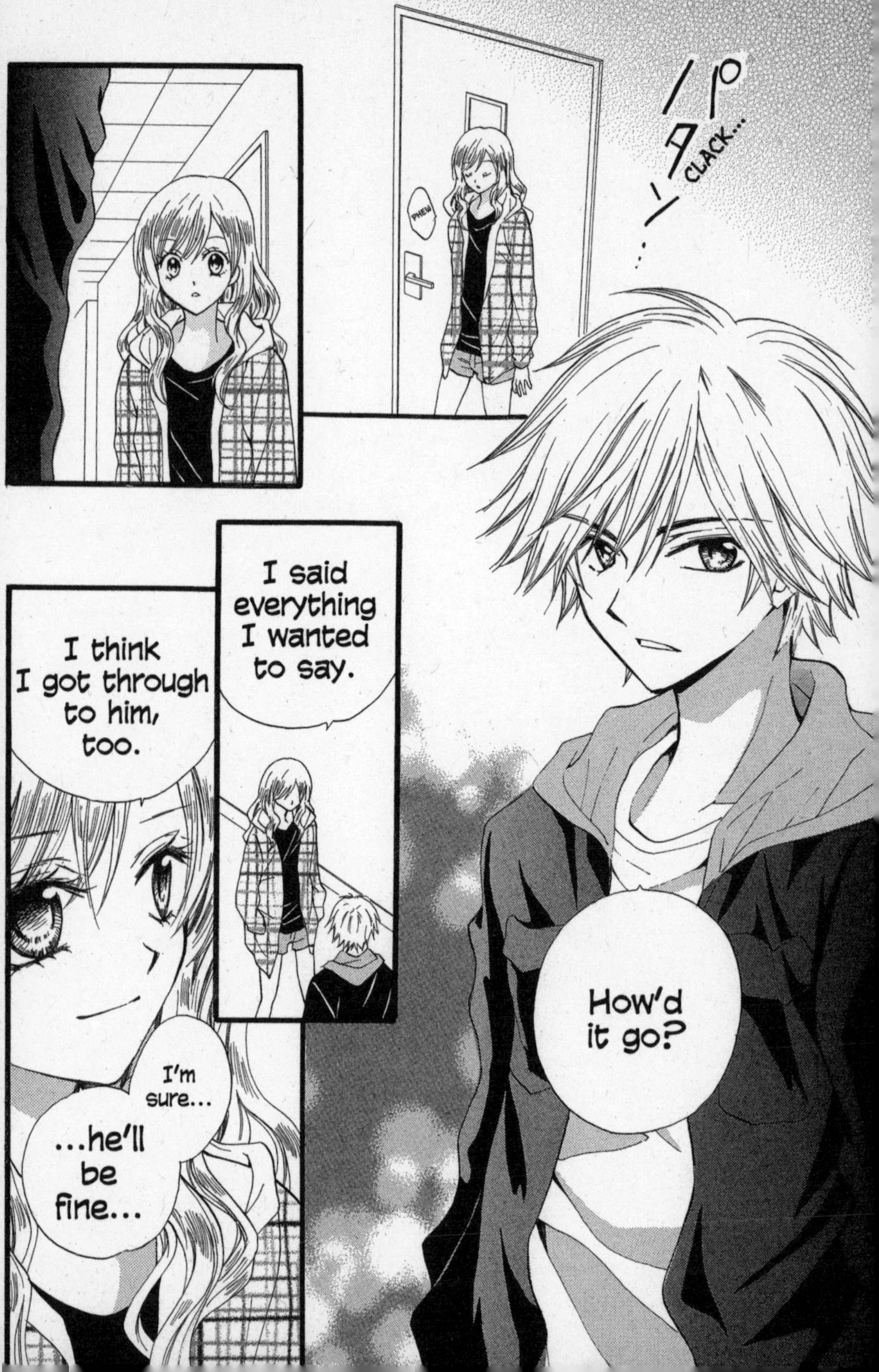
CLACK...
PHEW
How'd it go?
I said everything I wanted to say.
I think I got through to him, too.
I'm sure...
...he'll be fine...

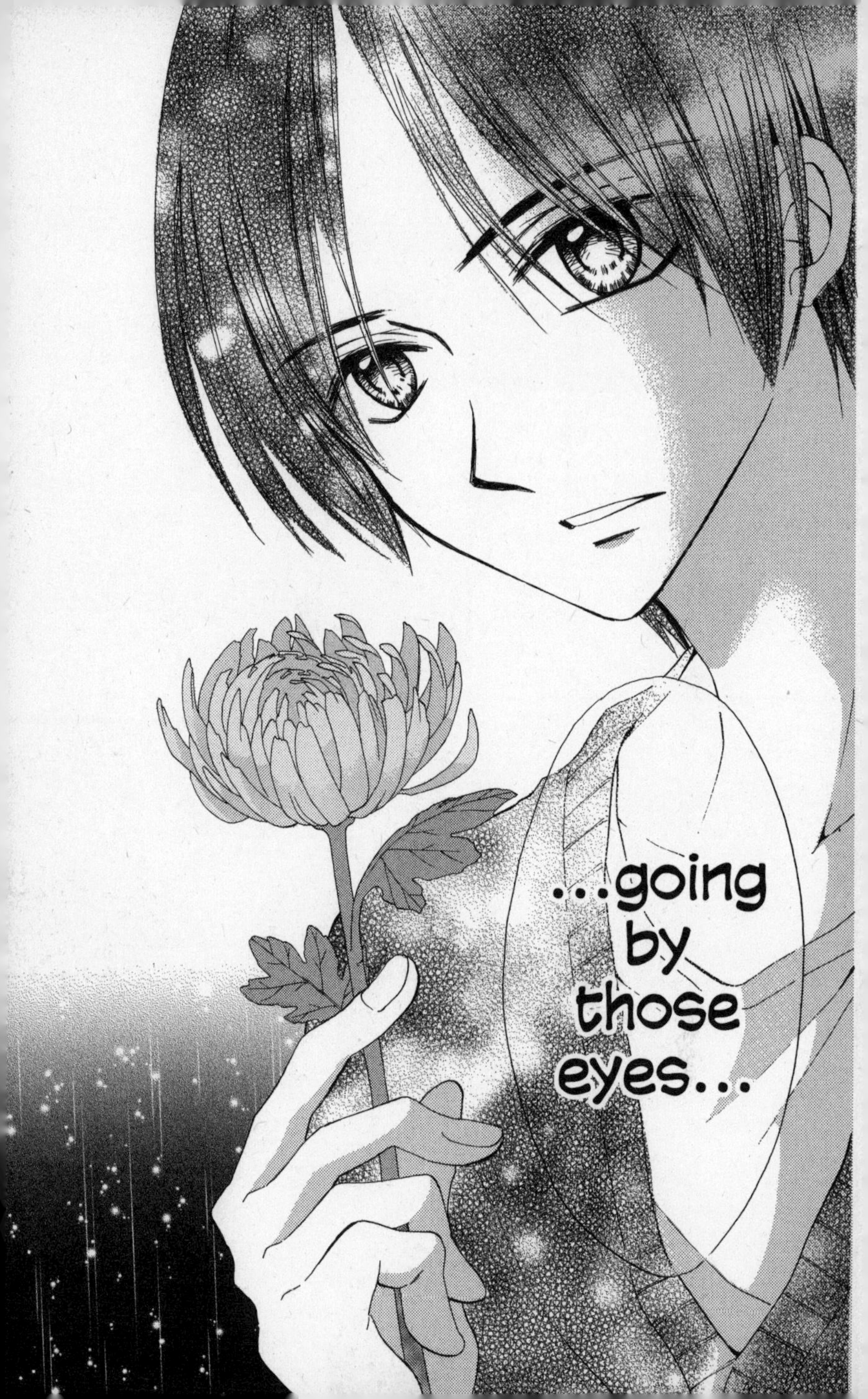
...going by those eyes...

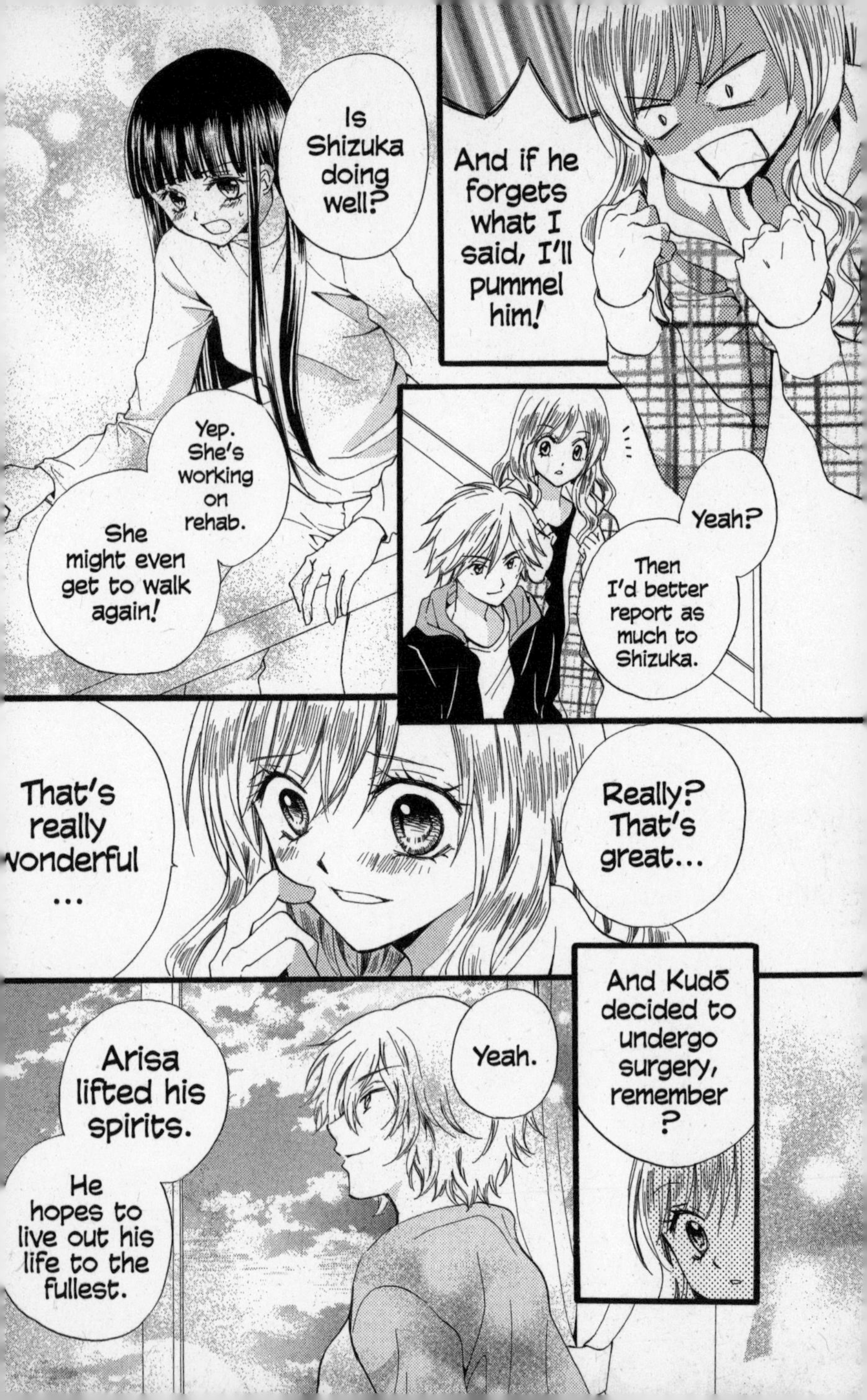
And if he forgets what I said, I'll pummel him!
Is Shizuka doing well?
Yep. She's working on rehab.
She might even get to walk again!
Yeah?
Then I'd better report as much to Shizuka.
Really? That's great...
That's really wonderful...
And Kudō decided to undergo surgery, remember?
Yeah.
Arisa lifted his spirits.
He hopes to live out his life to the fullest.

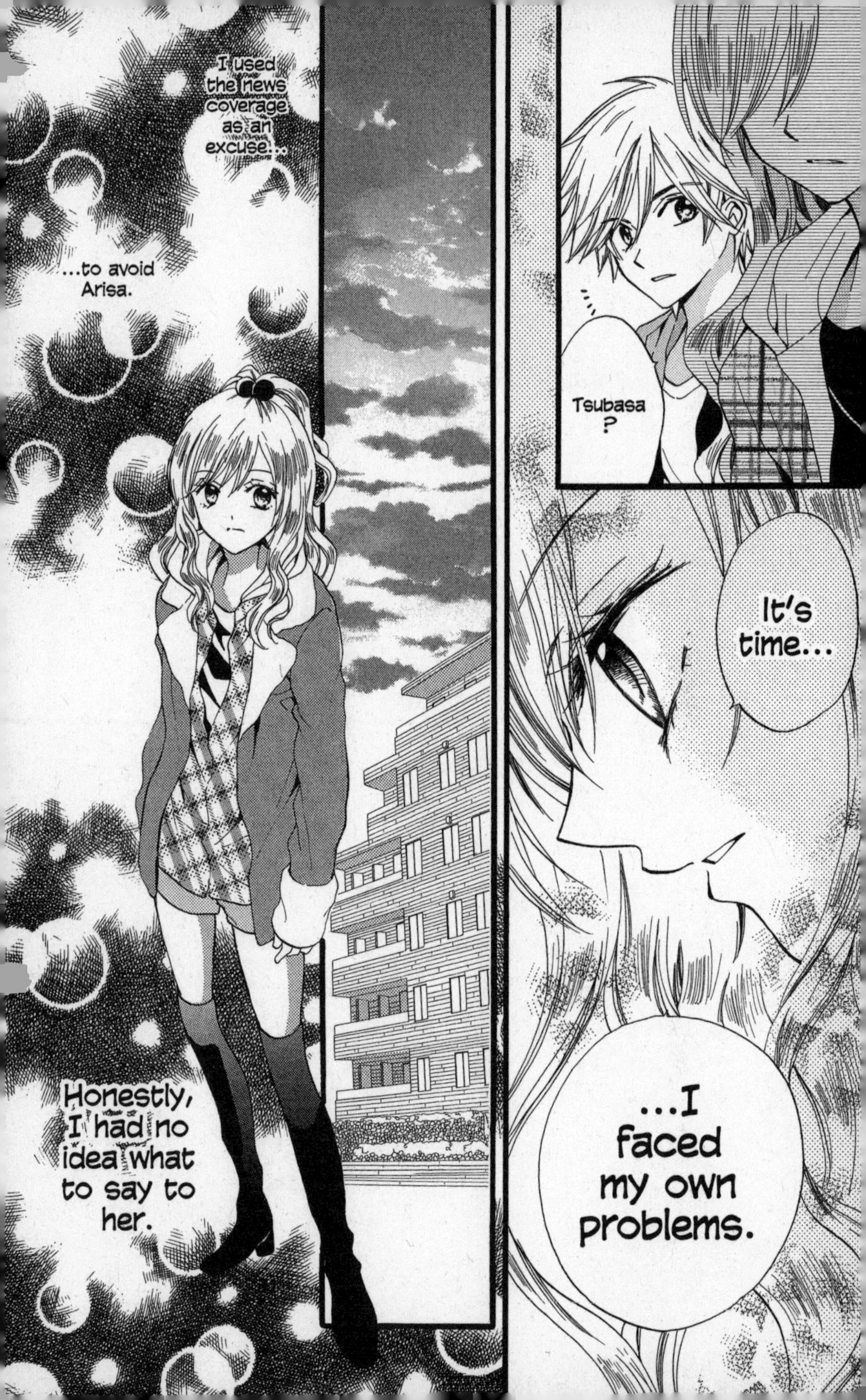
Tsubasa?
It's time...
...I faced my own problems.
I used the news coverage as an excuse...
...to avoid Arisa.
Honestly, I had no idea what to say to her.

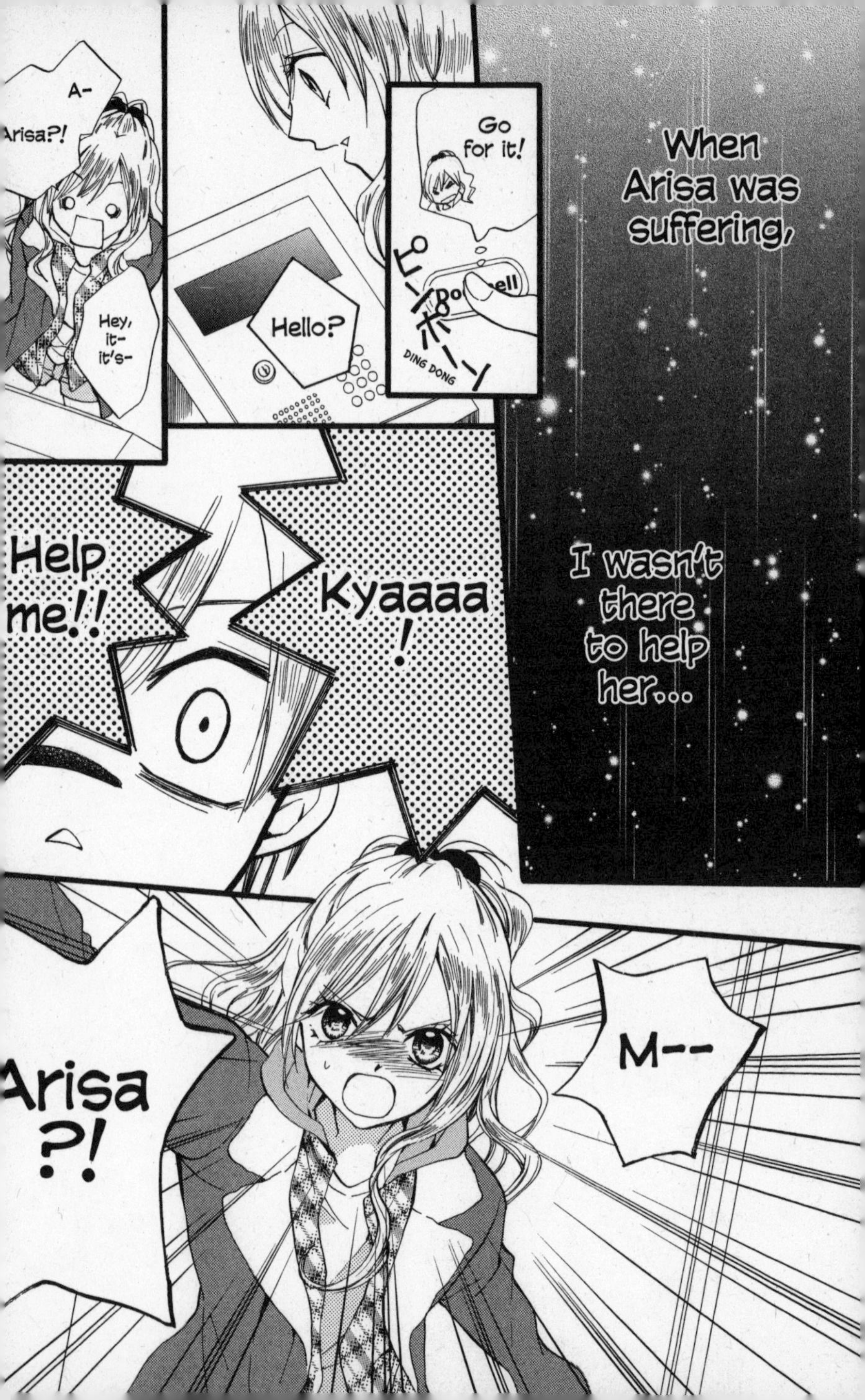
When Arisa was suffering,
I wasn't there to help her...
Go for it!
ピーンポーン
DING DONG
Hello?
A- Arisa?!
Hey, it- it's-
Kyaaaa!
Help me!!
M--
Arisa?!

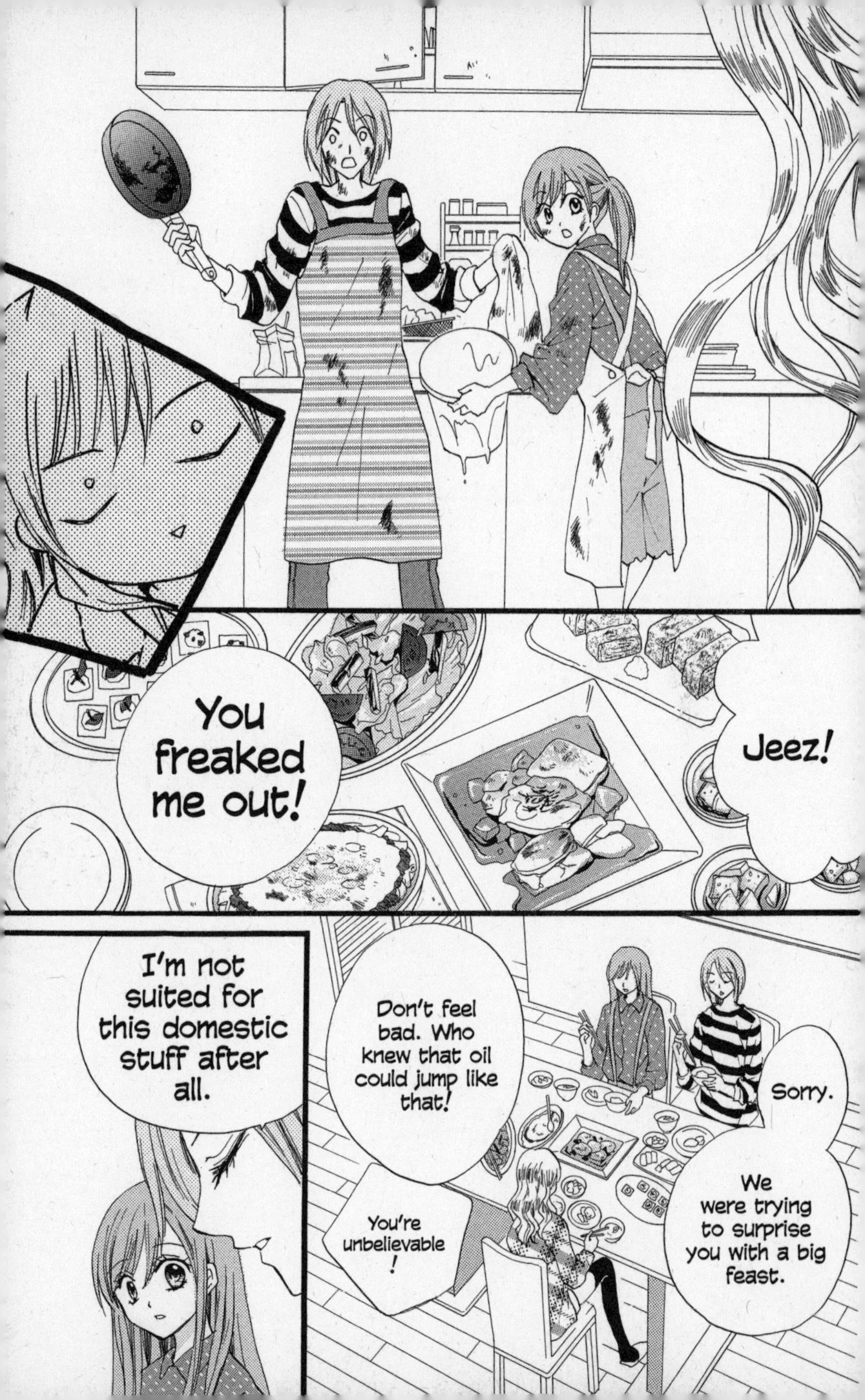
Jeez!
You freaked me out!
Sorry.
We were trying to surprise you with a big feast.
Don't feel bad. Who knew that oil could jump like that!
You're unbelievable!
I'm not suited for this domestic stuff after all.

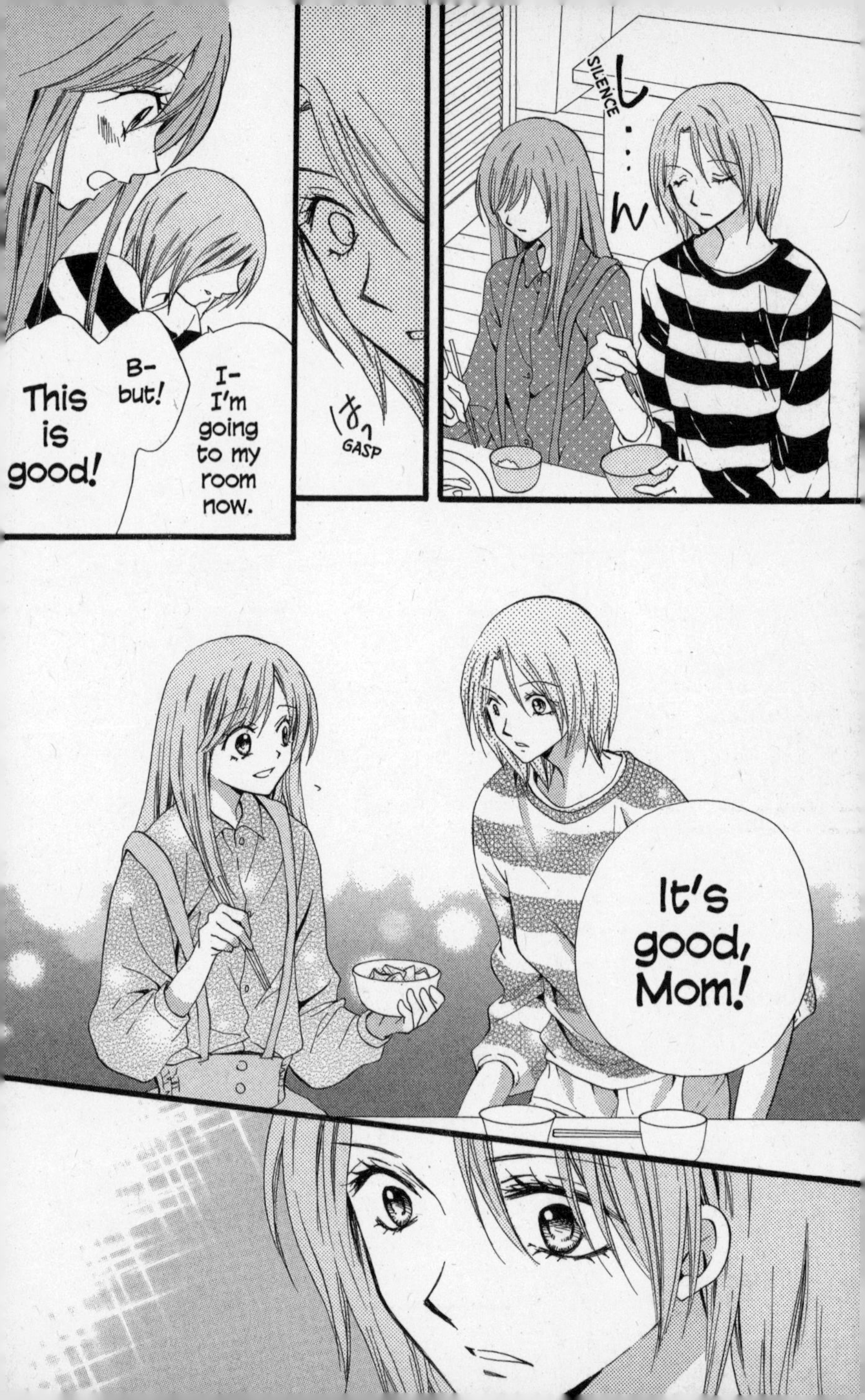
SILENCE
GASP
I- I'm going to my room now.
B-but!
This is good!
It's good, Mom!

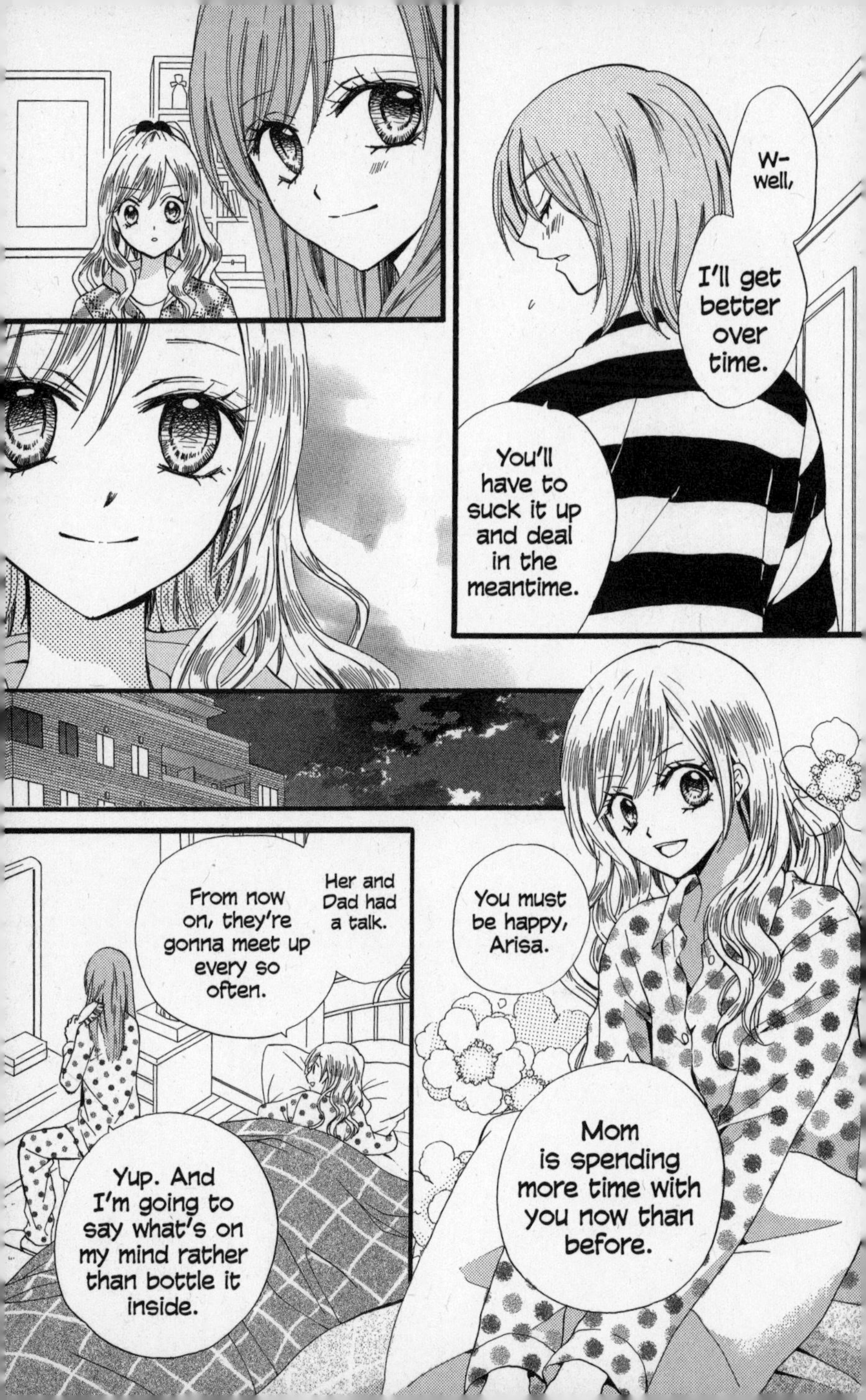
W-well,
I'll get better over time.
You'll have to suck it up and deal in the meantime.
You must be happy, Arisa.
Mom is spending more time with you now than before.
Her and Dad had a talk.
From now on, they're gonna meet up every so often.
Yup. And I'm going to say what's on my mind rather than bottle it inside.

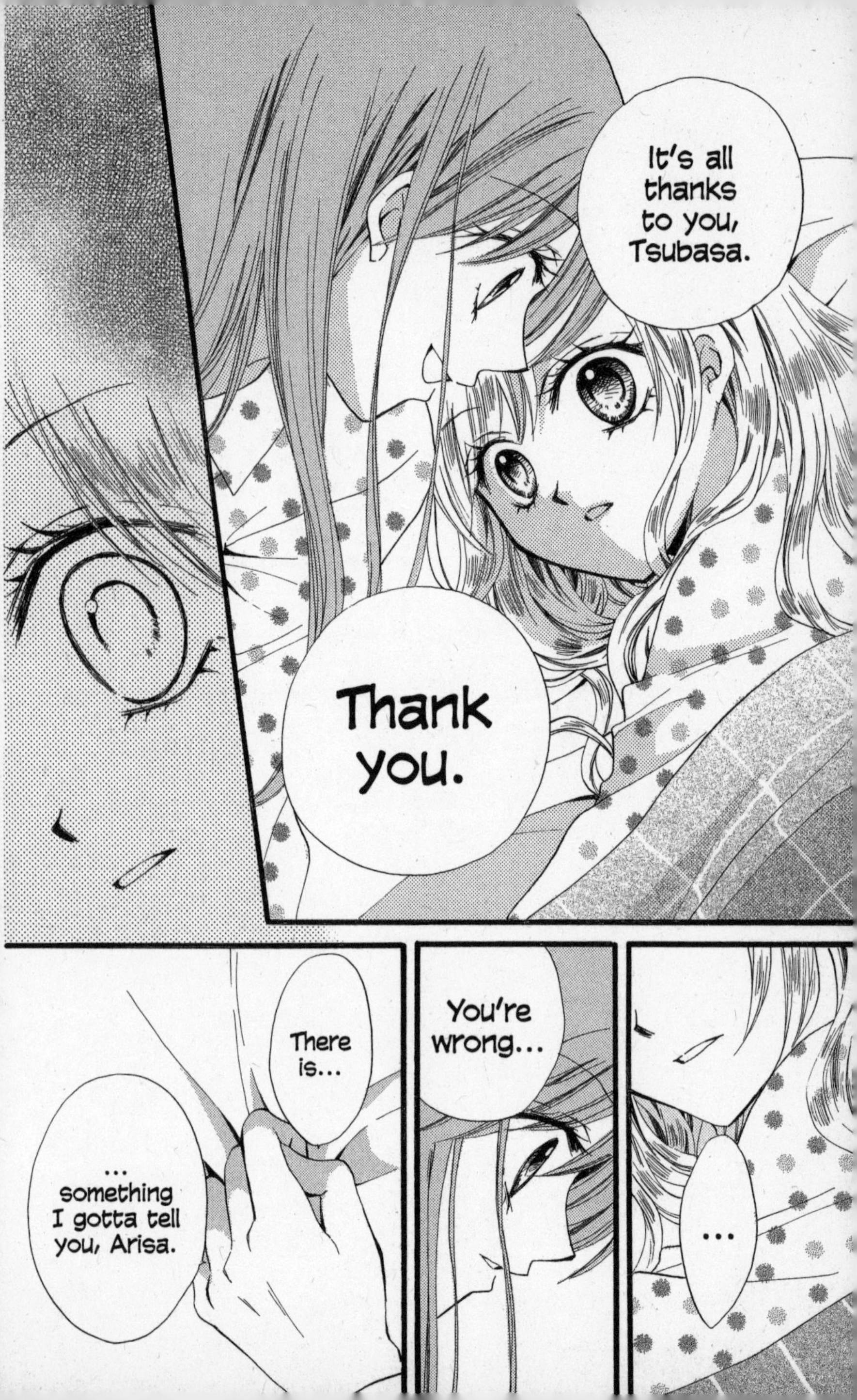
It's all thanks to you, Tsubasa.
Thank you.
...
You're wrong...
There is...
... something I gotta tell you, Arisa.

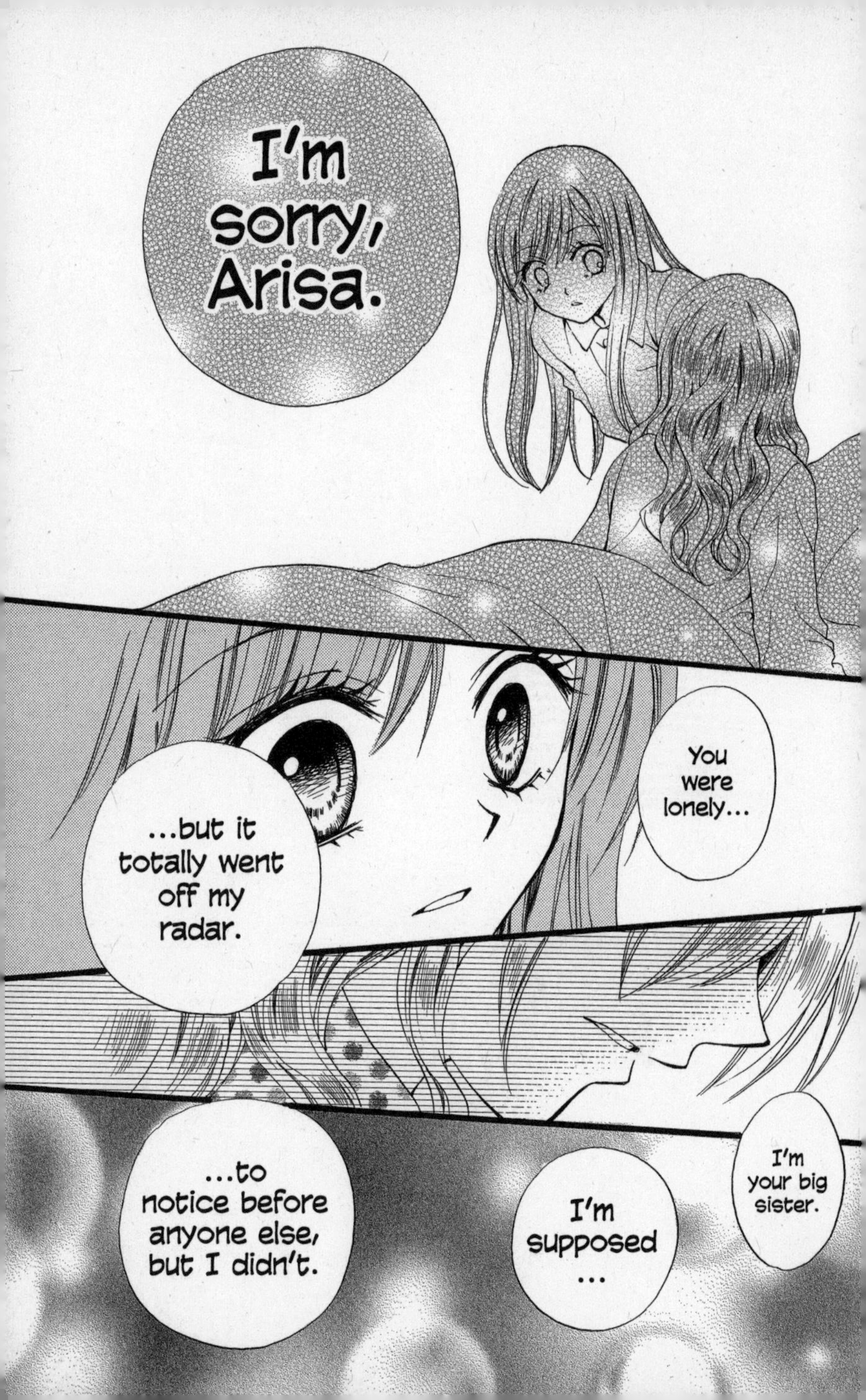
I'm sorry, Arisa.
You were lonely...
...but it totally went off my radar.
I'm your big sister.
I'm supposed...
...to notice before anyone else, but I didn't.

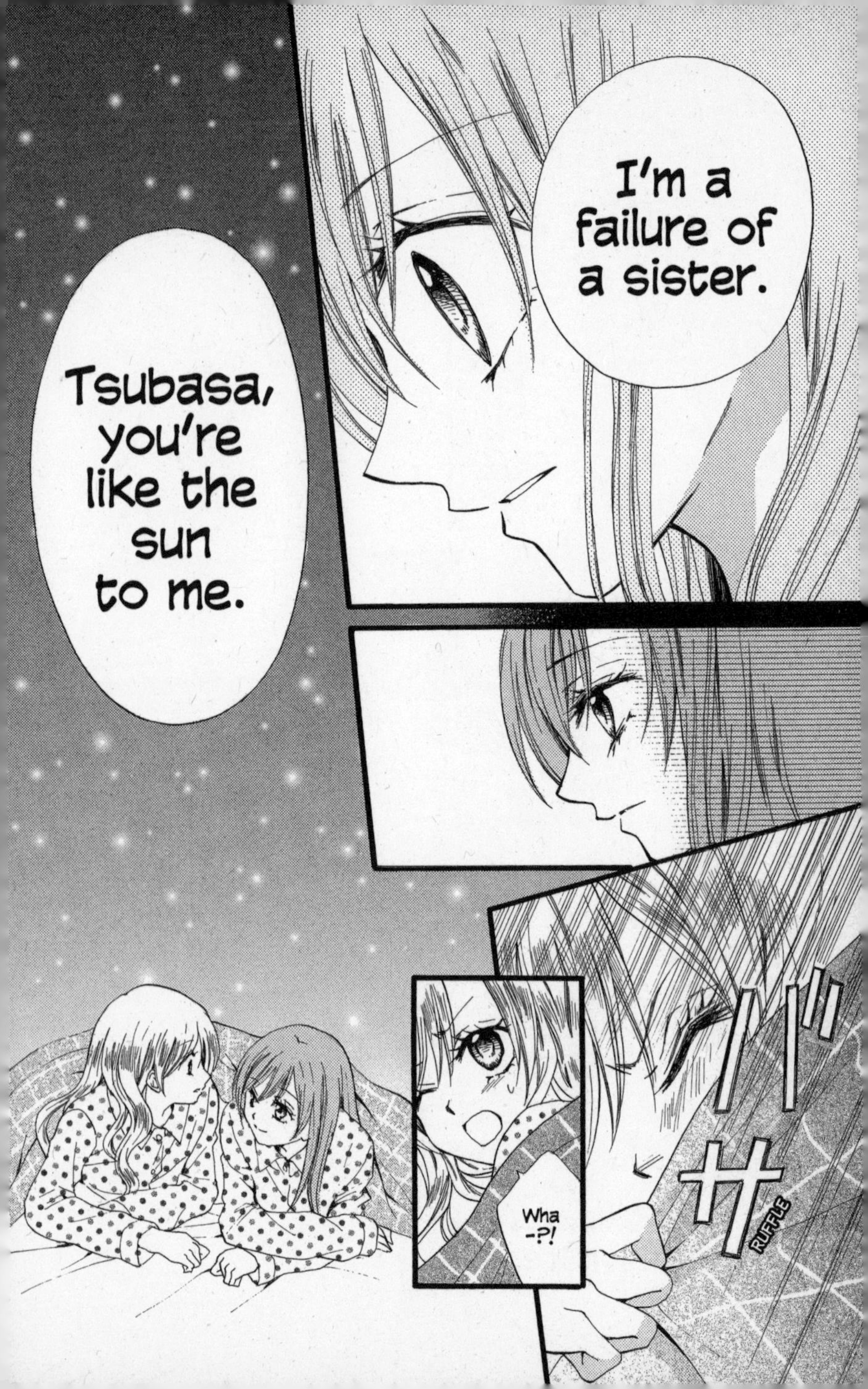
I'm a failure of a sister.
RUFFLE
Wha -?!
Tsubasa, you're like the sun to me.

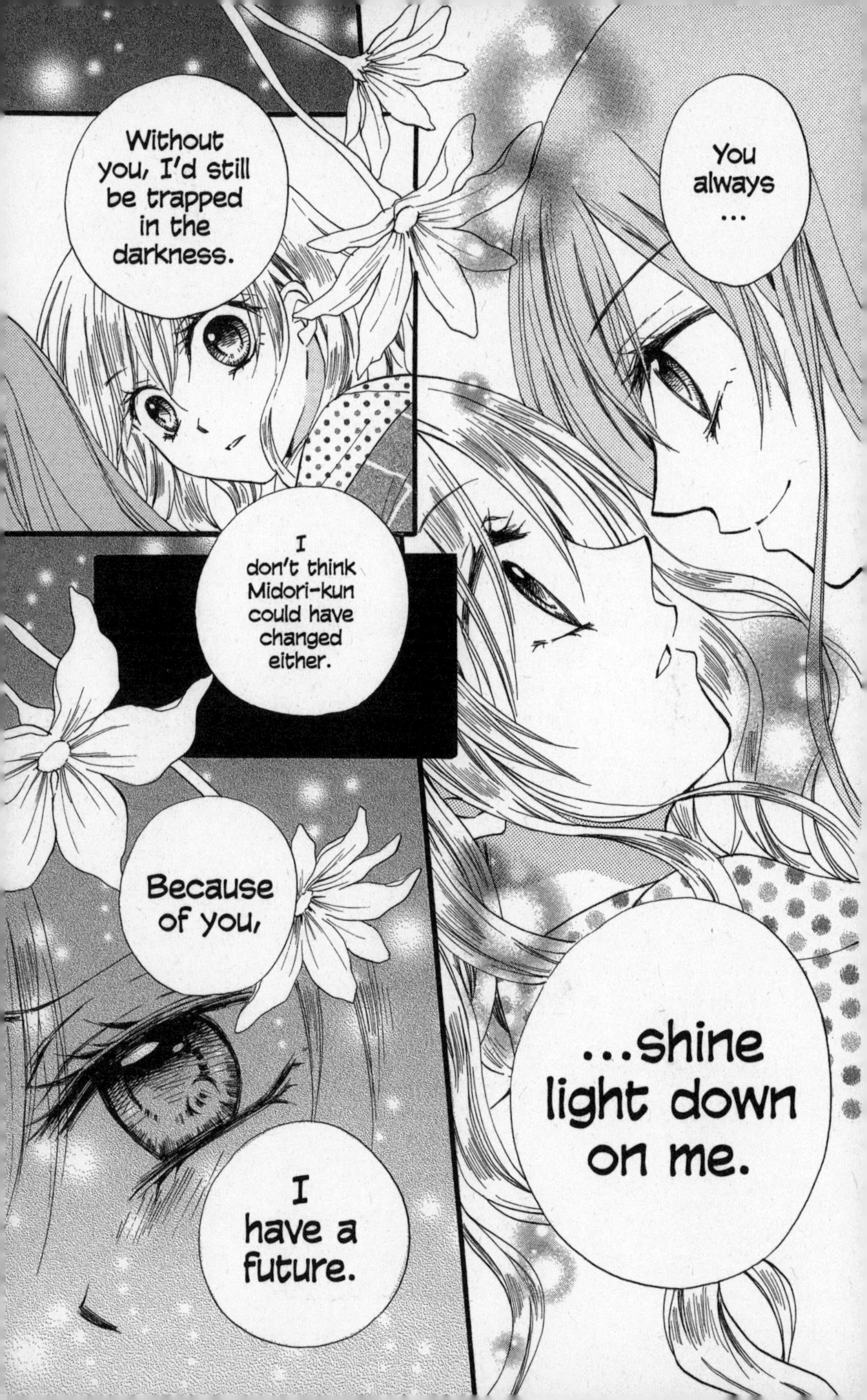
You always ...
...shine light down on me.
Without you, I'd still be trapped in the darkness.
I don't think Midori-kun could have changed either.
Because of you,
I have a future.

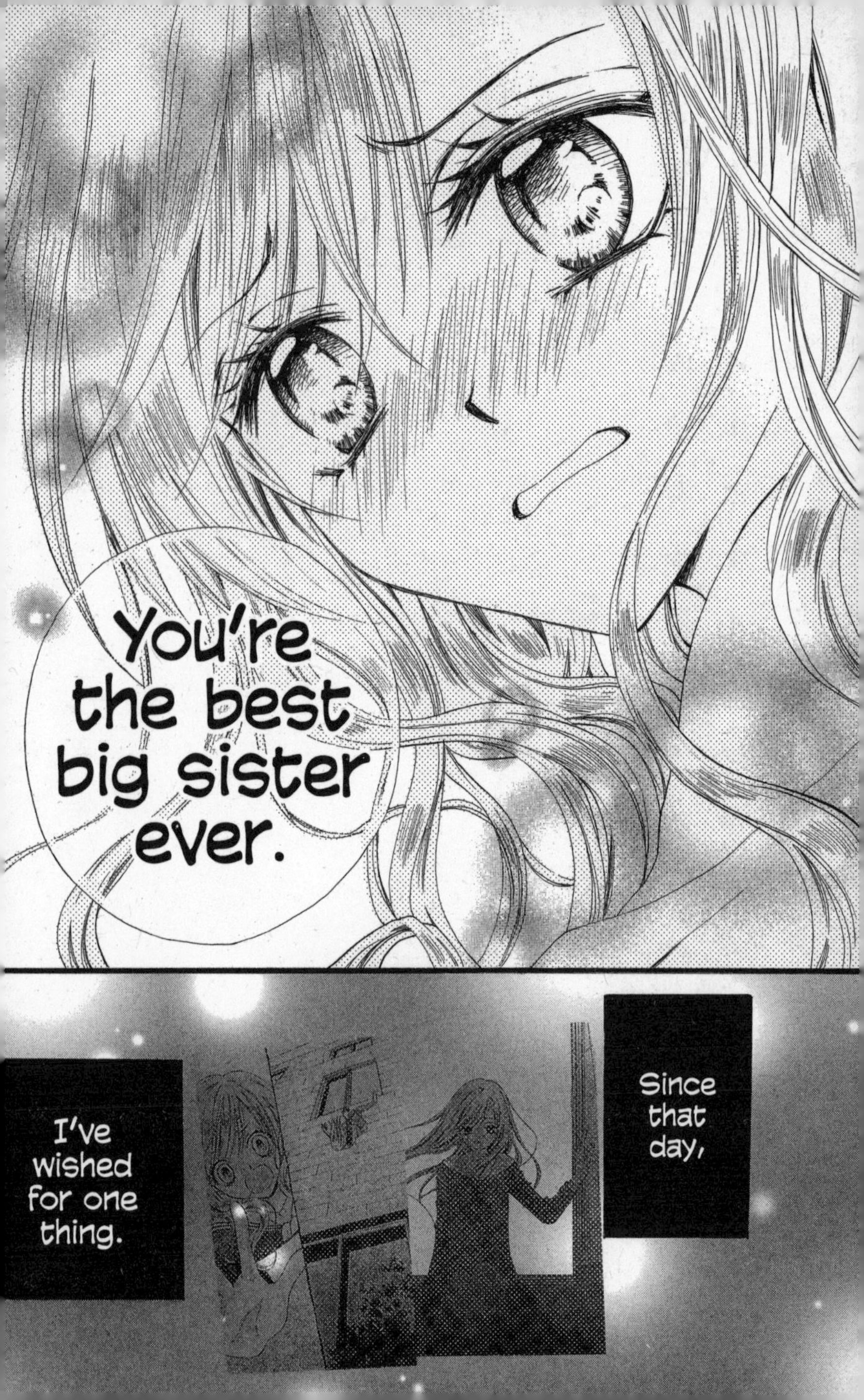
You're the best big sister ever.
Since that day,
I've wished for one thing.

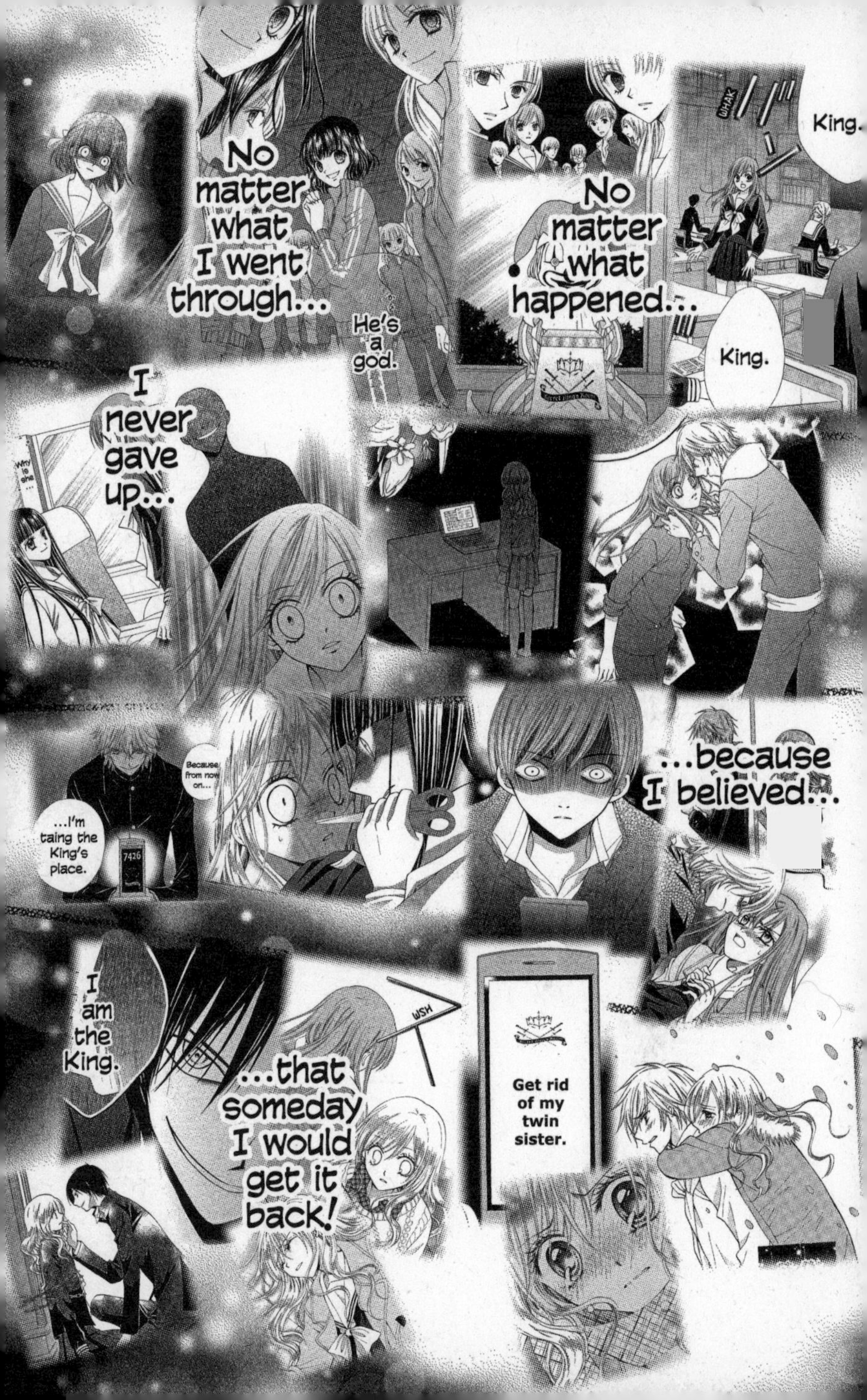
King.
WHAK
King.
No matter what happened...
No matter what I went through...
He's a god.
I never gave up...
Why is she ...
...because I believed...
Because from now on...
...I'm taing the King's place.
Get rid of my twin sister.
WSH
...that someday I would get it back!
I am the King.

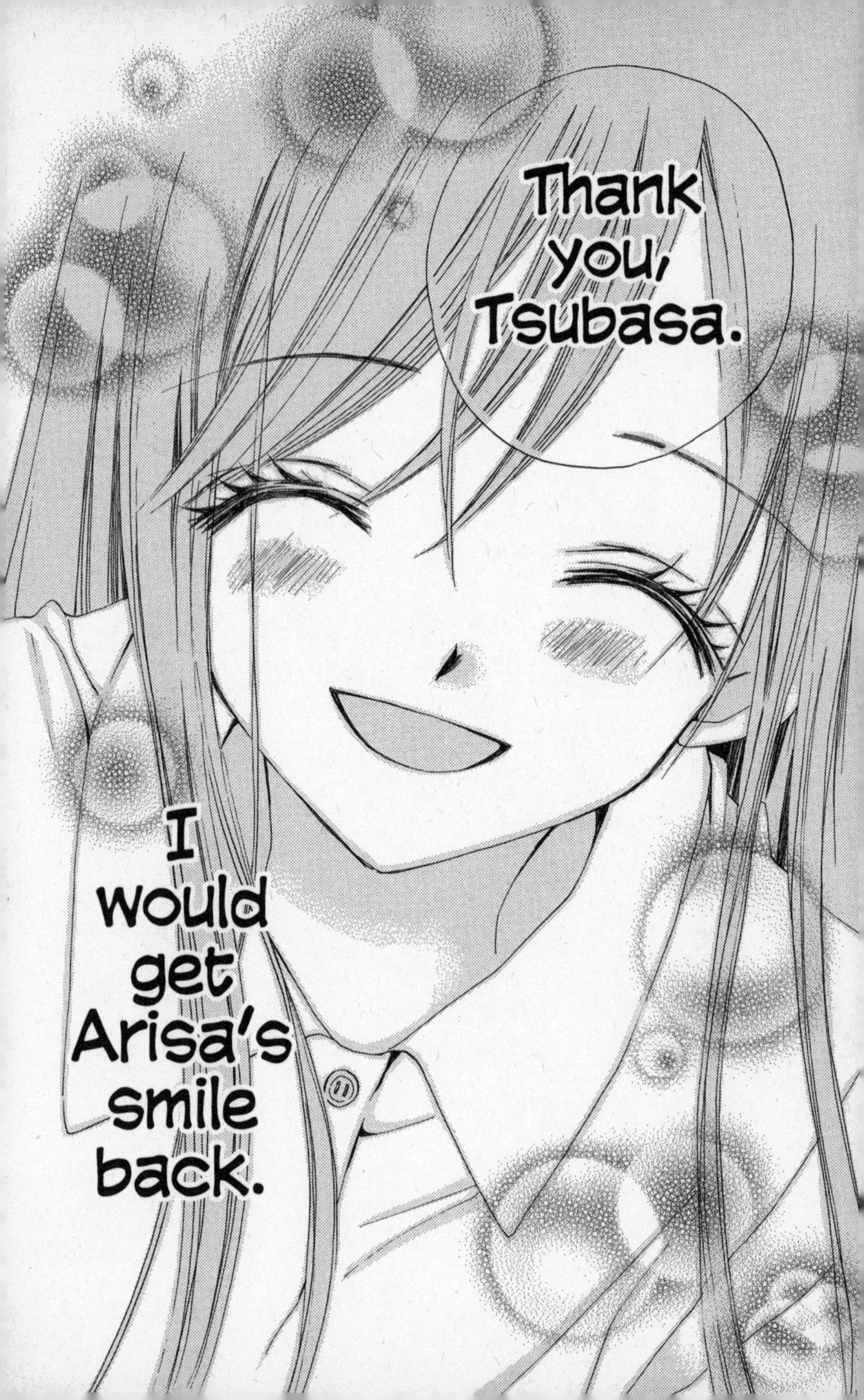
Thank you, Tsubasa.
I would get Arisa's smile back.

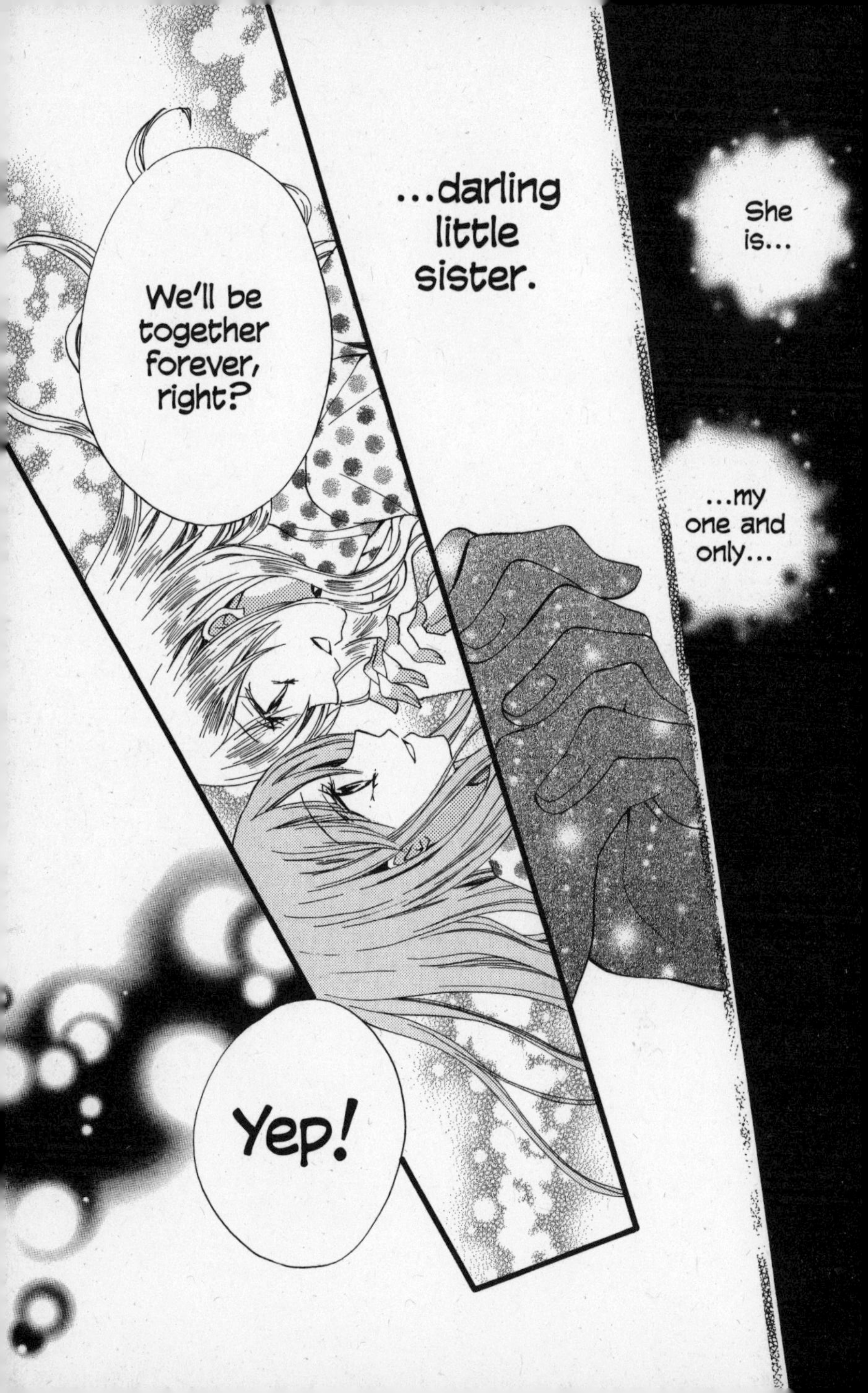
She is...
...my one and only...
...darling little sister.
We'll be together forever, right?
Yep!

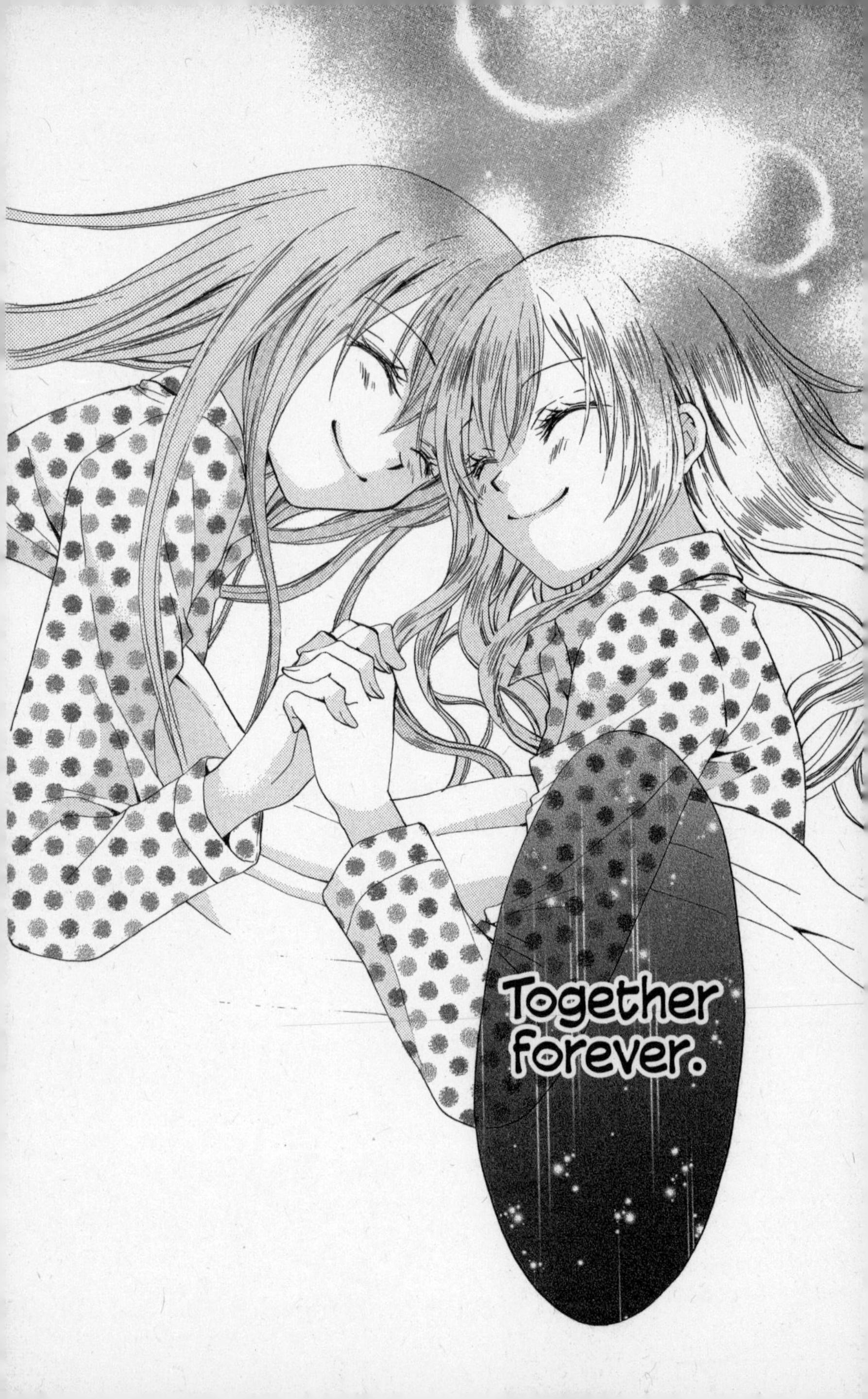
Together forever.

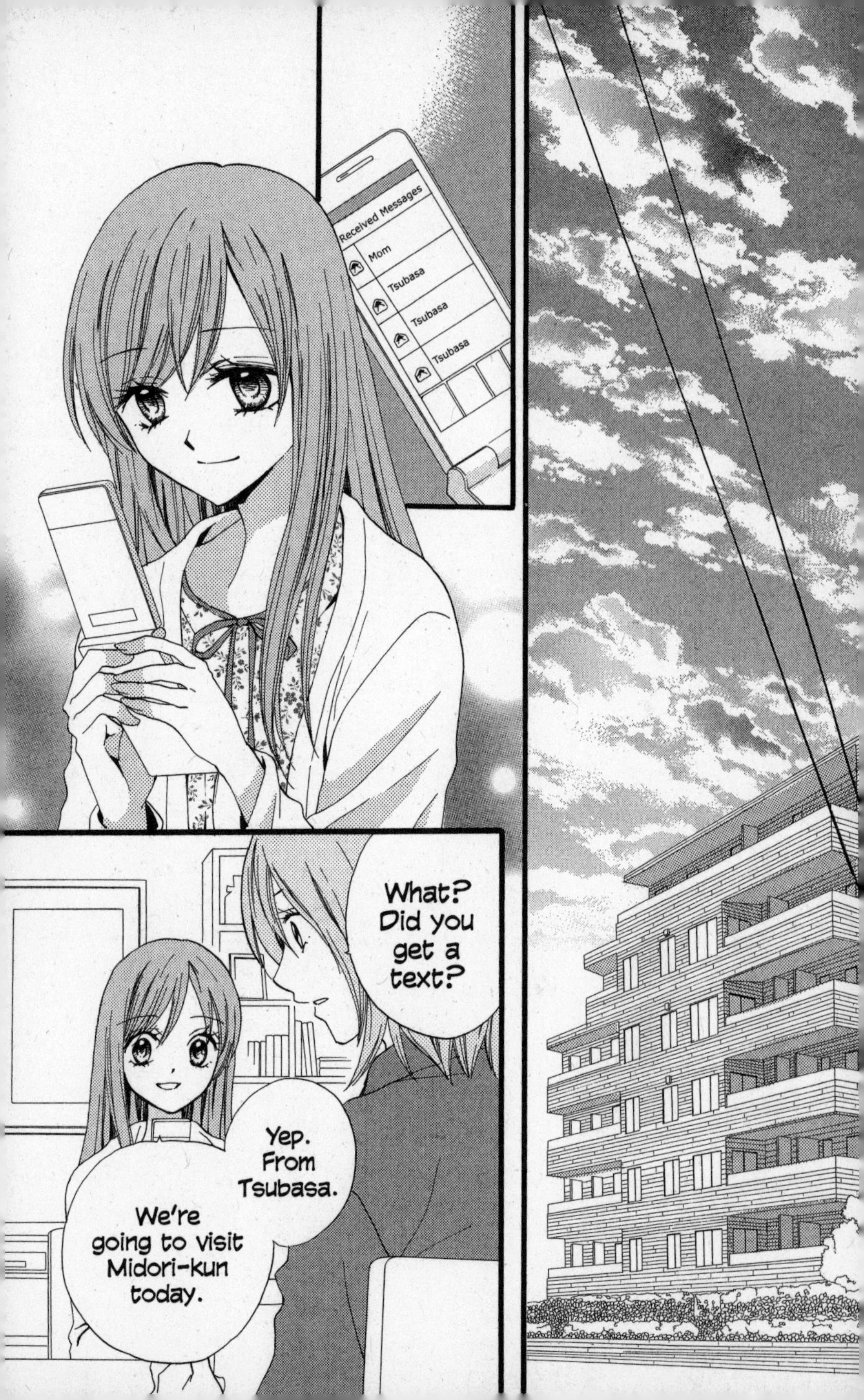
Received Messages
Mom
Tsubasa
Tsubasa
Tsubasa
What? Did you get a text?
Yep. From Tsubasa.
We're going to visit Midori-kun today.

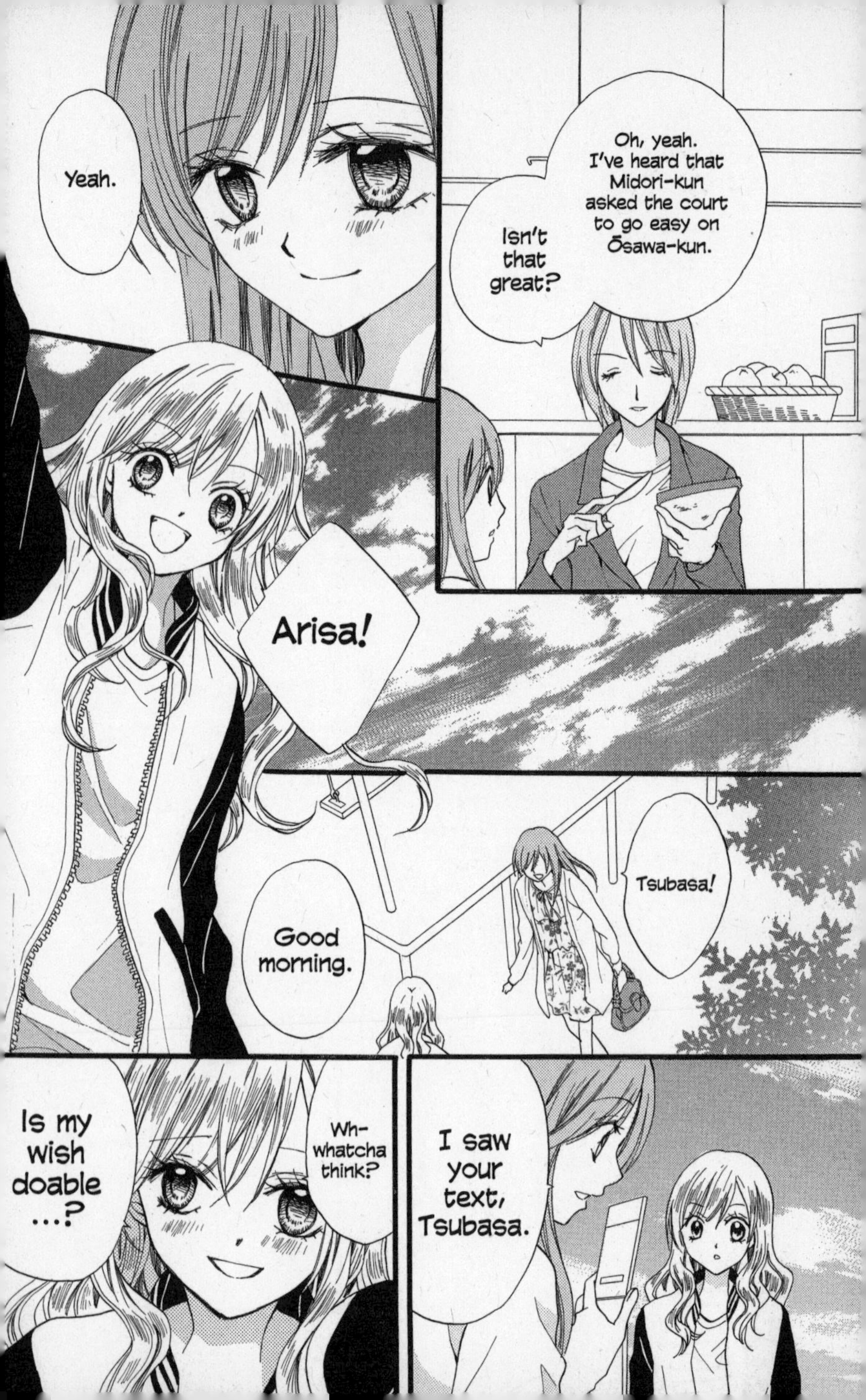
Oh, yeah. I've heard that Midori-kun asked the court to go easy on Ōsawa-kun.
Isn't that great?
Yeah.
Arisa!
Tsubasa!
Good morning.
I saw your text, Tsubasa.
Wh-whatcha think?
Is my wish doable ...?

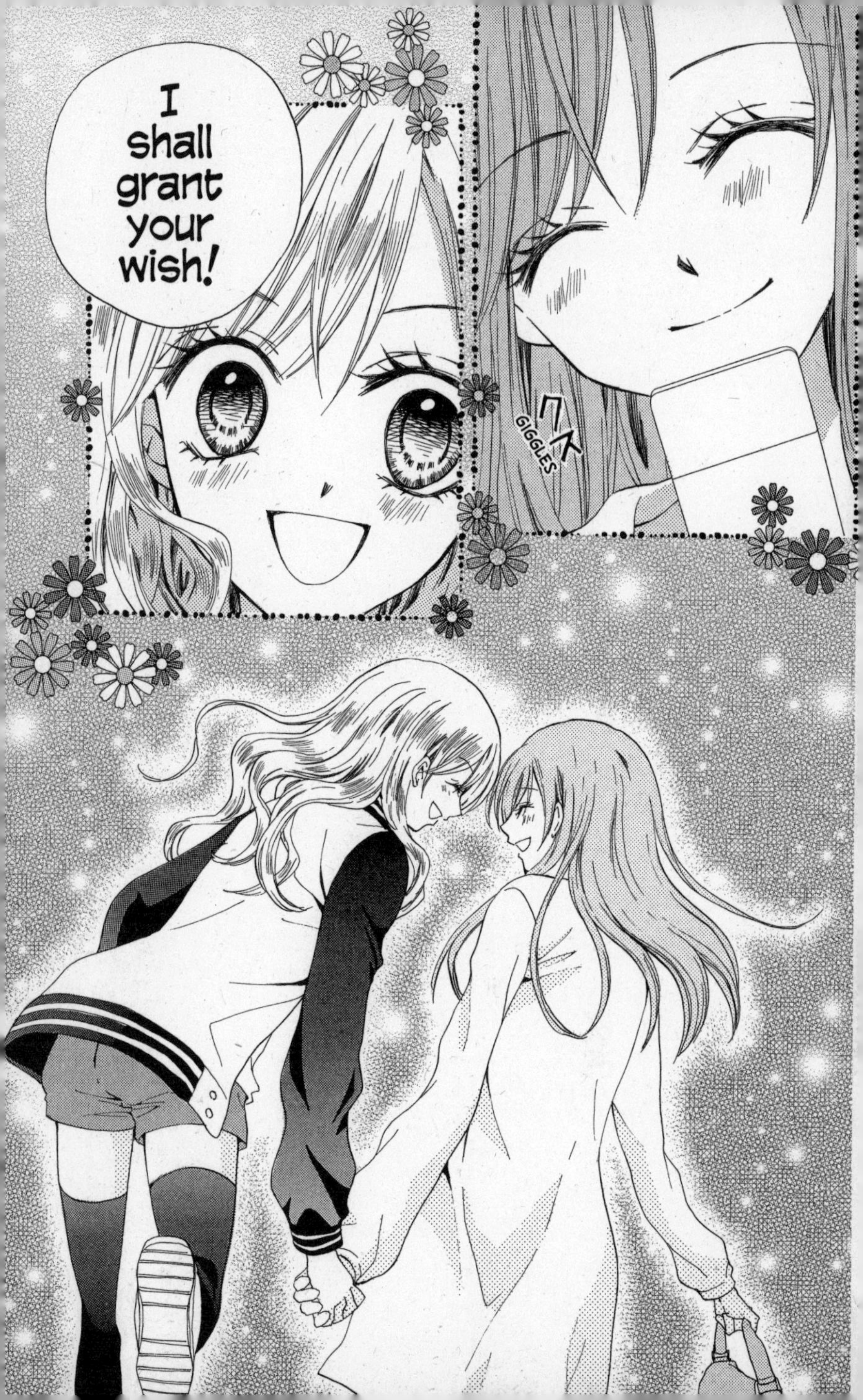
GIGGLES
I shall grant your wish!

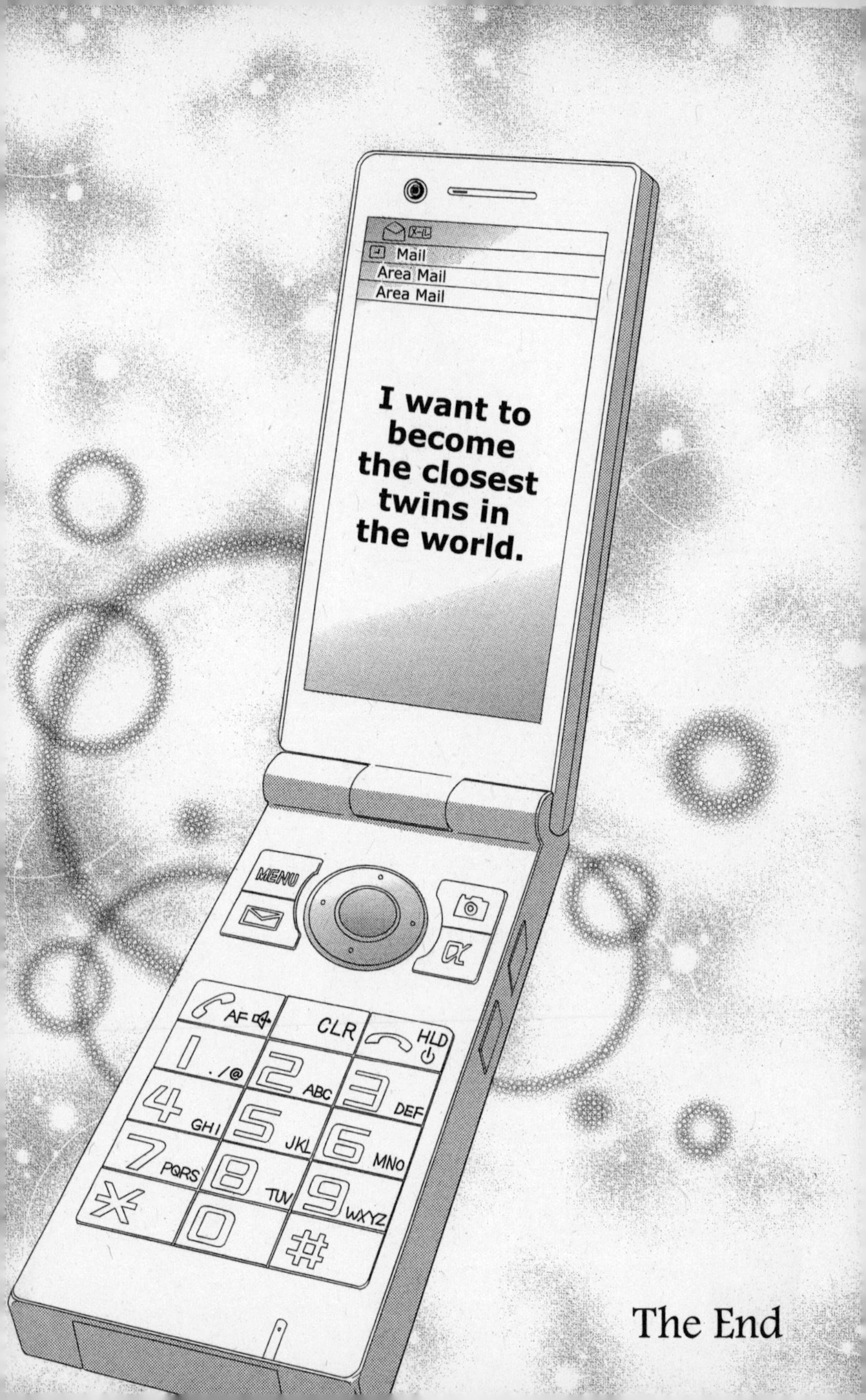
Mail
Area Mail
Area Mail
I want to become the closest twins in the world.
The End

Special Thanks

T. NAKAMURA
H. KISHIMOTO
M. NAKATA
M. MIYAJI

&
Takeda-sama, Kawamoto-sama
and Yonemura-sama of the
Nakayoshi editorial dept.
&
"hive"
Tadashi Hisamochi-sama
and
Seiko Tsuchihashi-sama
&
"Red rooster"
Takashi Shimoyama-sama
&
Ginnansha-sama

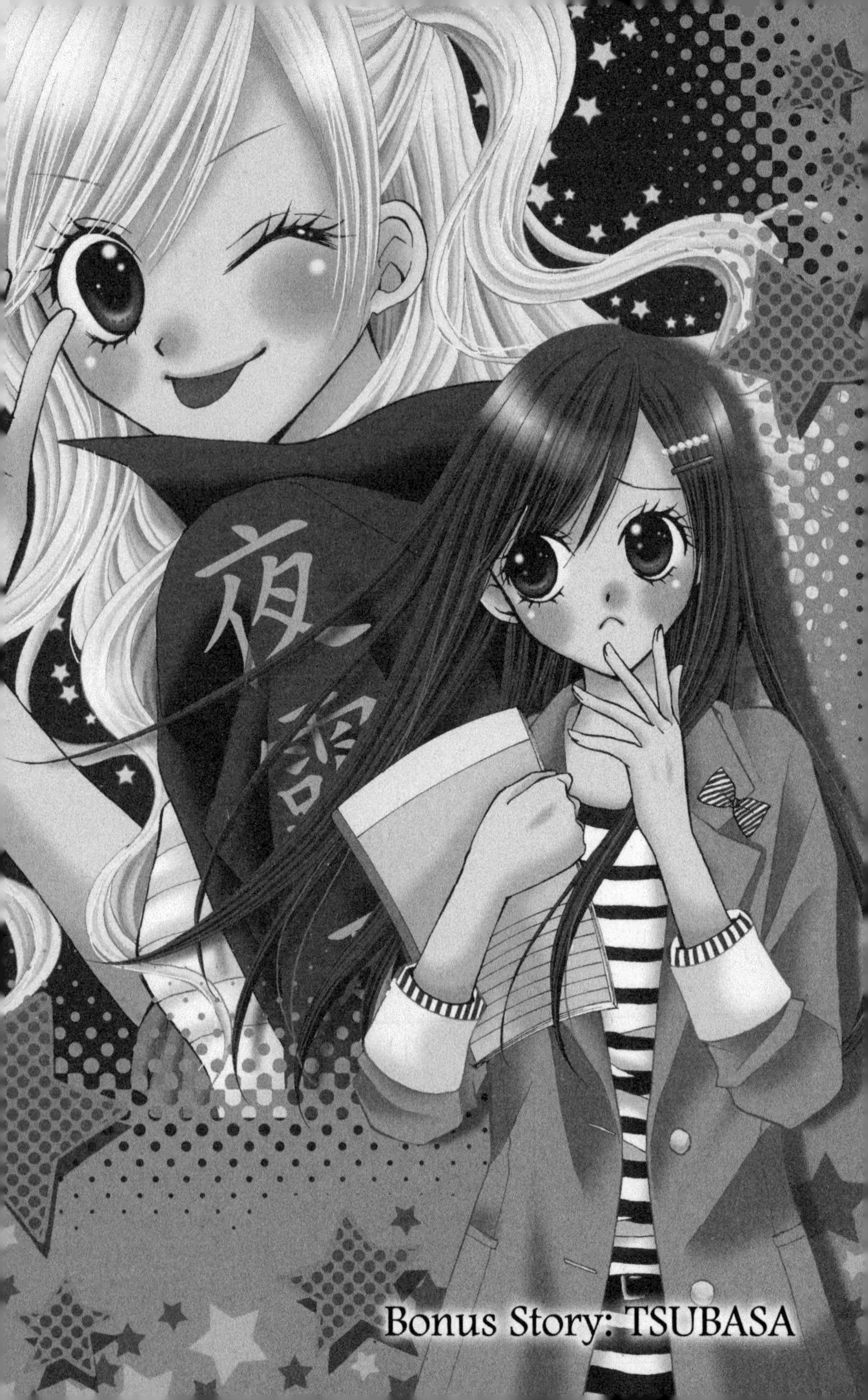
Bonus Story: TSUBASA

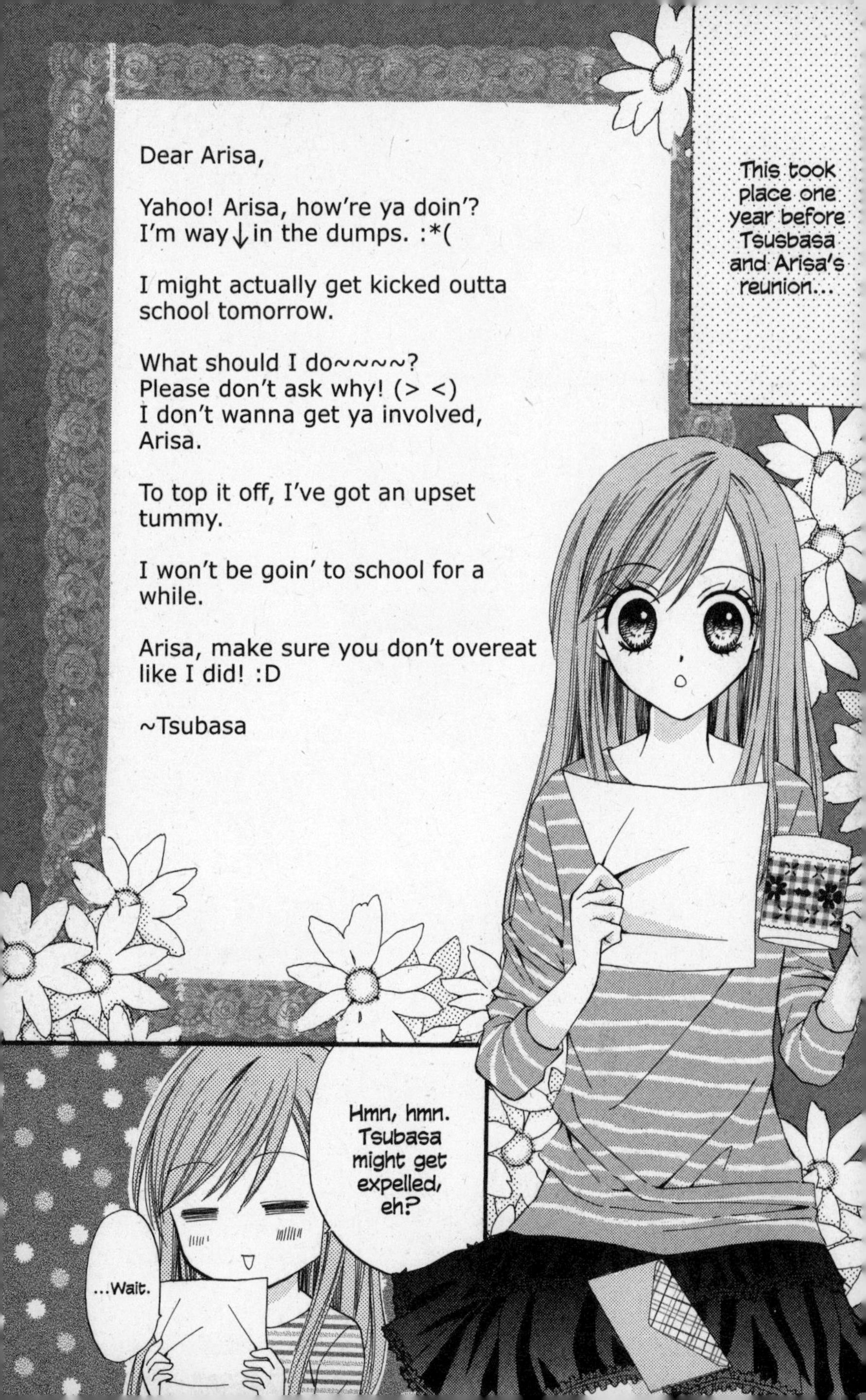
This took place one year before Tsubasa and Arisa's reunion...
Dear Arisa,
Yahoo! Arisa, how're ya doin'?
I'm way↓in the dumps. :*(
I might actually get kicked outta school tomorrow.
What should I do~~~~?
Please don't ask why! (> <)
I don't wanna get ya involved, Arisa.
To top it off, I've got an upset tummy.
I won't be goin' to school for a while.
Arisa, make sure you don't overeat like I did! :D
~Tsubasa
Hmn, hmn. Tsubasa might get expelled, eh?
...Wait.

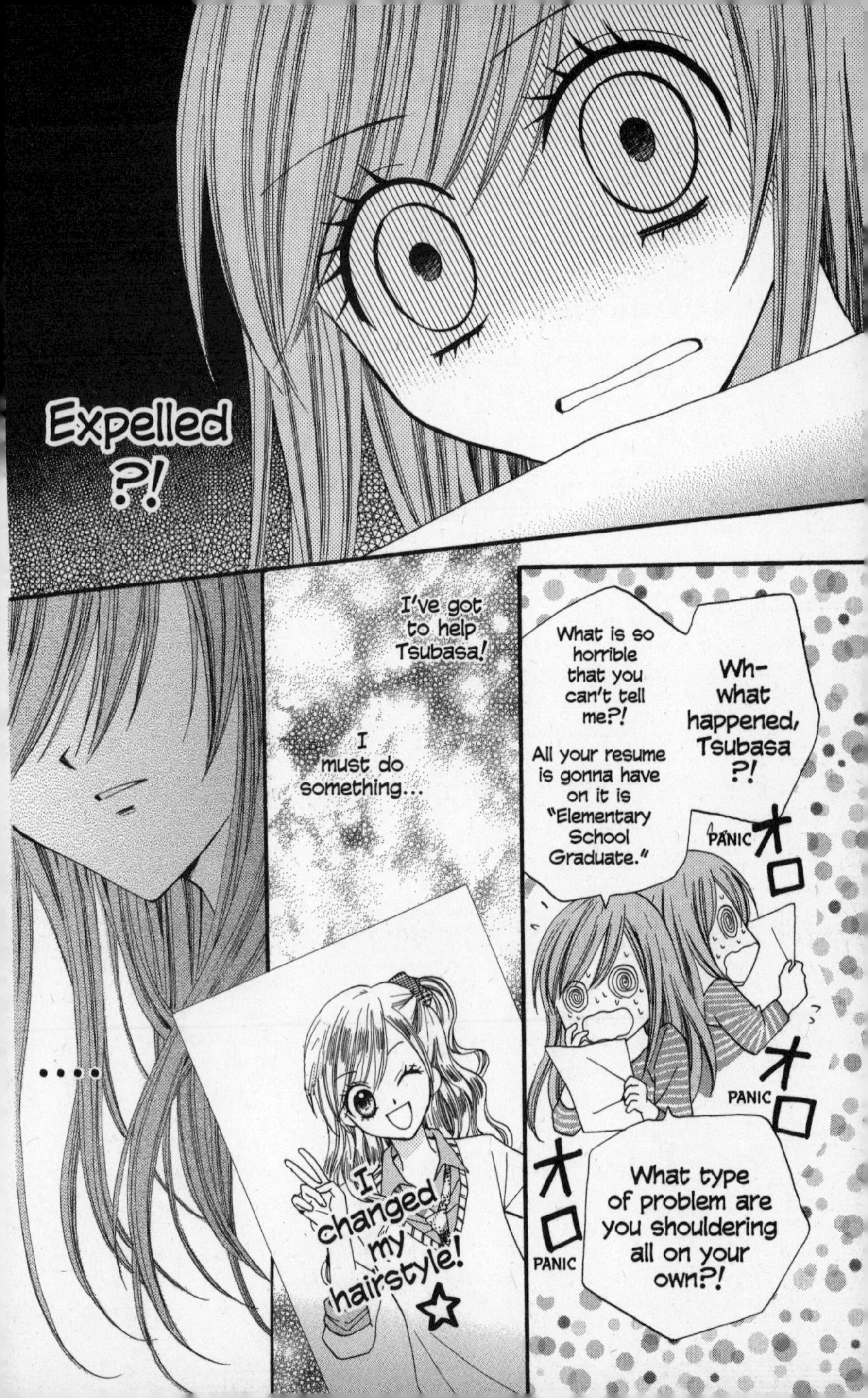
Expelled ?!
Wh- what happened, Tsubasa ?!
What is so horrible that you can't tell me?!
All your resume is gonna have on it is "Elementary School Graduate."
PANIC
PANIC
What type of problem are you shouldering all on your own?!
PANIC
I've got to help Tsubasa!
I must do something...
I changed my hairstyle! ☆
....

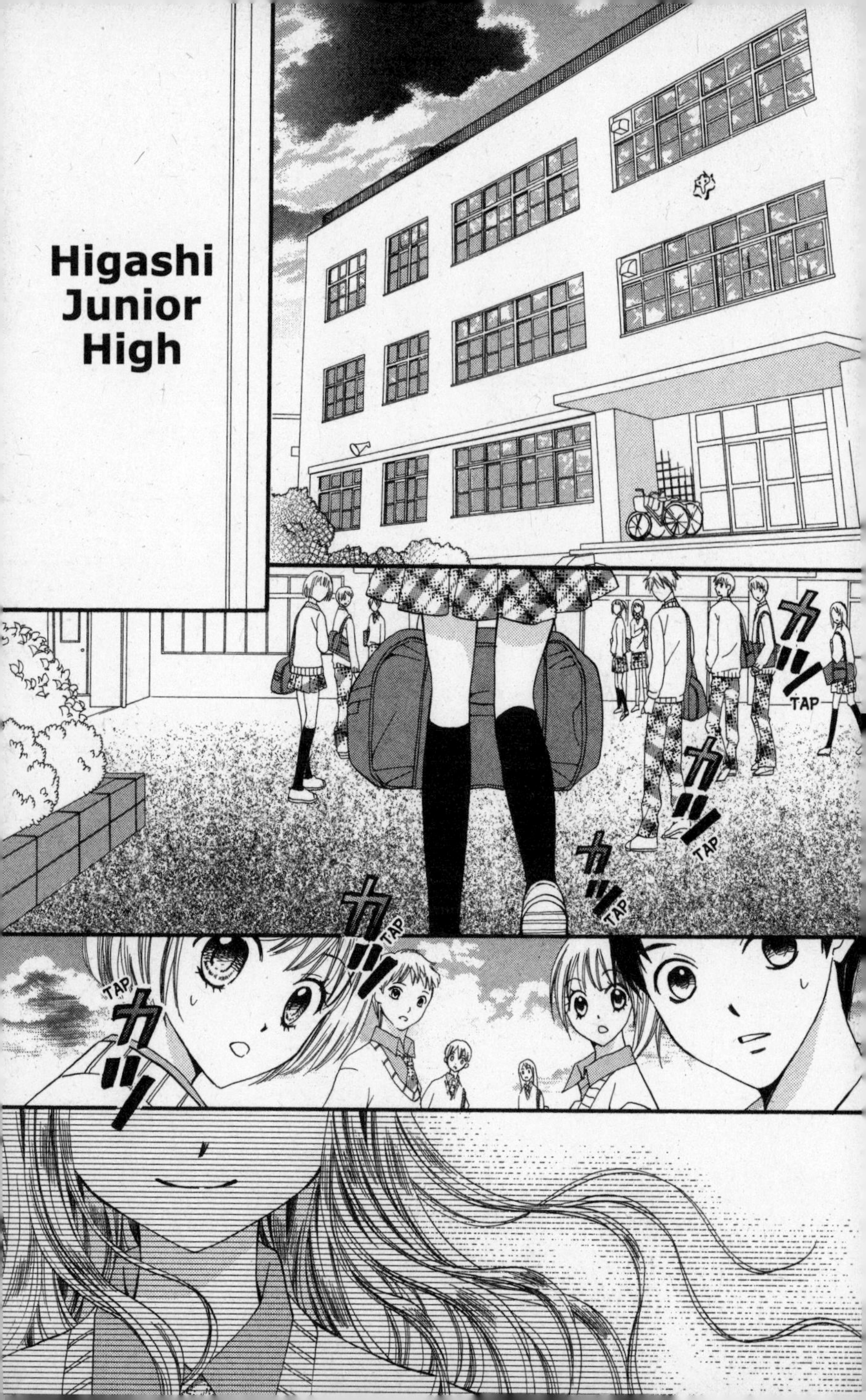
Higashi Junior High
TAP
TAP
TAP
TAP
TAP

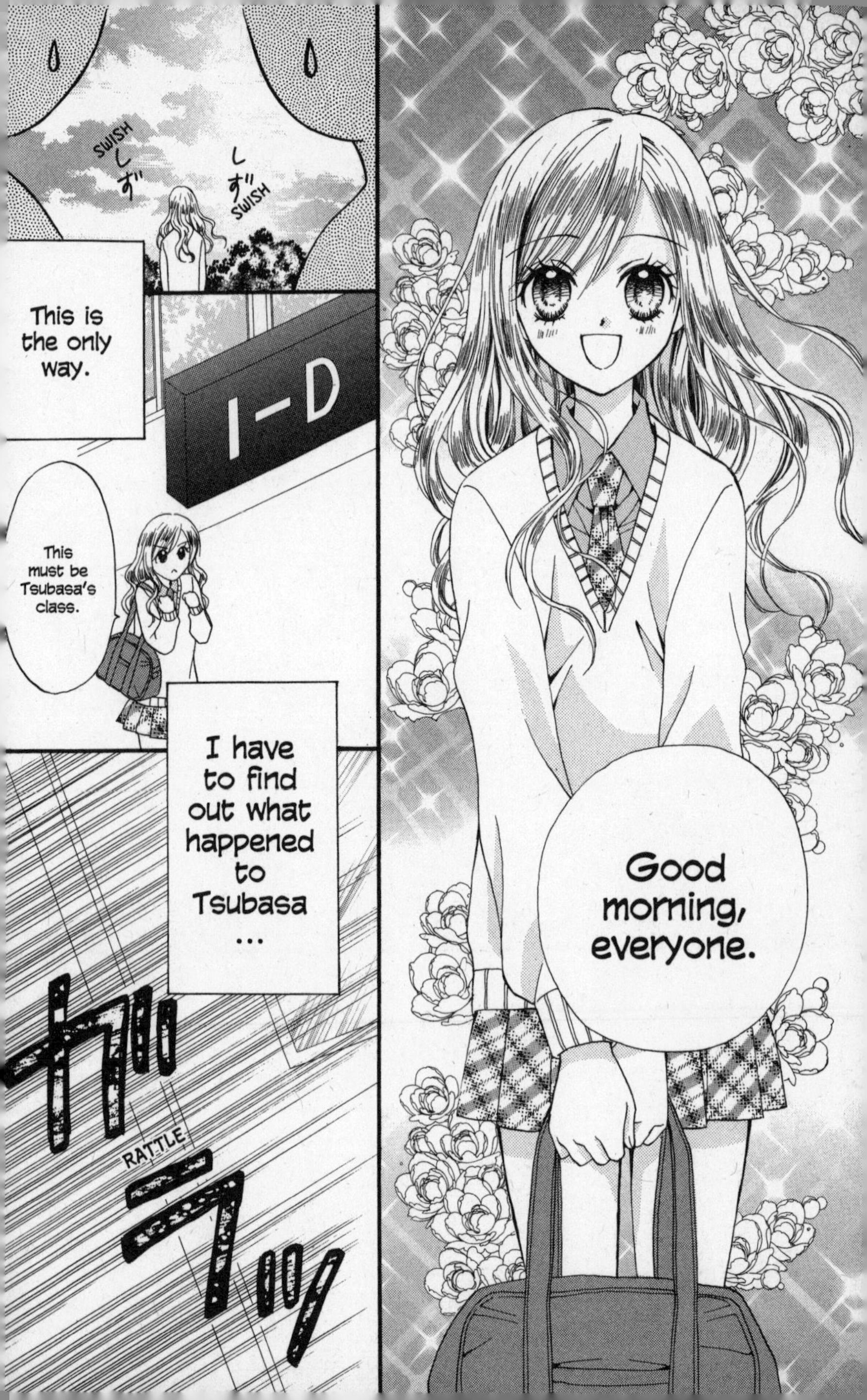
Good morning, everyone.
SWISH
しず
しず
SWISH
This is the only way.
I-D
This must be Tsubasa's class.
I have to find out what happened to Tsubasa ...
ガラッ
RATTLE

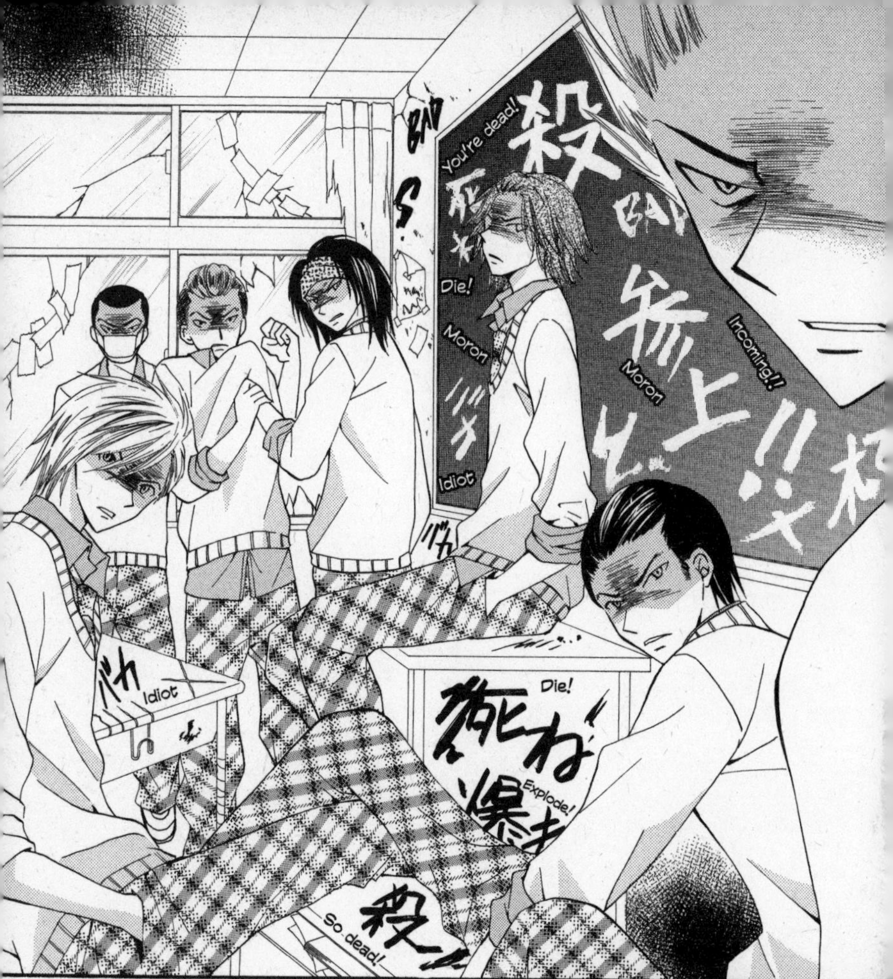
Incoming!!
Moron
You're dead!
Die!
Moron
Idiot
Die!
Explode!
So dead!
Idiot
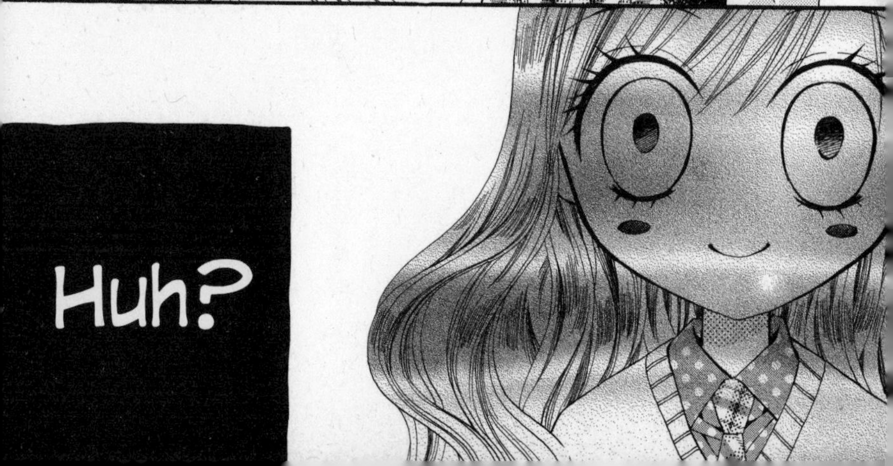
Huh?

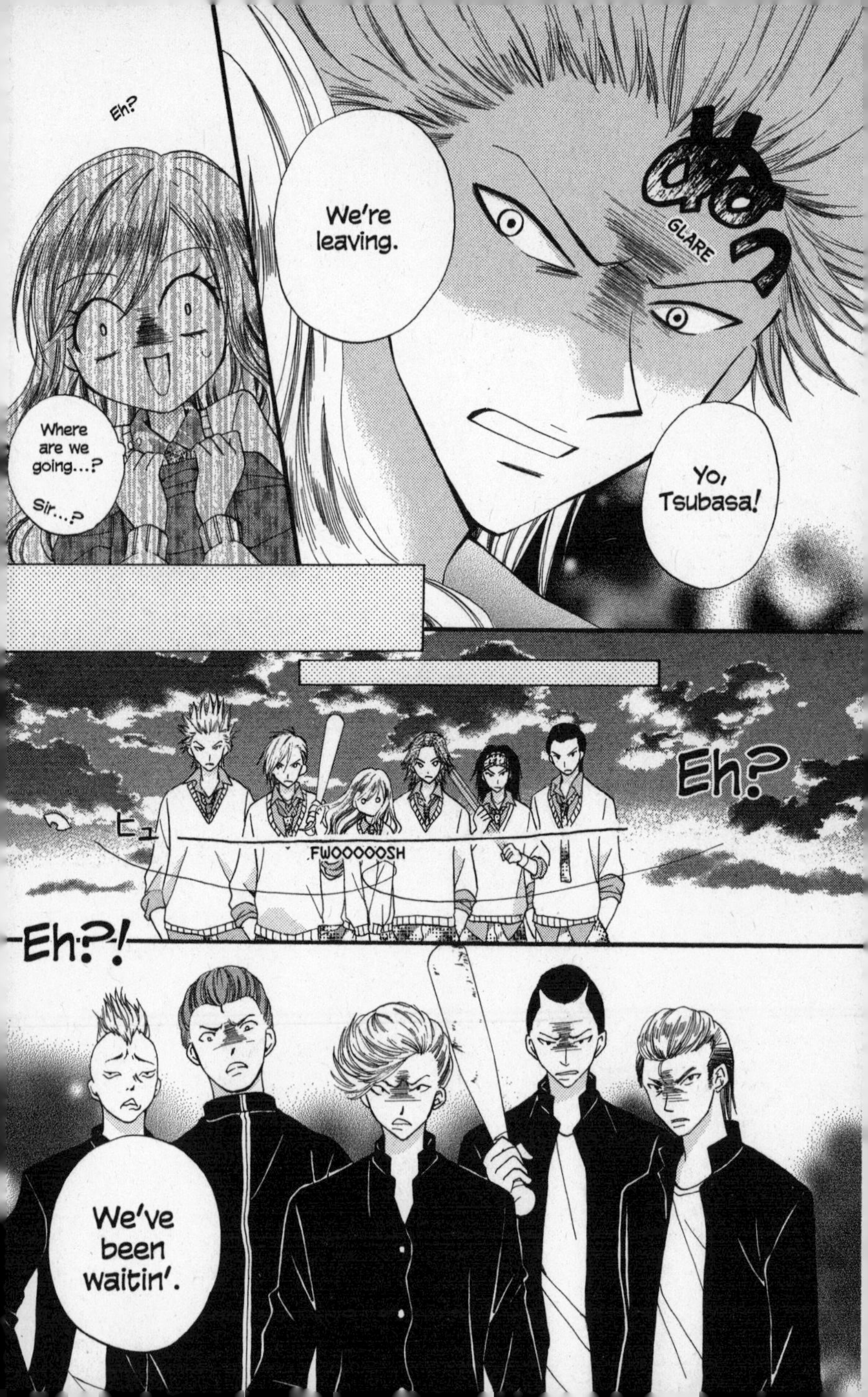
GLARE
We're leaving.
Yo, Tsubasa!
Eh?
Where are we going...?
Sir...?
Eh?
FWOOOOOSH
Eh?!
We've been waitin'.

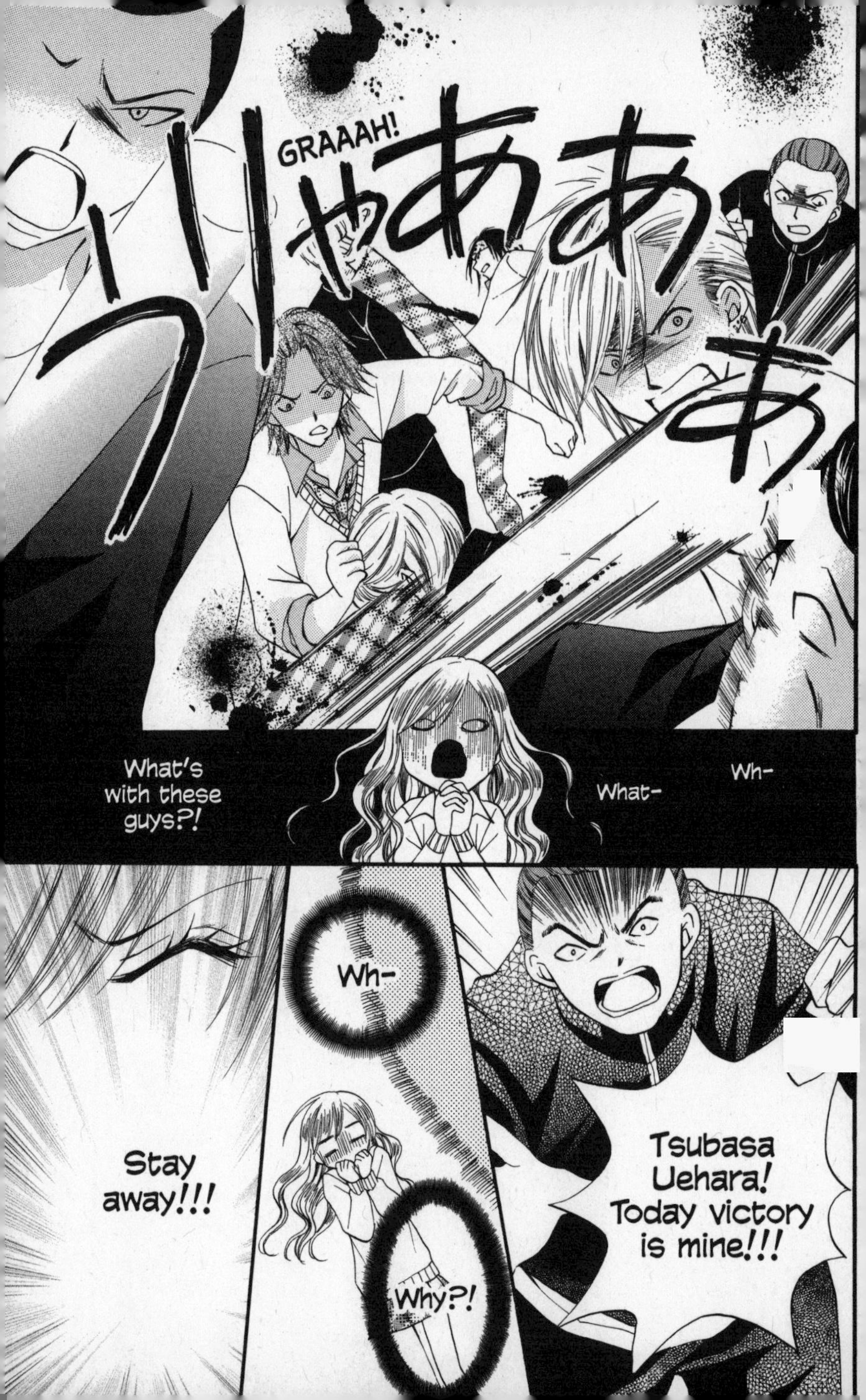
GRAAAH!
Wh-
What-
What's with these guys?!
Tsubasa Uehara! Today victory is mine!!!
Wh-
Why?!
Stay away!!!

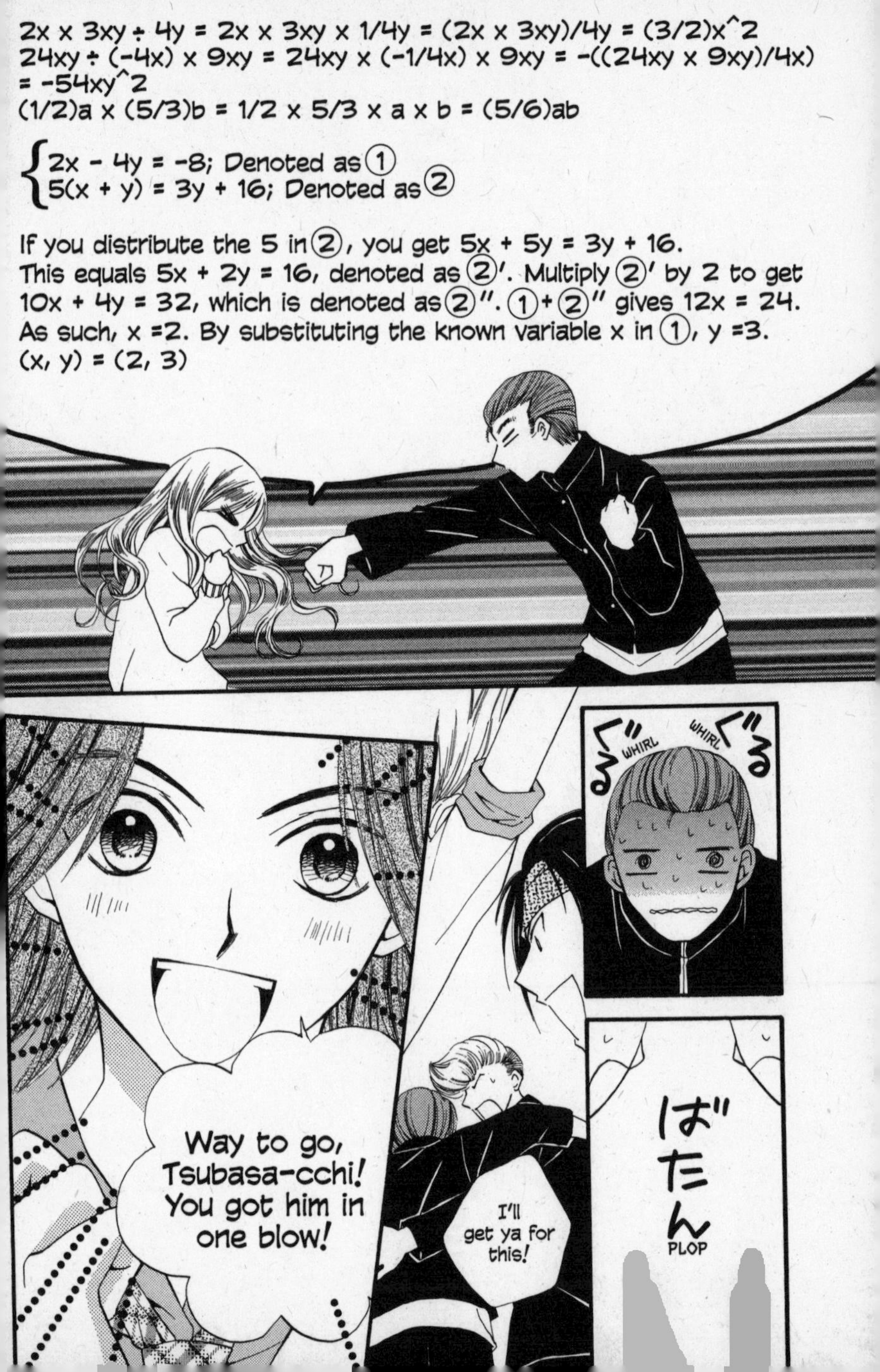
2x x 3xy ÷ 4y = 2x x 3xy x 1/4y = (2x x 3xy)/4y = (3/2)x^2
24xy ÷ (-4x) x 9xy = 24xy x (-1/4x) x 9xy = -((24xy x 9xy)/4x) = -54xy^2
(1/2)a x (5/3)b = 1/2 x 5/3 x a x b = (5/6)ab
{2x - 4y = -8; Denoted as ①
5(x + y) = 3y + 16; Denoted as ②
If you distribute the 5 in ②, you get 5x + 5y = 3y + 16. This equals 5x + 2y = 16, denoted as ②′. Multiply ②′ by 2 to get 10x + 4y = 32, which is denoted as ②″. ①+②″ gives 12x = 24. As such, x =2. By substituting the known variable x in ①, y =3. (x, y) = (2, 3)
ぐる WHIRL
ぐる WHIRL
ばたん
PLOP
I'll get ya for this!
Way to go, Tsubasa-cchi! You got him in one blow!

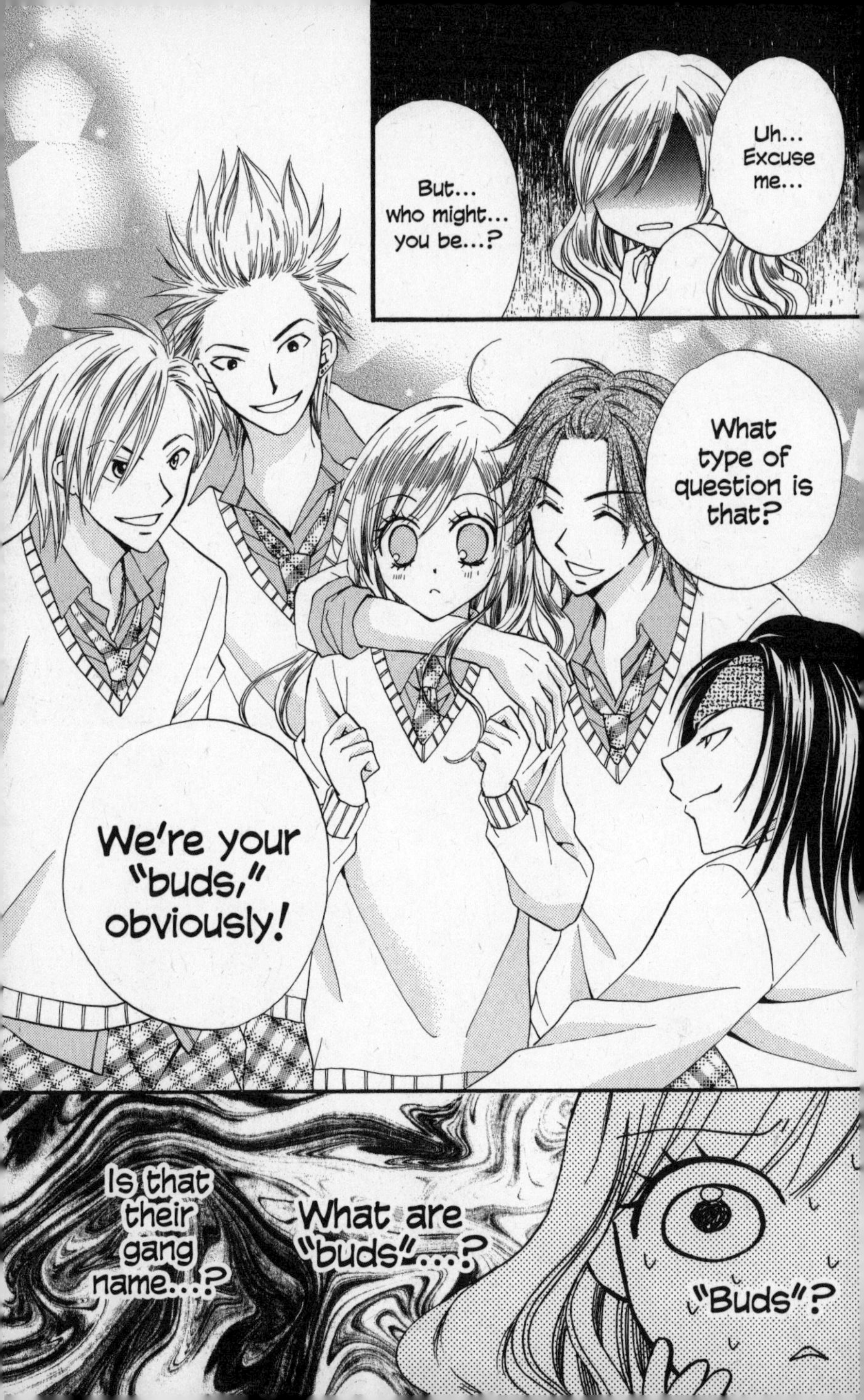
Uh... Excuse me...
But... who might... you be...?
What type of question is that?
We're your "buds," obviously!
"Buds"?
What are "buds"...?
Is that their gang name...?

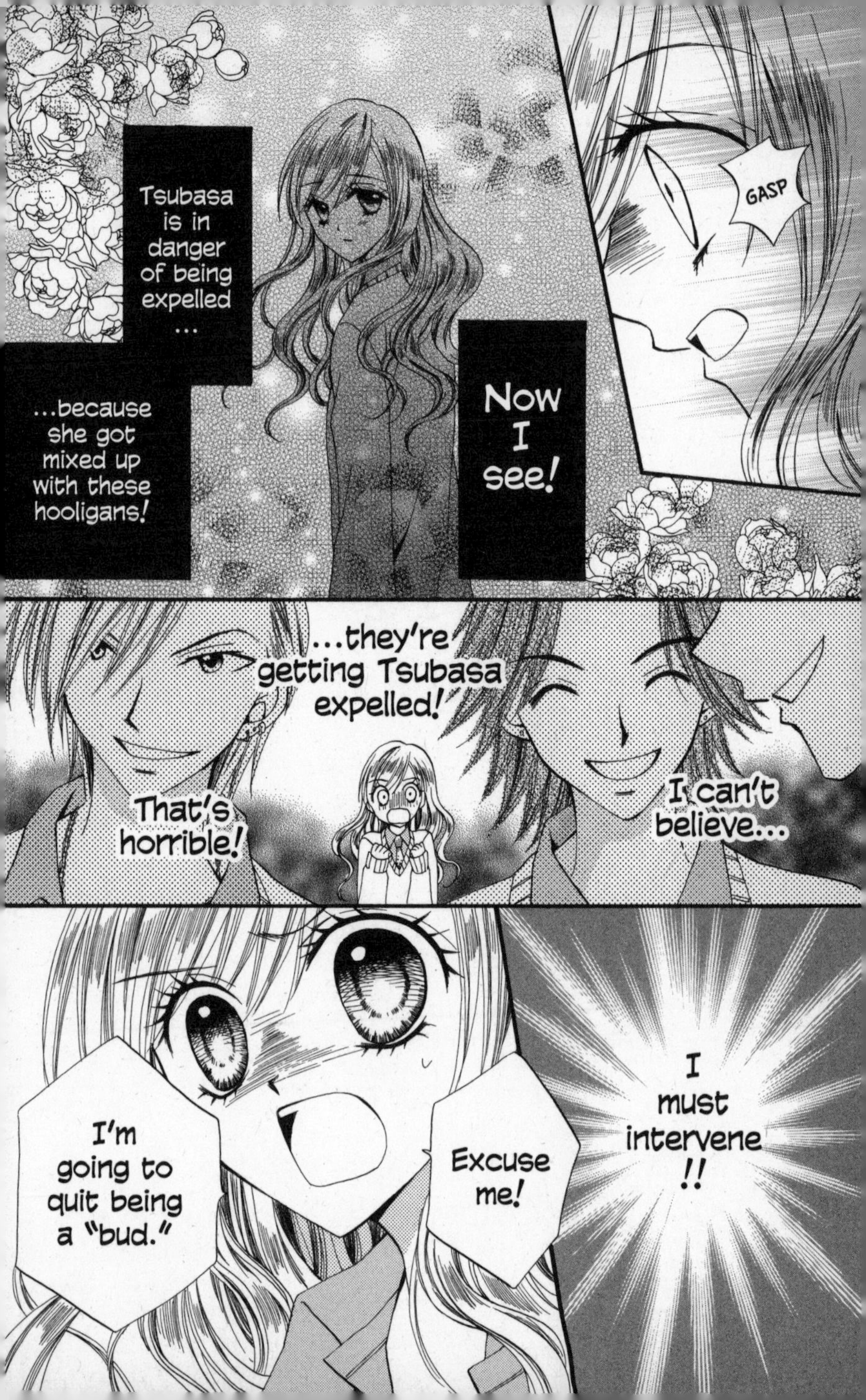

GASP
Now I see!
Tsubasa is in danger of being expelled...
...because she got mixed up with these hooligans!
I can't believe...
...they're getting Tsubasa expelled!
That's horrible!
I must intervene!!
Excuse me!
I'm going to quit being a "bud."

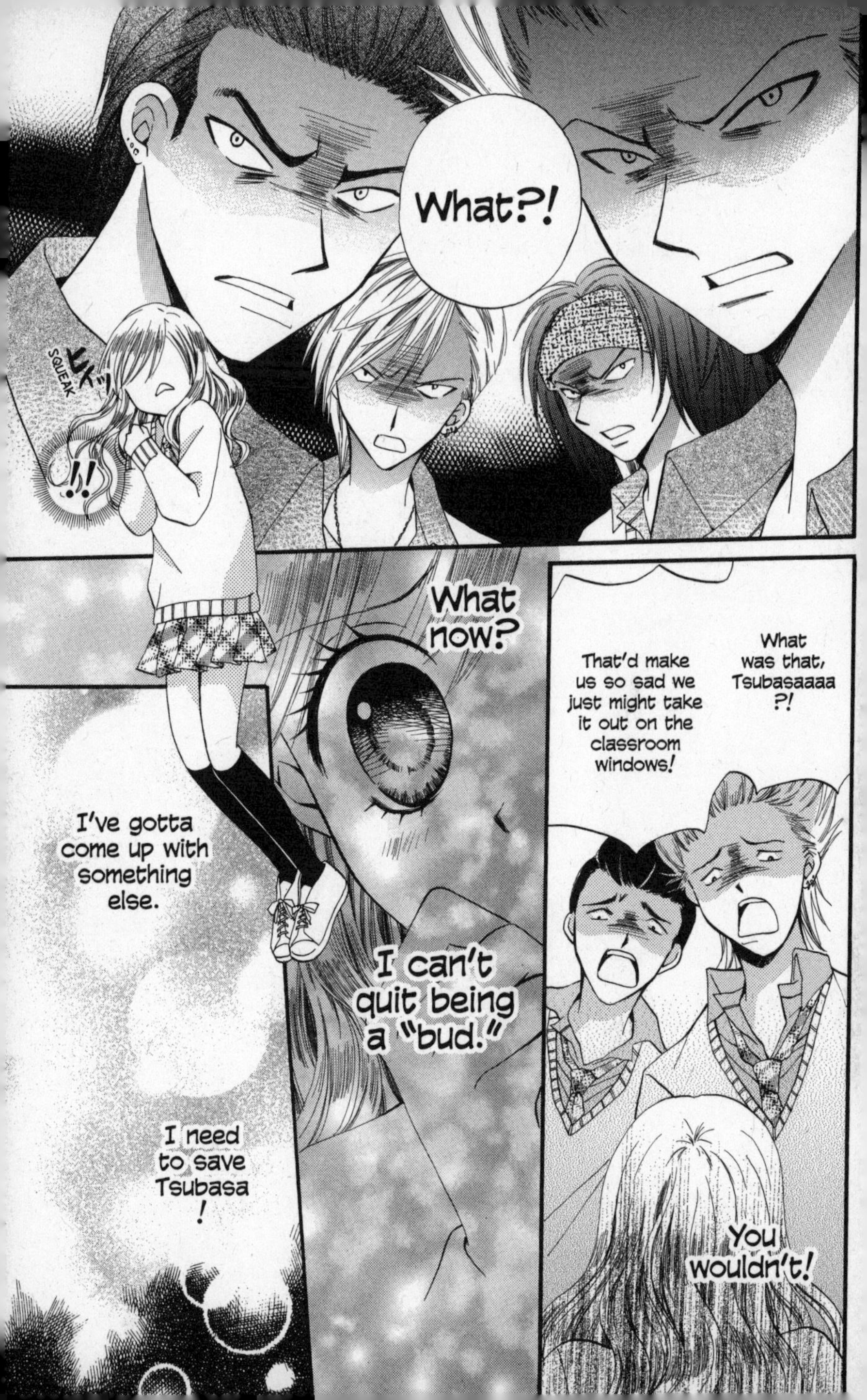
What?!
ヒッ
SQUEAK
!!
What was that, Tsubasaaaa?!
That'd make us so sad we just might take it out on the classroom windows!
You wouldn't!
What now?
I can't quit being a "bud."
I've gotta come up with something else.
I need to save Tsubasa!

te: A Dog of Flanders was written in 1872 by Marie Louise de la Ramée.

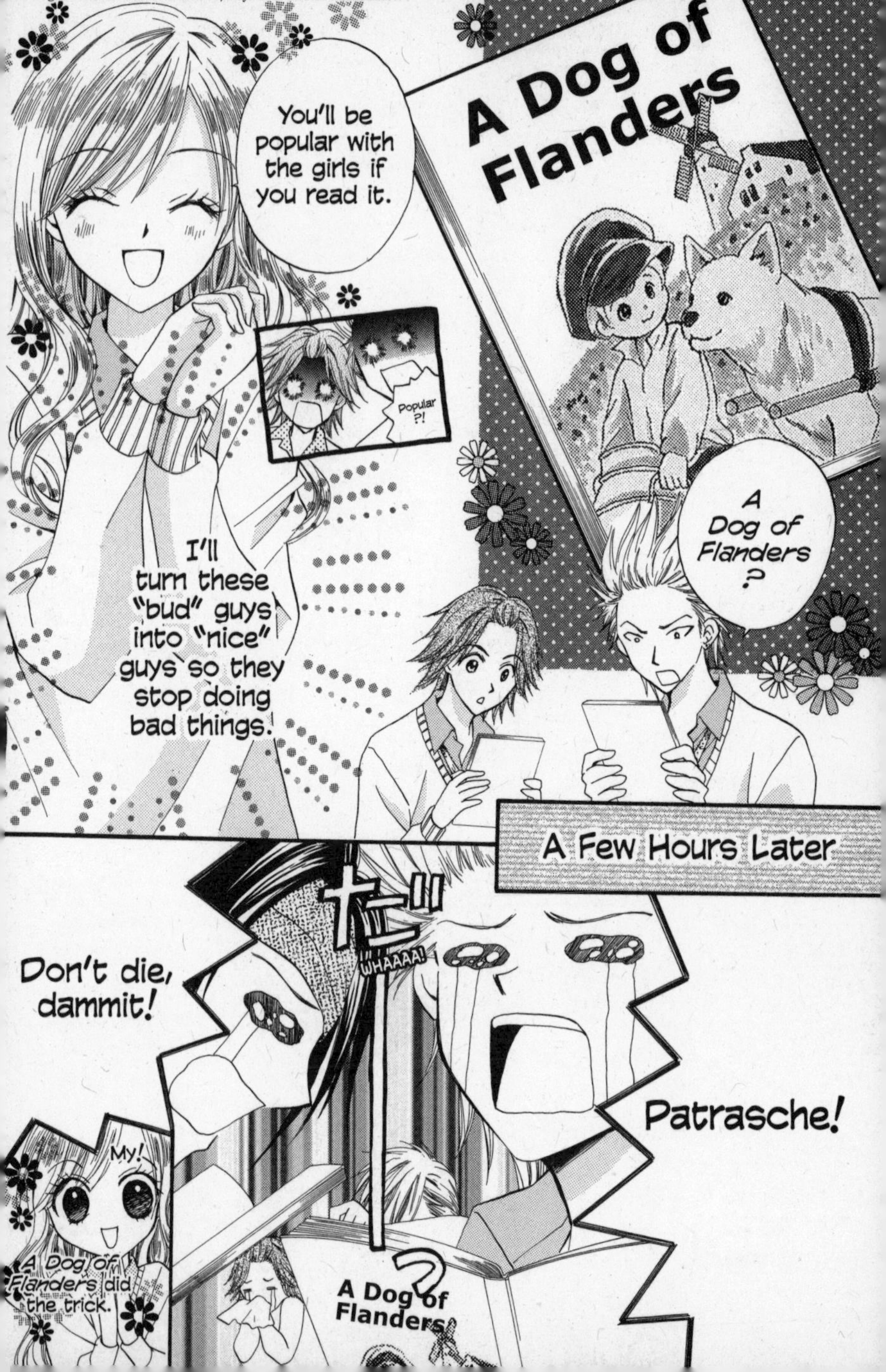

A Dog of Flanders
A Dog of Flanders?
You'll be popular with the girls if you read it.
Popular?!
I'll turn these "bud" guys into "nice" guys so they stop doing bad things.
A Few Hours Later
Patrasche!
WHAAAA!
Don't die, dammit!
A Dog of Flanders
My!
A Dog of Flanders did the trick.

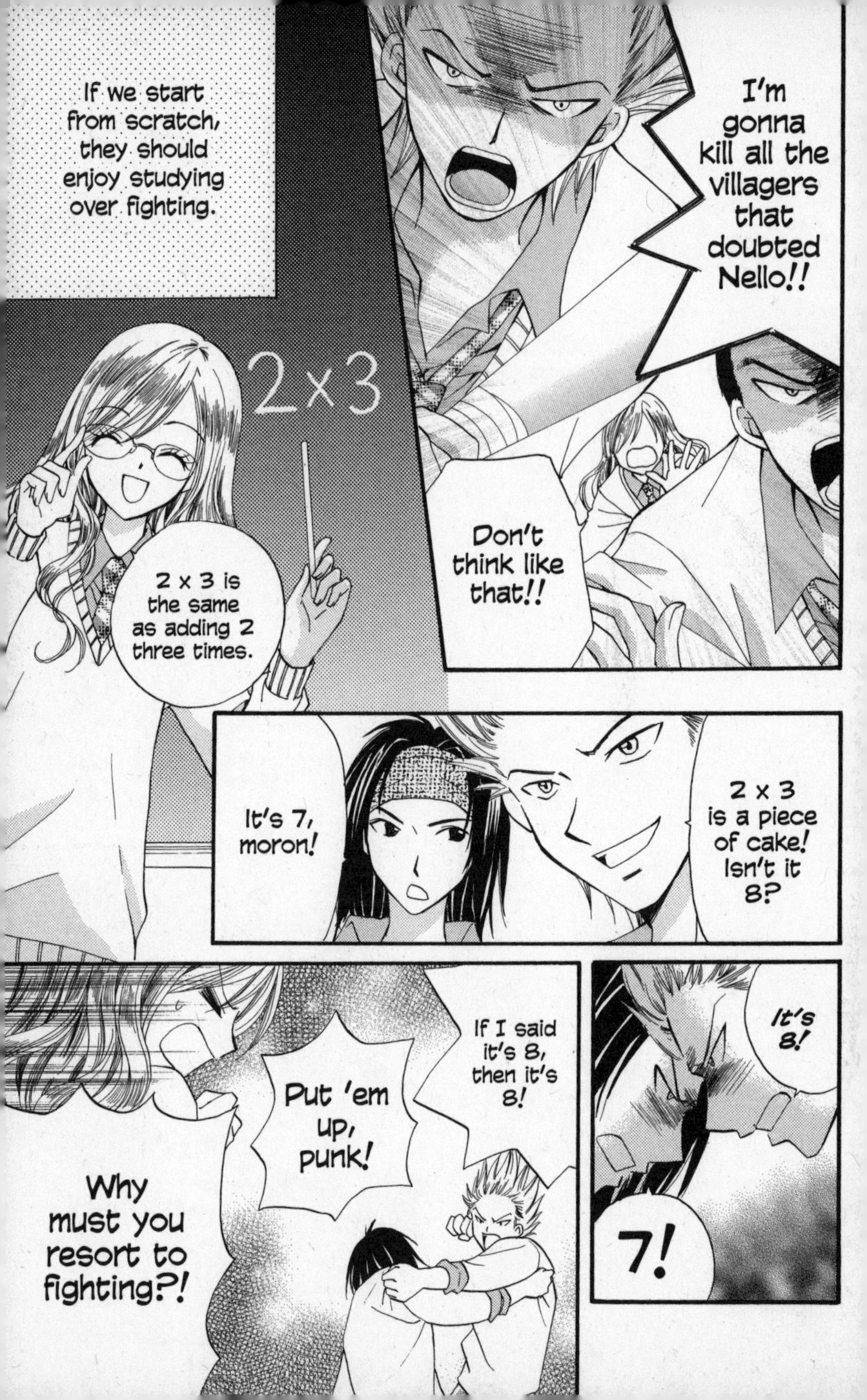
I'm gonna kill all the villagers that doubted Nello!!
Don't think like that!!
2 x 3 is a piece of cake! Isn't it 8?
It's 7, moron!
If we start from scratch, they should enjoy studying over fighting.
2x3
2 x 3 is the same as adding 2 three times.
It's 8!
7!
If I said it's 8, then it's 8!
Put 'em up, punk!
Why must you resort to fighting?!

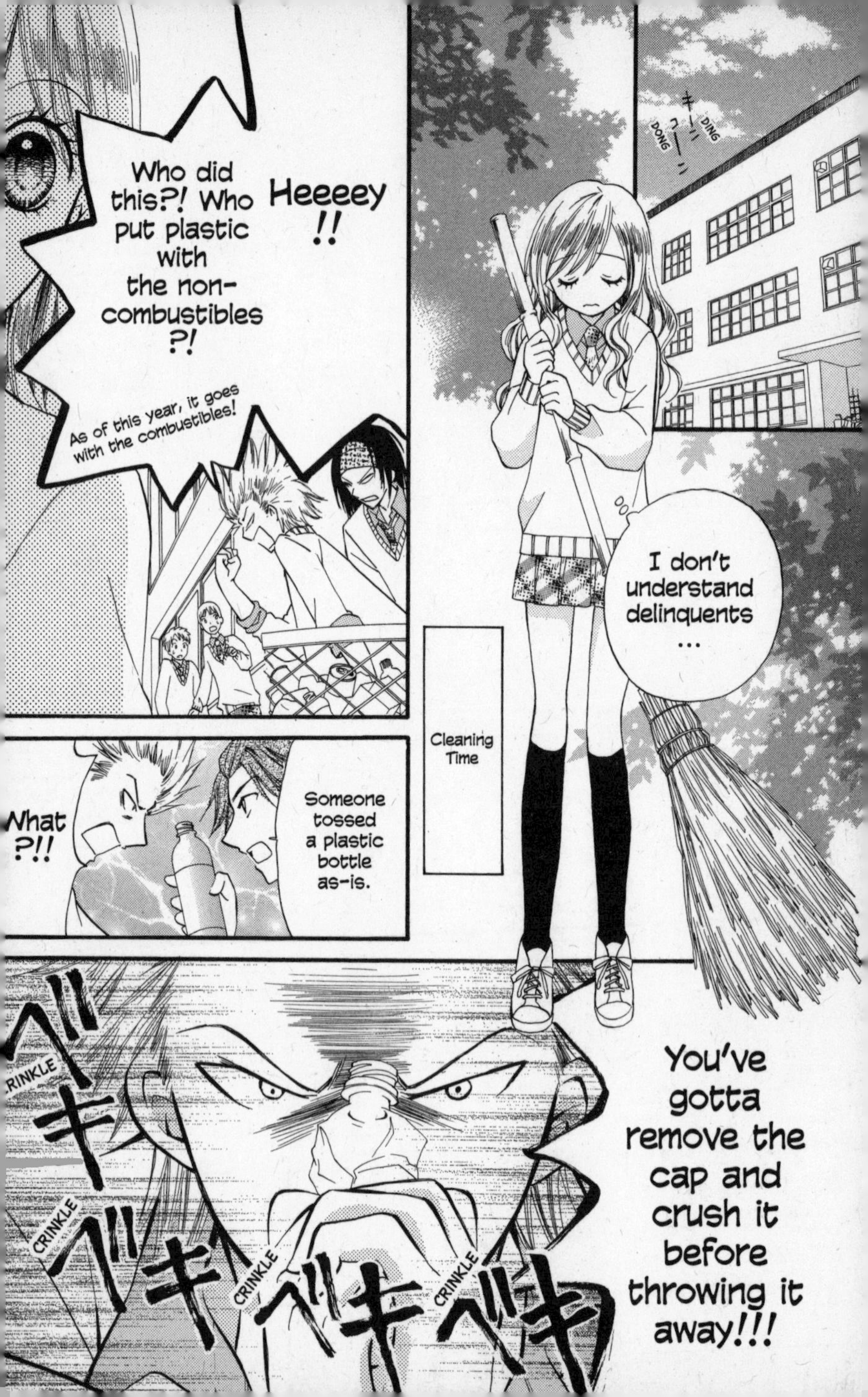

DING
DONG
I don't understand delinquents...
Cleaning Time
Heeeey!!
Who did this?! Who put plastic with the non-combustibles?!
As of this year, it goes with the combustibles!
Someone tossed a plastic bottle as-is.
What?!!
You've gotta remove the cap and crush it before throwing it away!!!
CRINKLE
CRINKLE
CRINKLE
CRINKLE

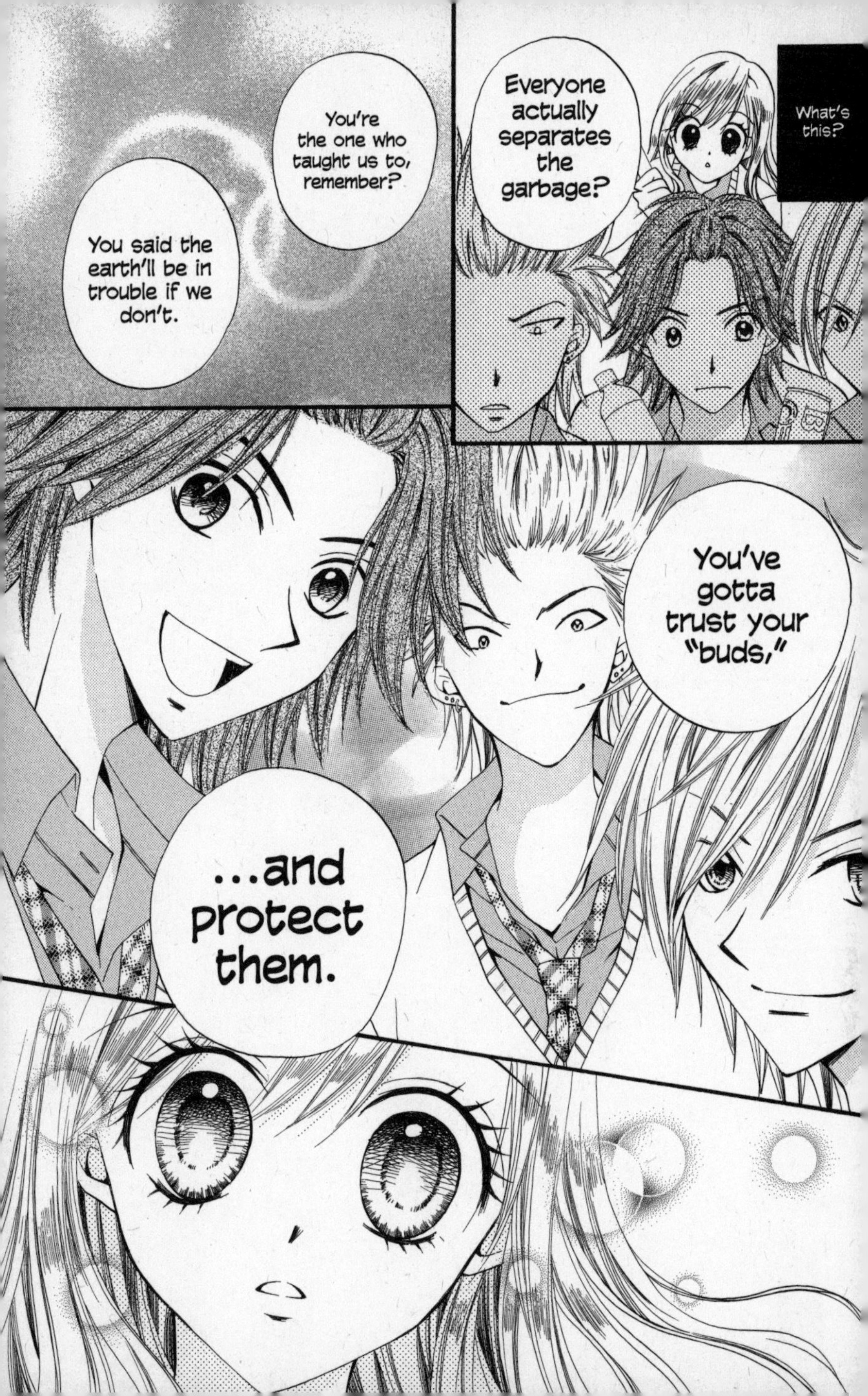
What's this?
Everyone actually separates the garbage?
You're the one who taught us to, remember?
You said the earth'll be in trouble if we don't.
You've gotta trust your "buds,"
...and protect them.

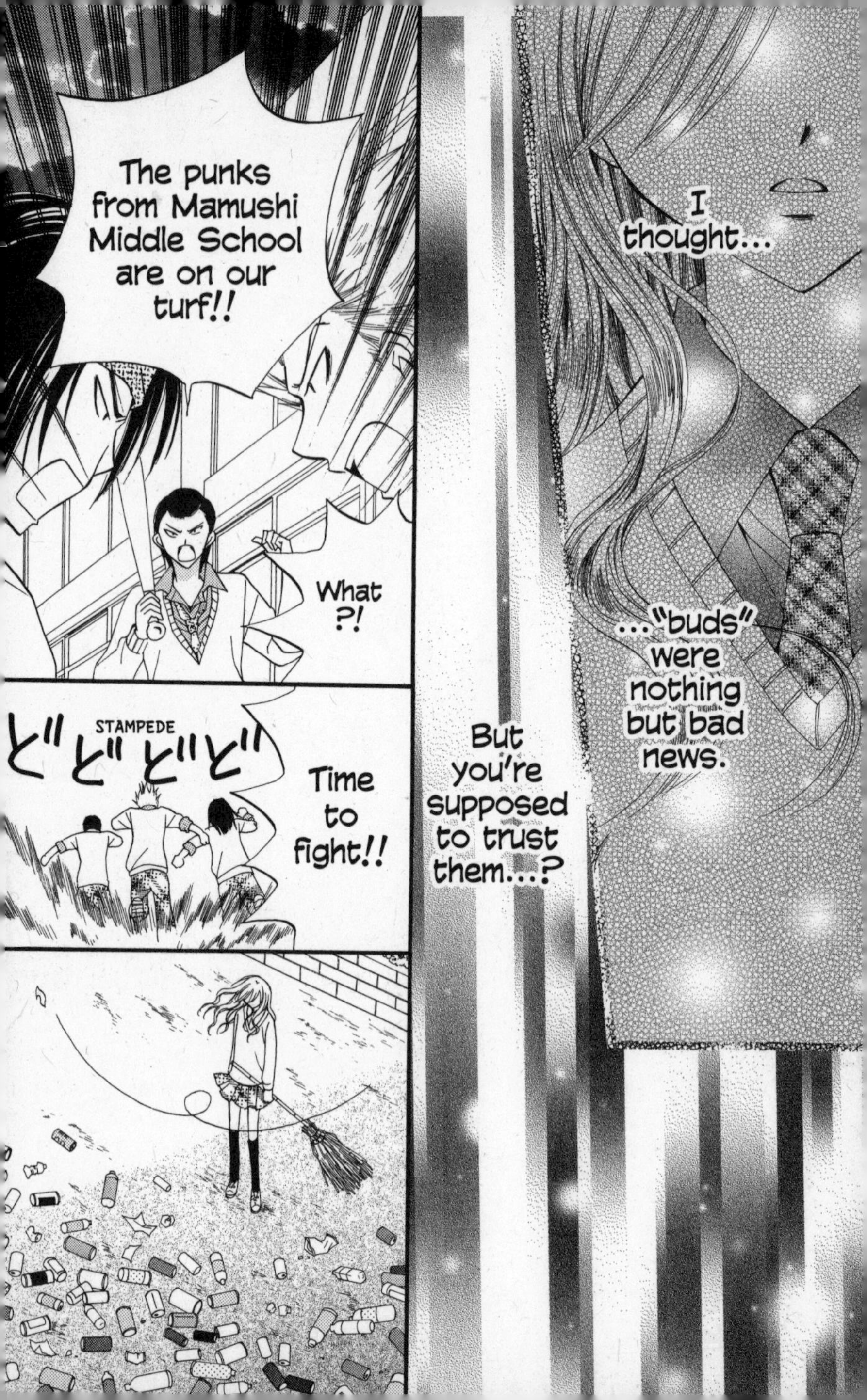
I thought...
..."buds" were nothing but bad news.
But you're supposed to trust them...?
The punks from Mamushi Middle School are on our turf!!
What?!
STAMPEDE
Time to fight!!

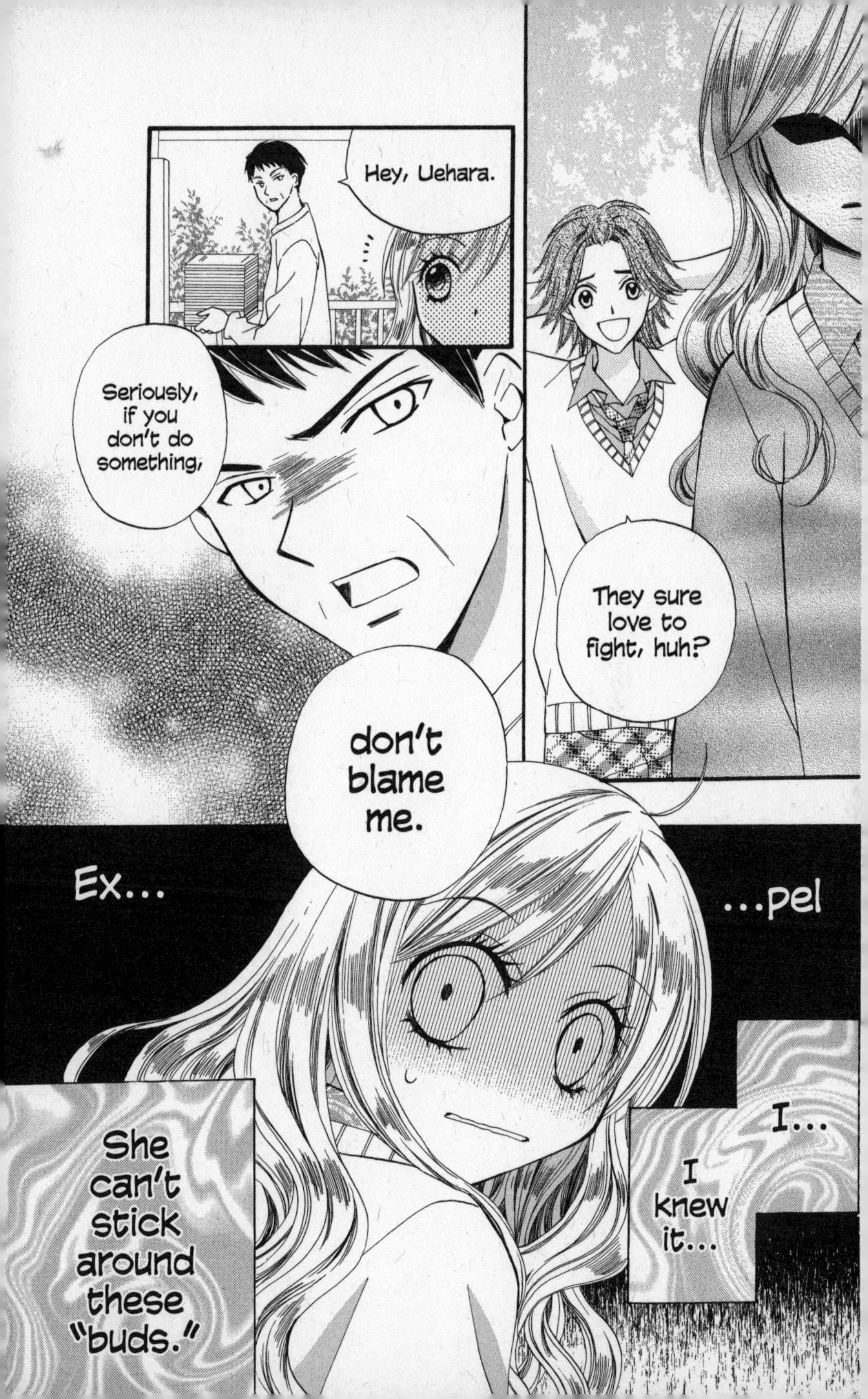
They sure love to fight, huh?
Hey, Uehara.
Seriously, if you don't do something,
don't blame me.
Ex...
...pel
I... I knew it...
She can't stick around these "buds."

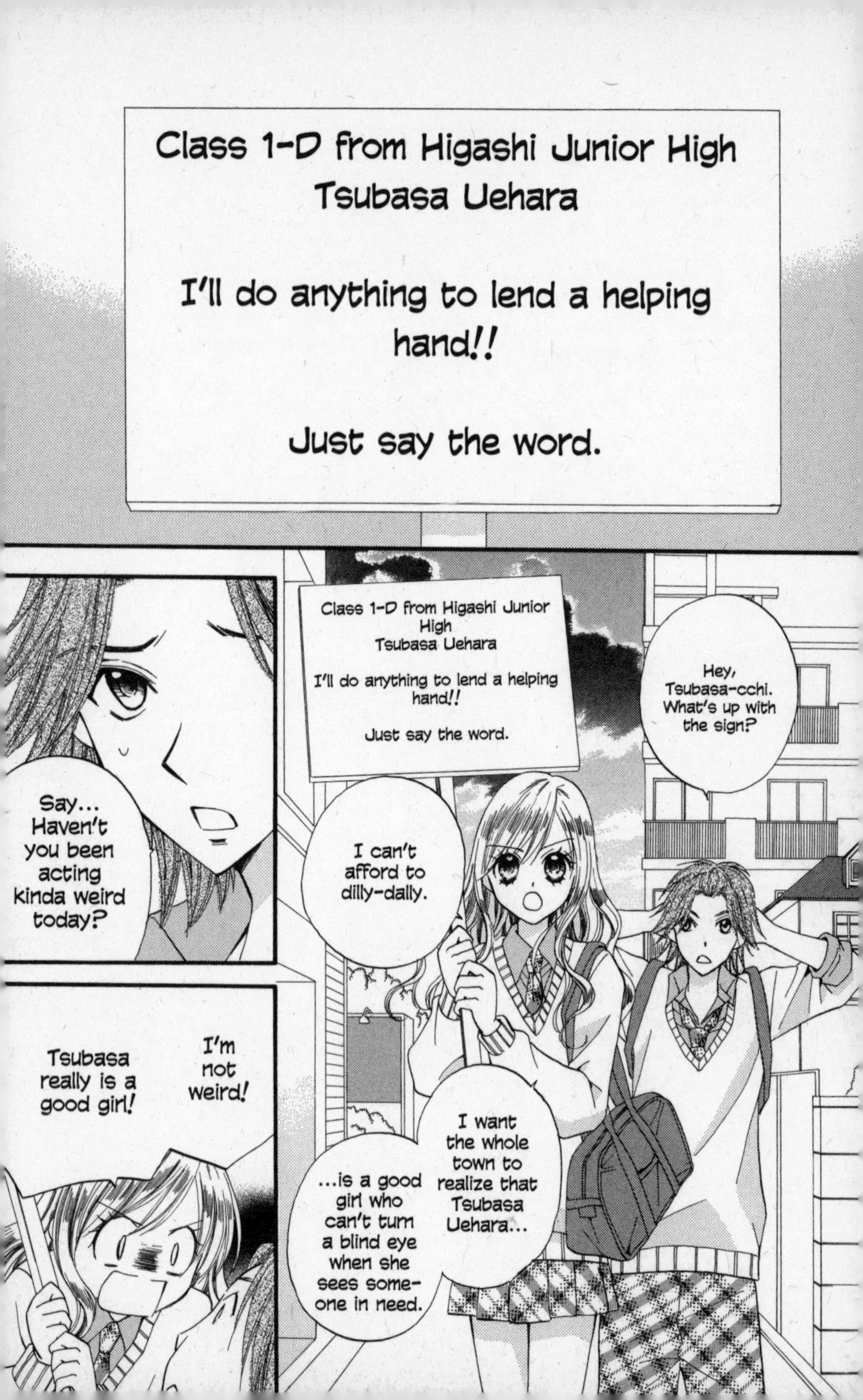
Class 1-D from Higashi Junior High
Tsubasa Uehara
I'll do anything to lend a helping hand!!
Just say the word.
Class 1-D from Higashi Junior High Tsubasa Uehara I'll do anything to lend a helping hand!! Just say the word.
Hey, Tsubasa-cchi. What's up with the sign?
I can't afford to dilly-dally.
I want the whole town to realize that Tsubasa Uehara...
...is a good girl who can't turn a blind eye when she sees someone in need.
Say... Haven't you been acting kinda weird today?
I'm not weird!
Tsubasa really is a good girl!

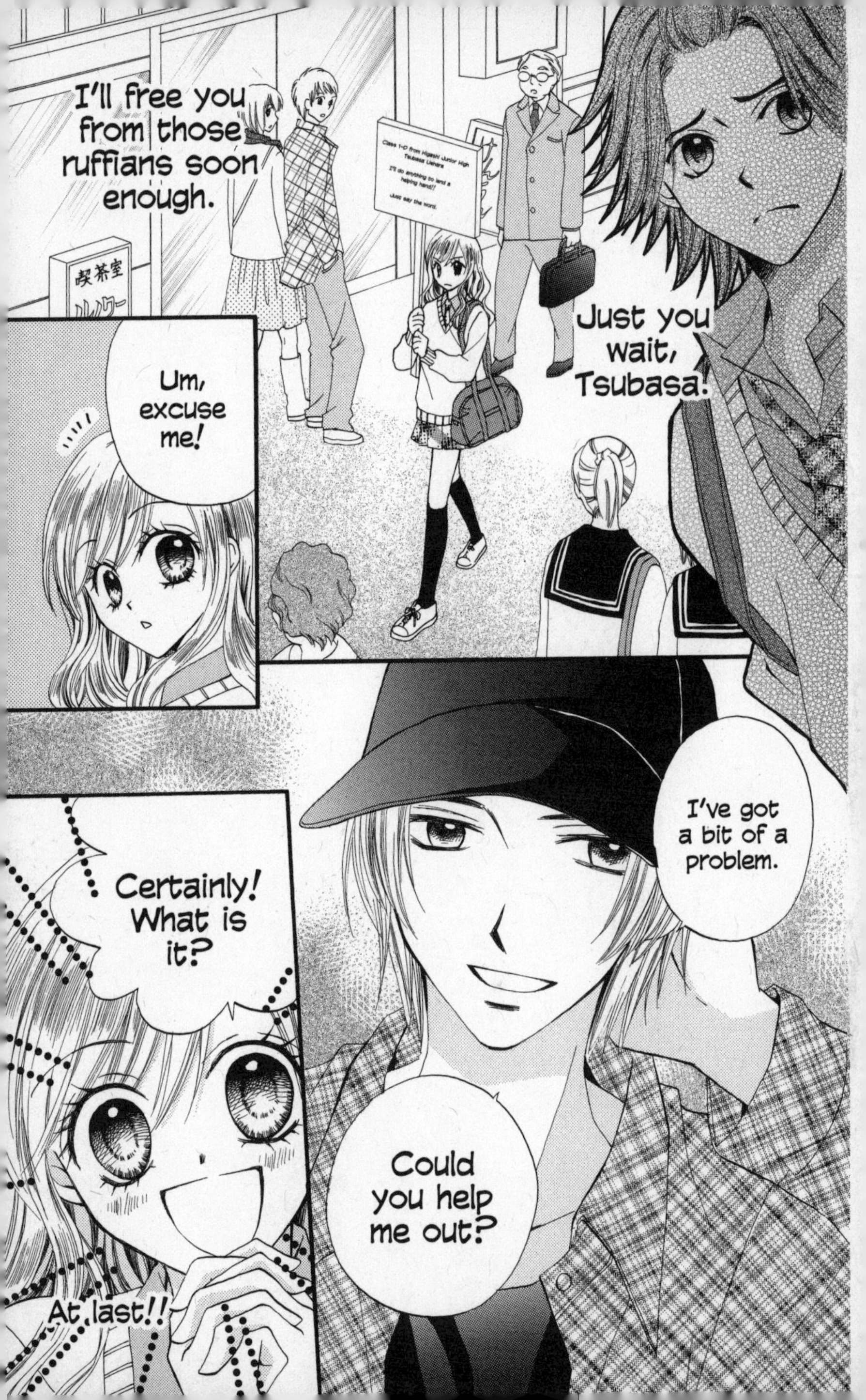
I'll free you from those ruffians soon enough.
Just you wait, Tsubasa.
Um, excuse me!
I've got a bit of a problem.
Could you help me out?
Certainly! What is it?
At last!!

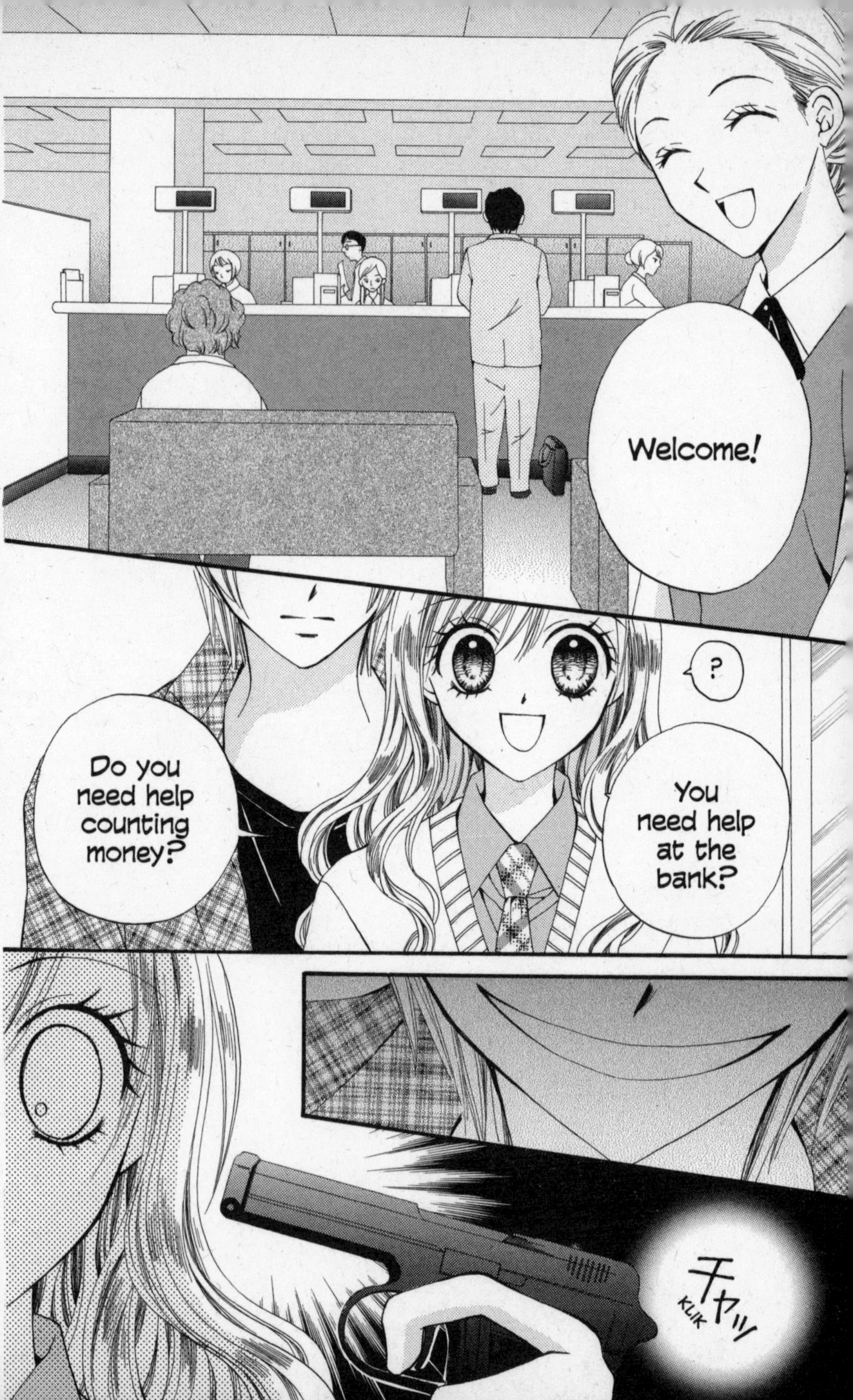
Welcome!
?
You need help at the bank?
Do you need help counting money?
チャッ
KLIK

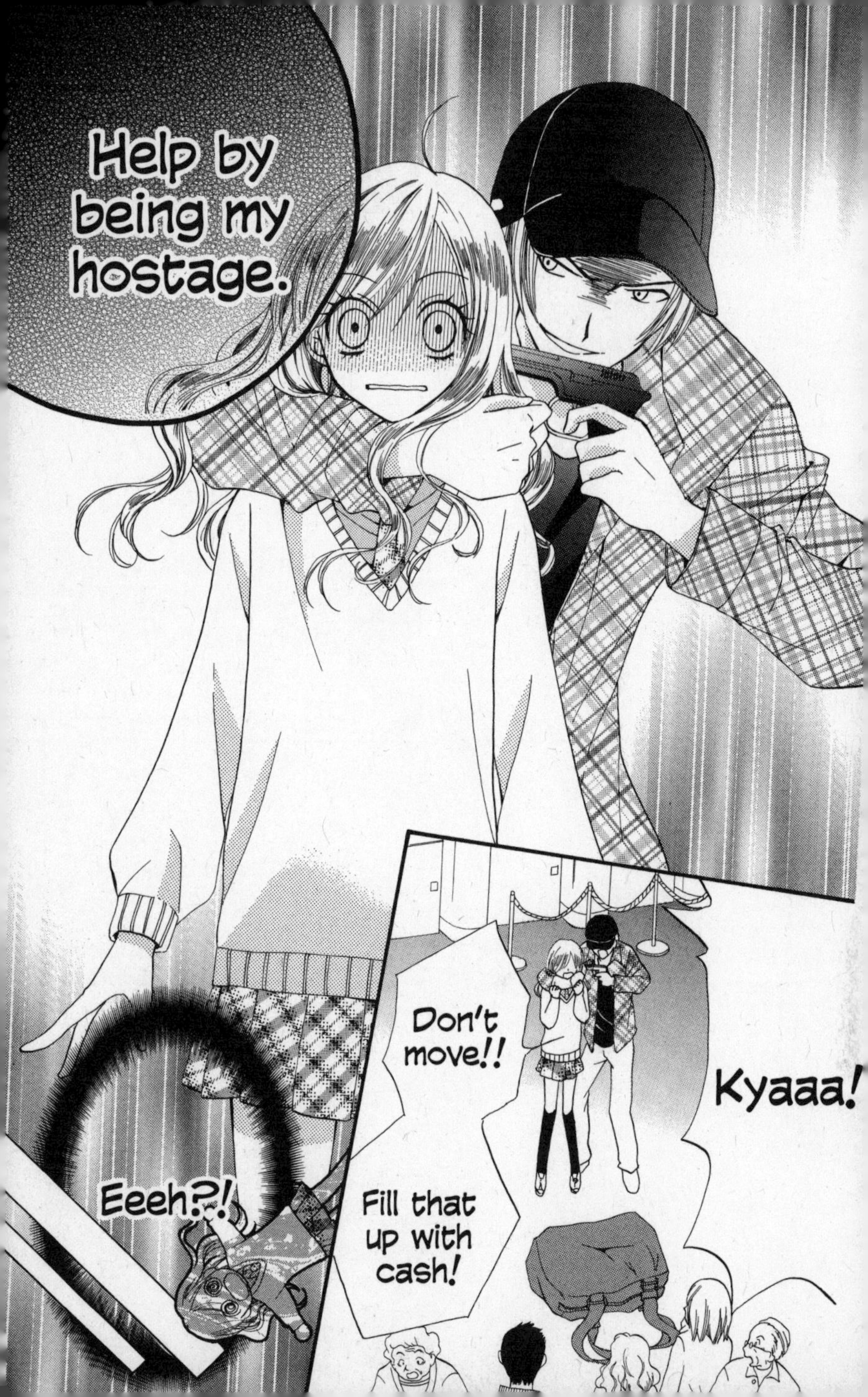
Help by being my hostage.
Eeeh?!
Kyaaa!
Don't move!!
Fill that up with cash!

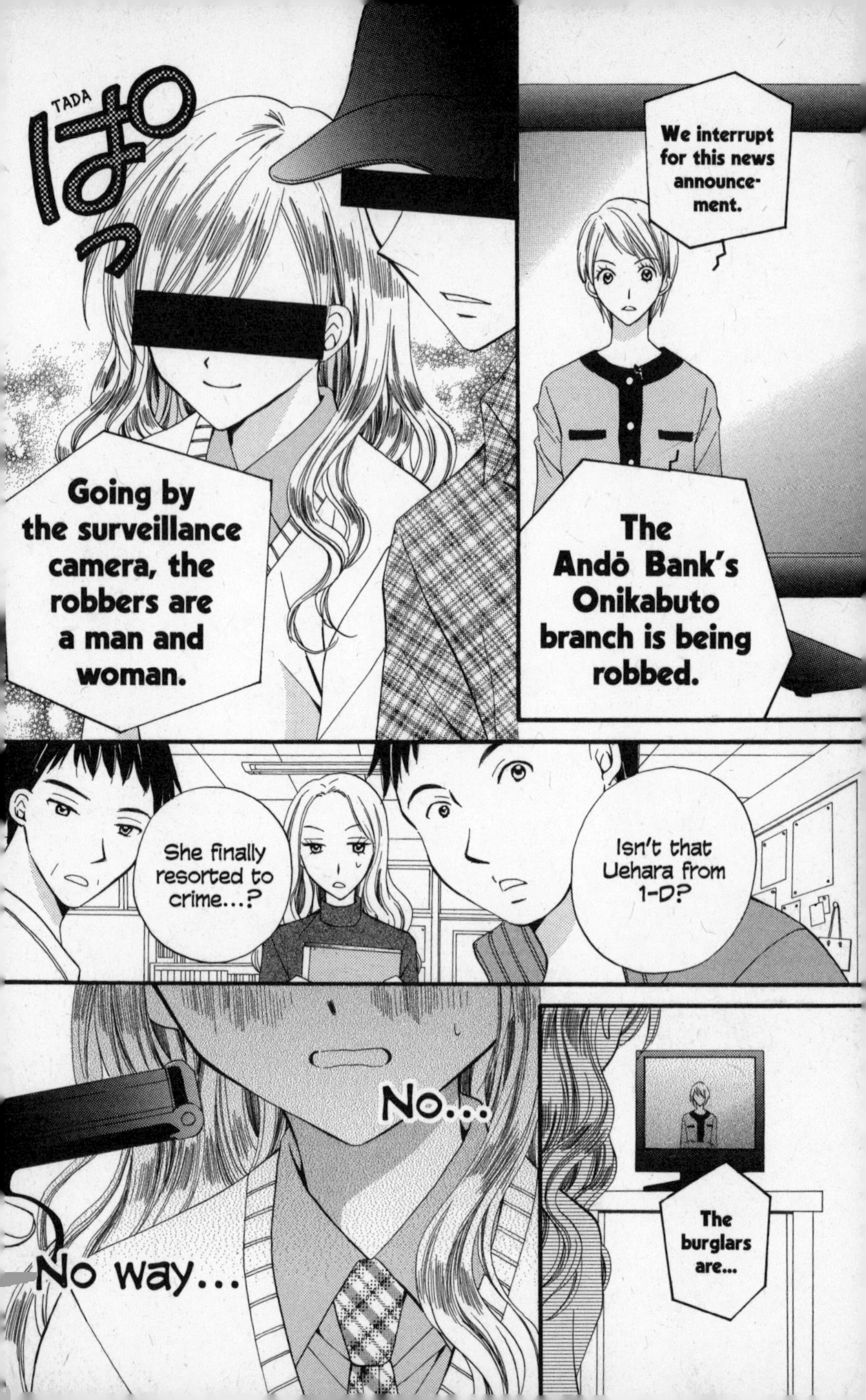

We interrupt for this news announce-ment.
The Andō Bank's Onikabuto branch is being robbed.
TADA
ぱっ
Going by the surveillance camera, the robbers are a man and woman.
Isn't that Uehara from 1-D?
She finally resorted to crime...?
The burglars are...
No...
No way...

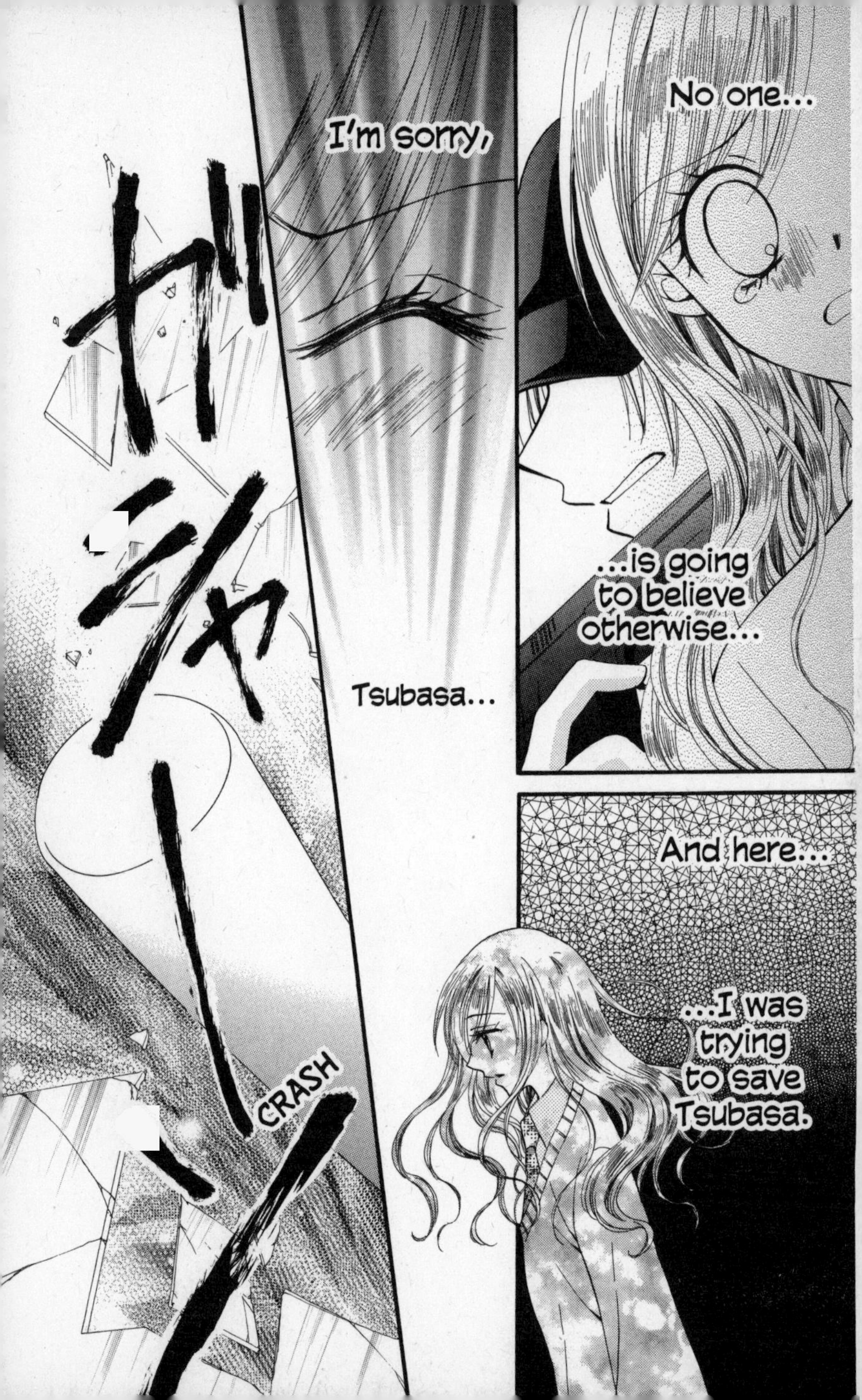
No one...
...is going to believe otherwise...
And here...
...I was trying to save Tsubasa.
I'm sorry,
Tsubasa...
ガシャーン
CRASH

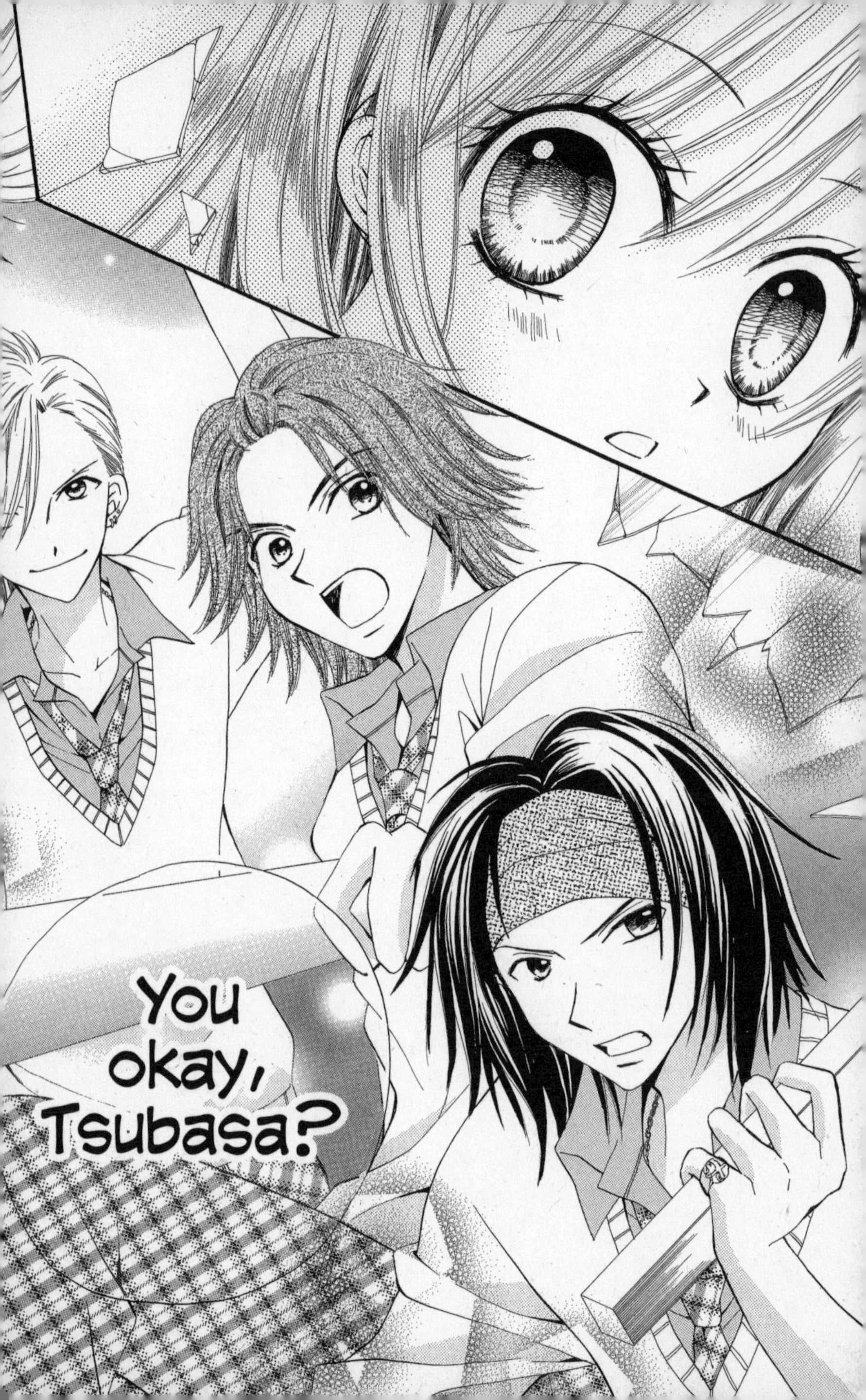
You okay, Tsubasa?

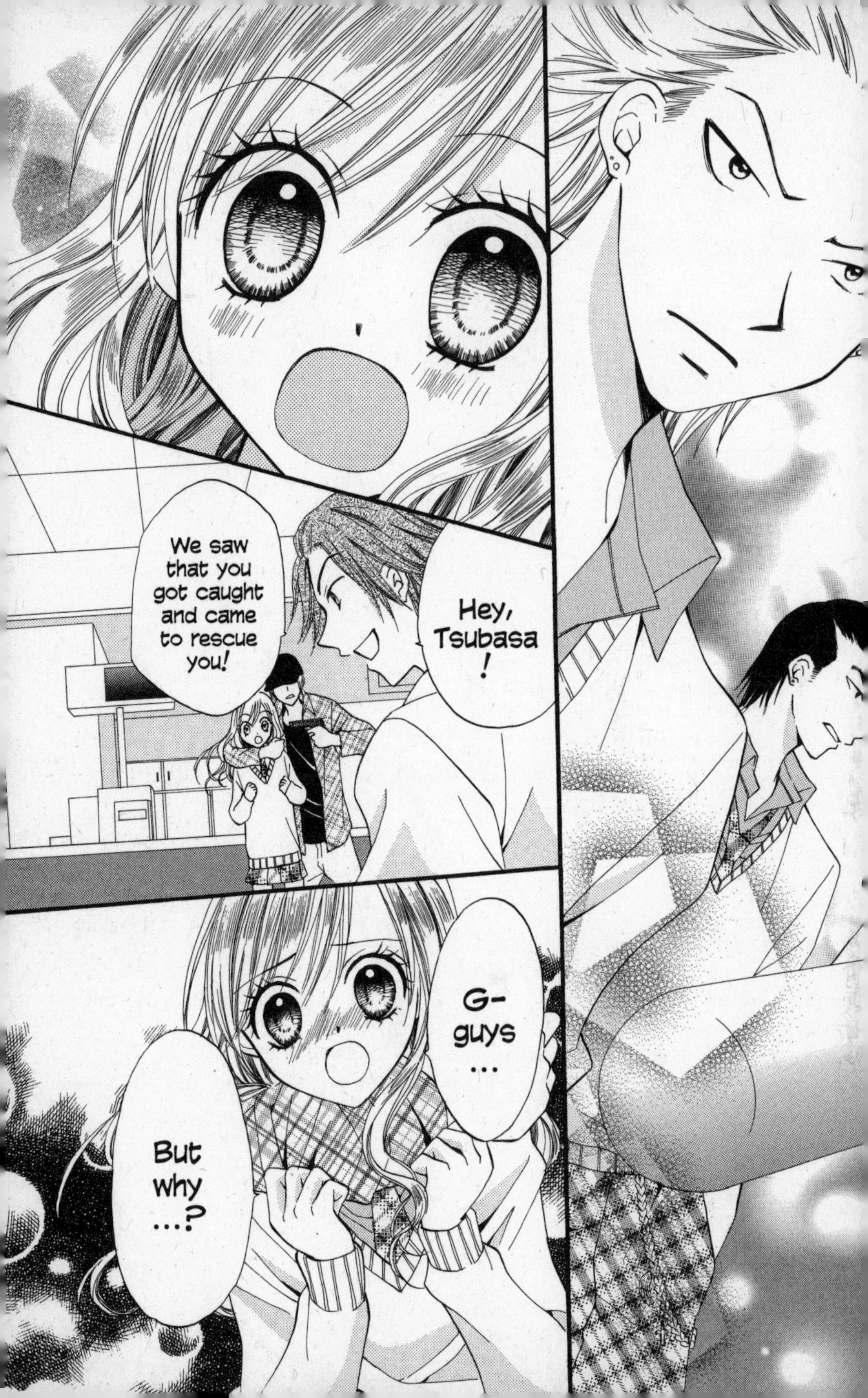
Hey, Tsubasa!
We saw that you got caught and came to rescue you!
G-guys...
But why...?

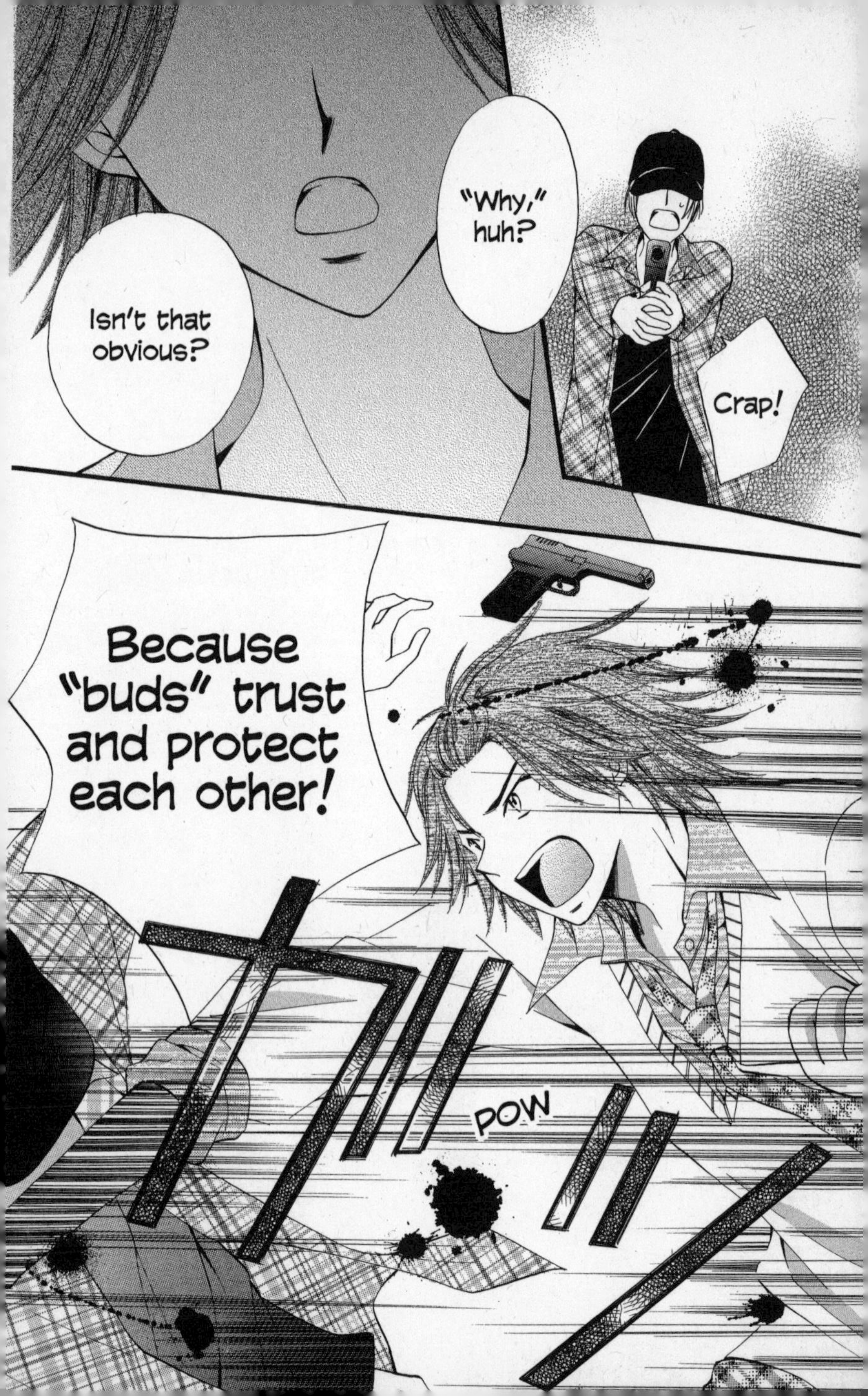
Crap!
"Why," huh?
Isn't that obvious?
Because "buds" trust and protect each other!
POW

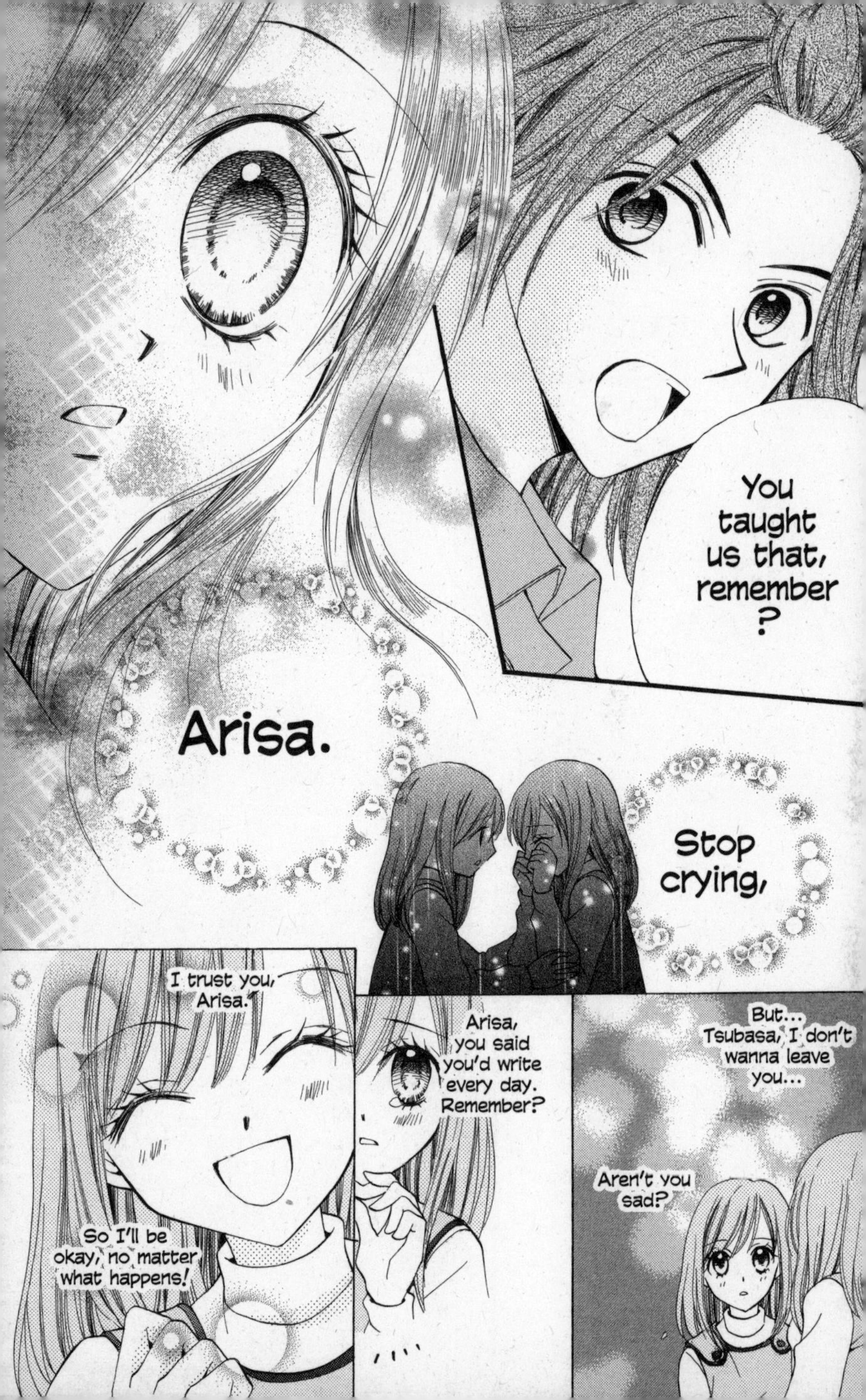

You taught us that, remember?
Stop crying,
Arisa.
But... Tsubasa, I don't wanna leave you...
Aren't you sad?
Arisa, you said you'd write every day. Remember?
I trust you, Arisa.
So I'll be okay, no matter what happens!

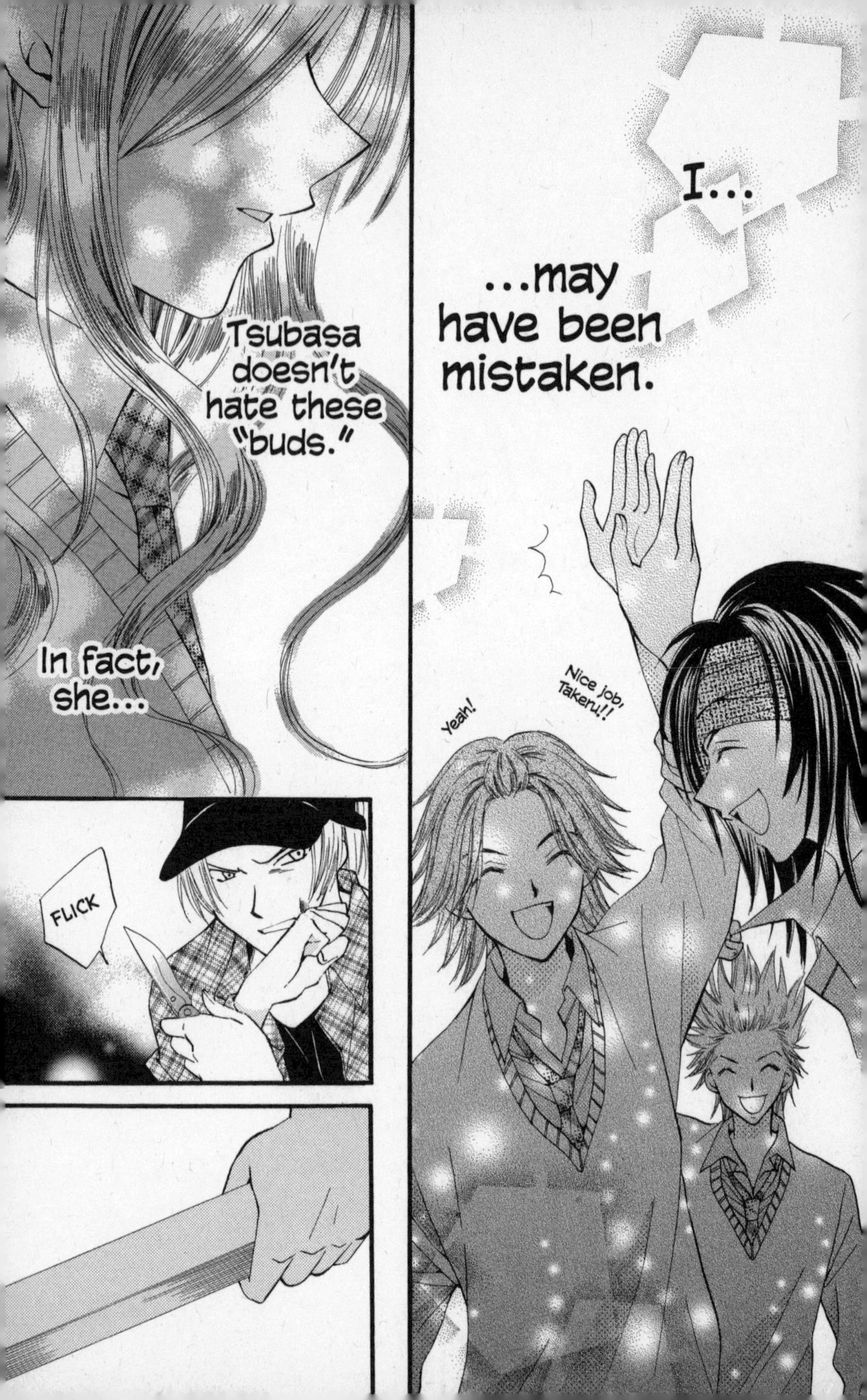
I...
...may have been mistaken.
Nice job, Takeru!!
Yeah!
Tsubasa doesn't hate these "buds."
In fact, she...
FLICK

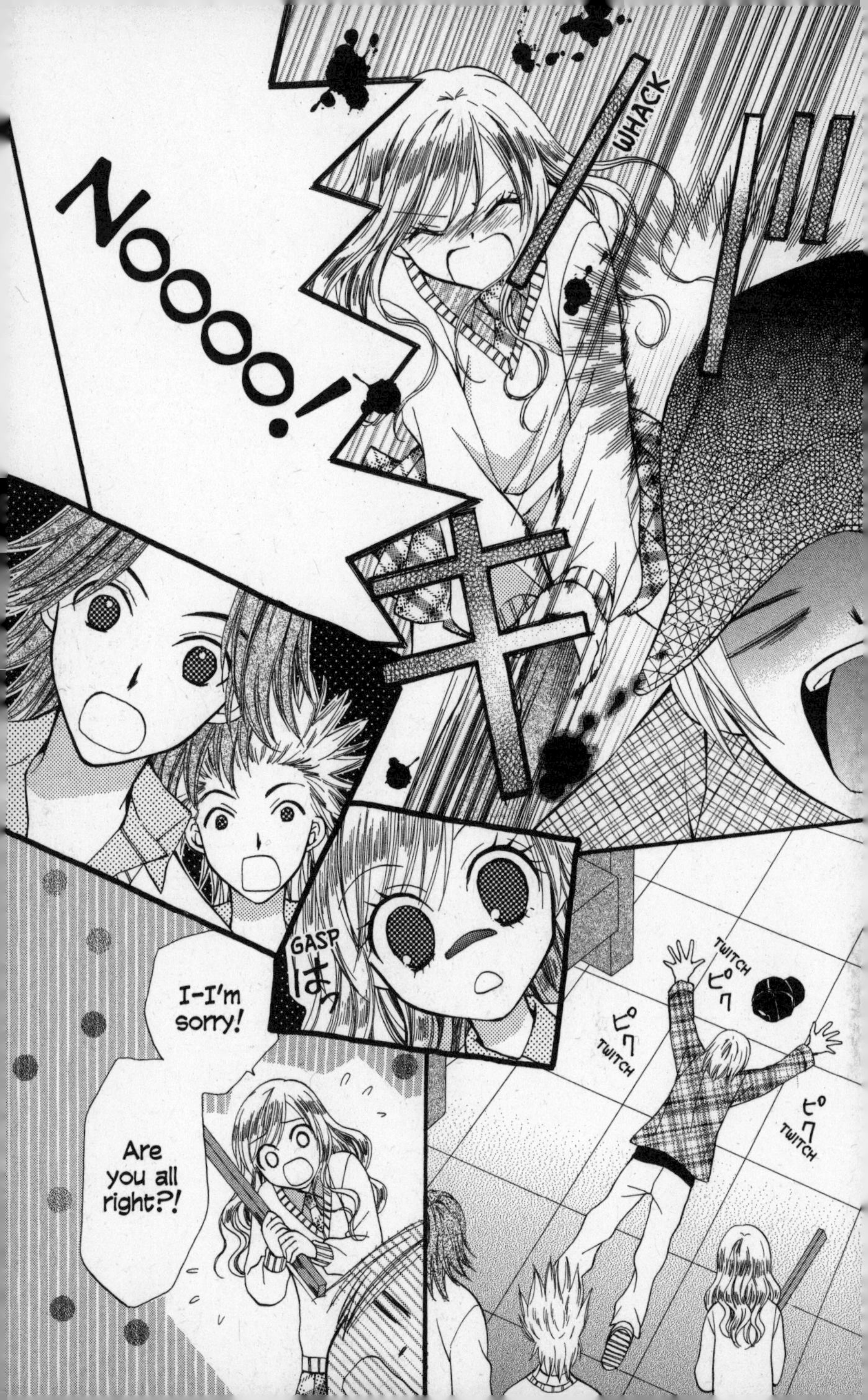
WHACK
NOOOO!
GASP
はっ
TWITCH
ピク
ピク
TWITCH
ピク
TWITCH
I-I'm sorry!
Are you all right?!

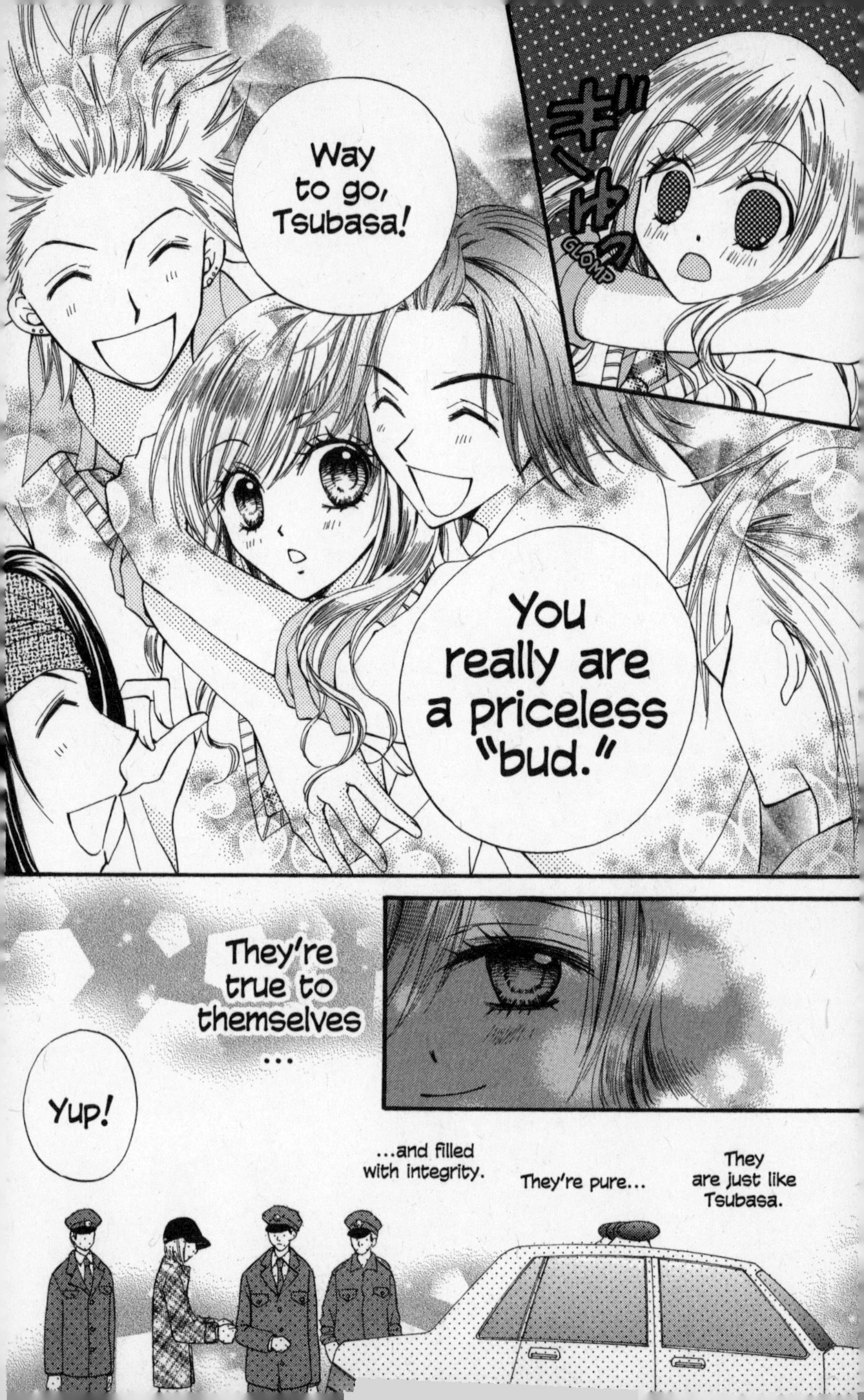
ぎゅっ
GLOMP
Way to go, Tsubasa!
You really are a priceless "bud."
They're true to themselves...
Yup!
They are just like Tsubasa.
They're pure...
...and filled with integrity.

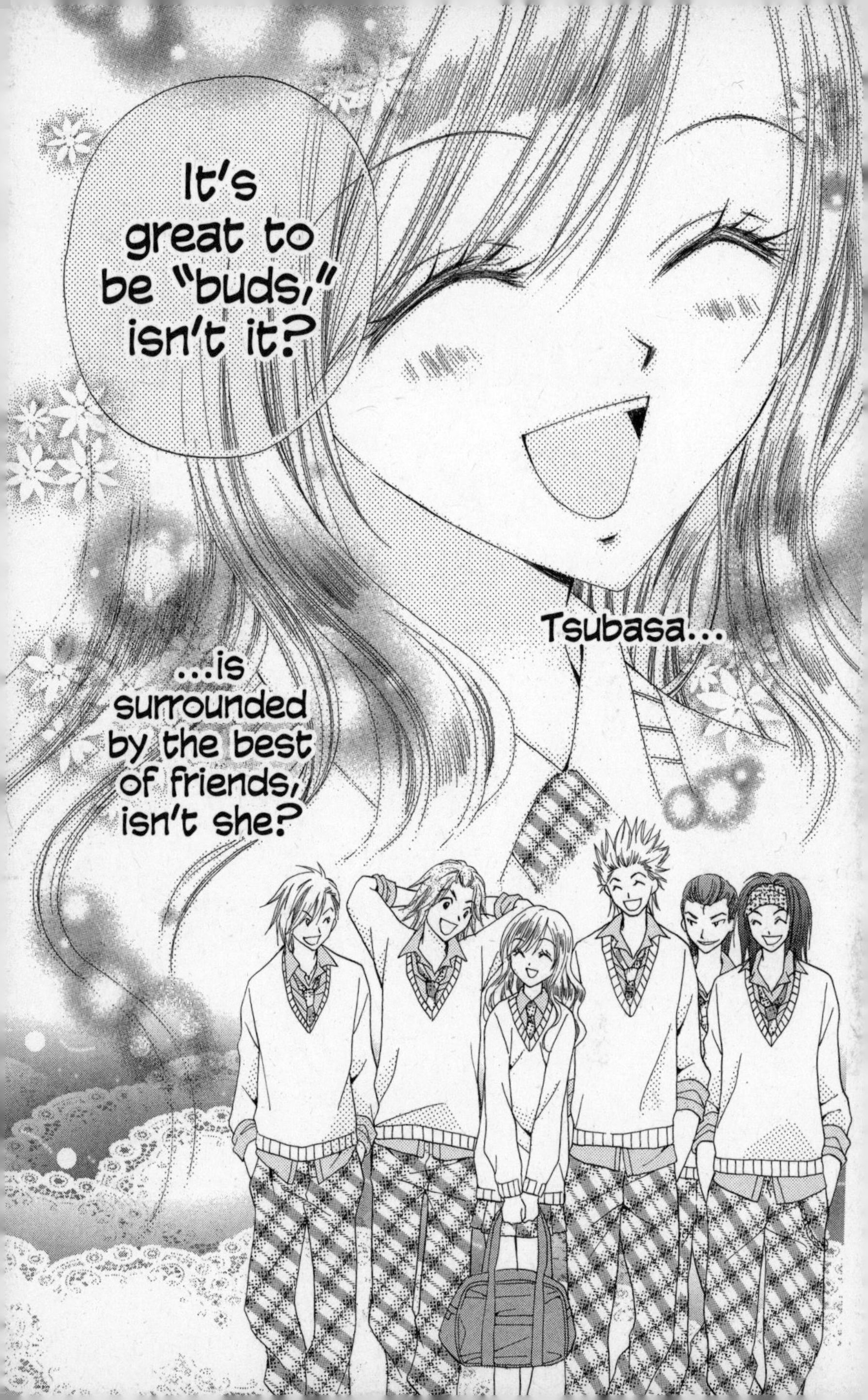
It's great to be "buds," isn't it?
Tsubasa...
...is surrounded by the best of friends, isn't she?

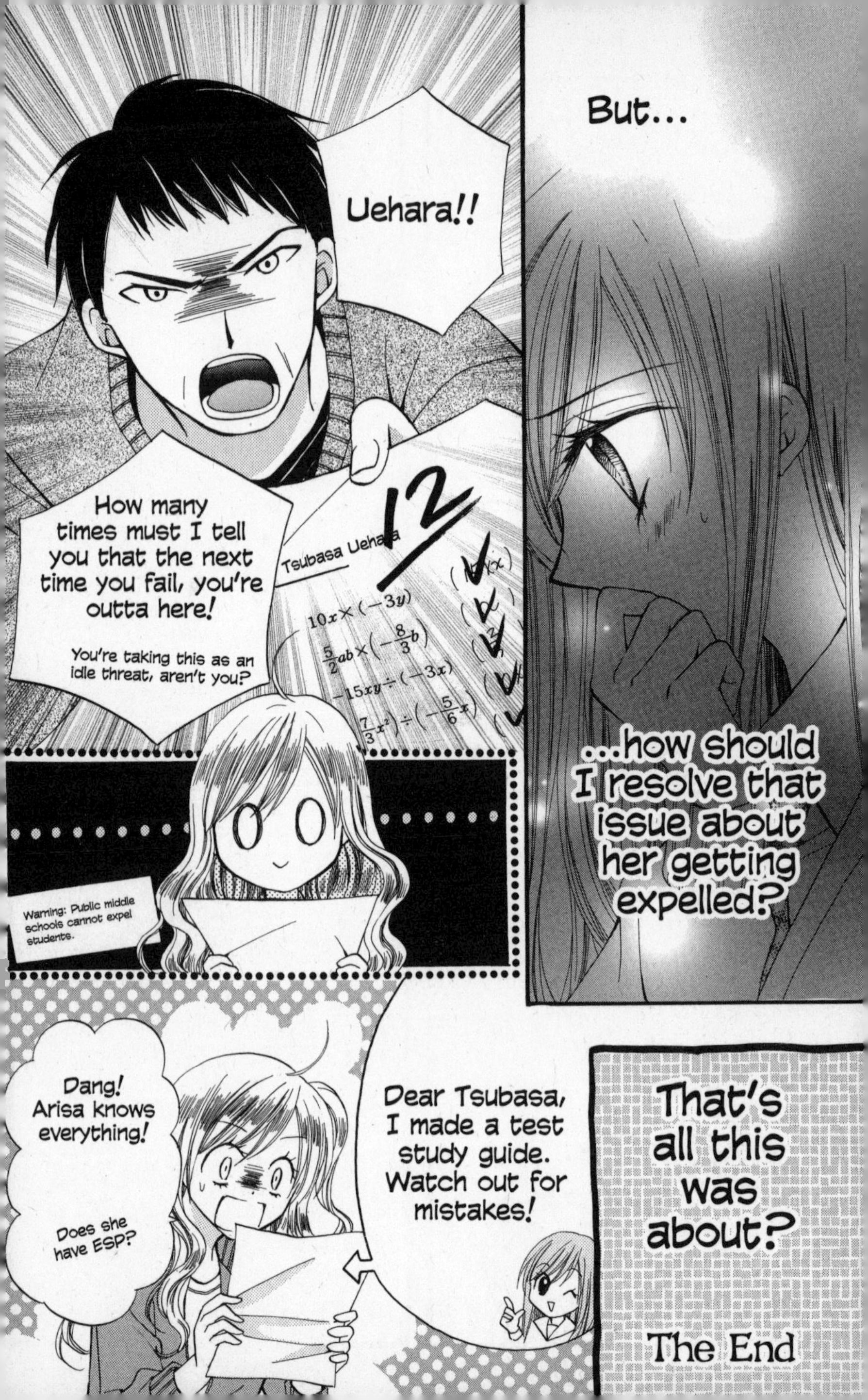
But...
...how should I resolve that issue about her getting expelled?
Uehara!!
12
Tsubasa Uehara
How many times must I tell you that the next time you fail, you're outta here!
You're taking this as an idle threat, aren't you?
Warning: Public middle schools cannot expel students.
That's all this was about?
The End
Dear Tsubasa, I made a test study guide. Watch out for mistakes!
Dang! Arisa knows everything!
Does she have ESP?

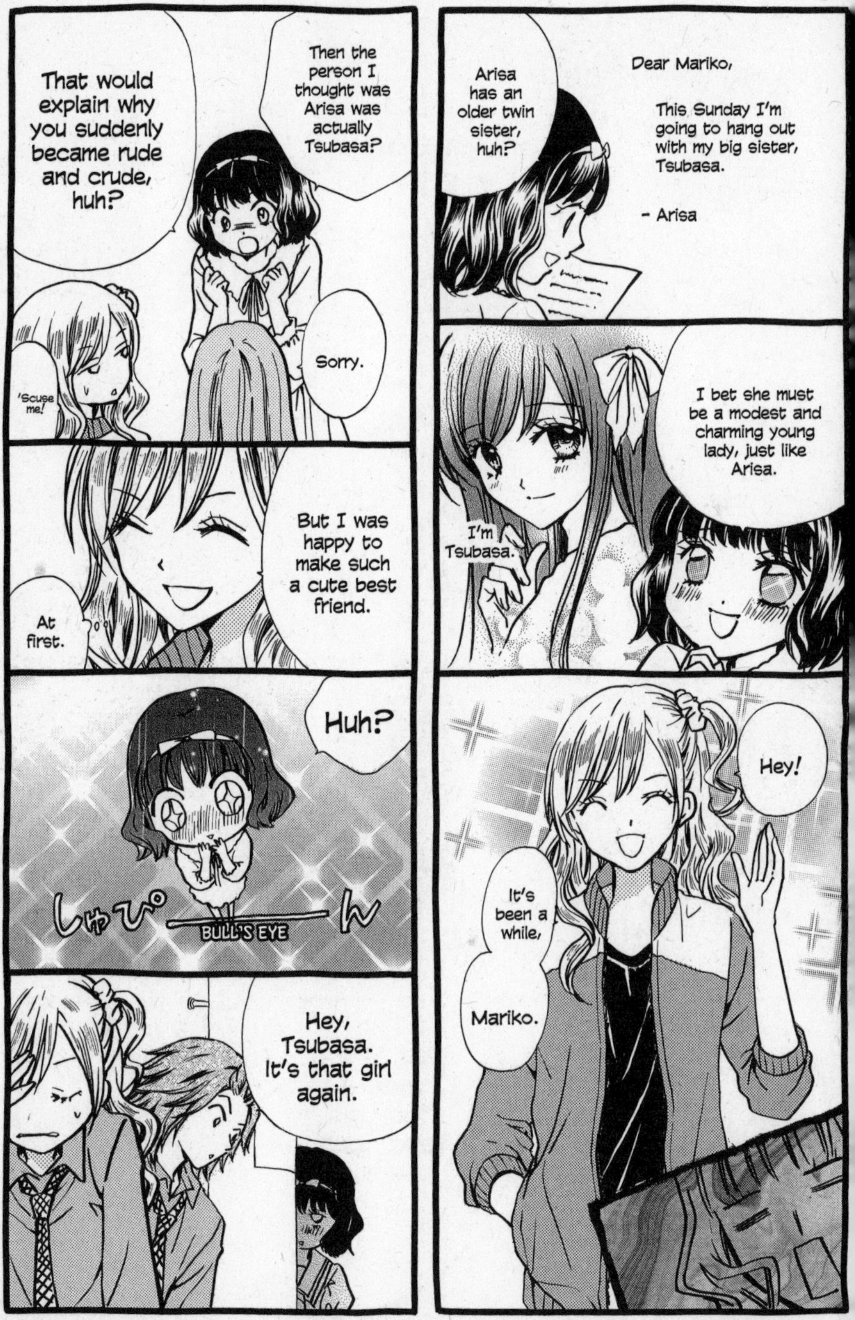
Dear Mariko,
This Sunday I'm going to hang out with my big sister, Tsubasa.
- Arisa
Arisa has an older twin sister, huh?
I bet she must be a modest and charming young lady, just like Arisa.
I'm Tsubasa.
Hey!
It's been a while,
Mariko.
Then the person I thought was Arisa was actually Tsubasa?
That would explain why you suddenly became rude and crude, huh?
Sorry.
'Scuse me!
But I was happy to make such a cute best friend.
At first.
Huh?
しゅぴーん
BULL'S EYE
Hey, Tsubasa. It's that girl again.

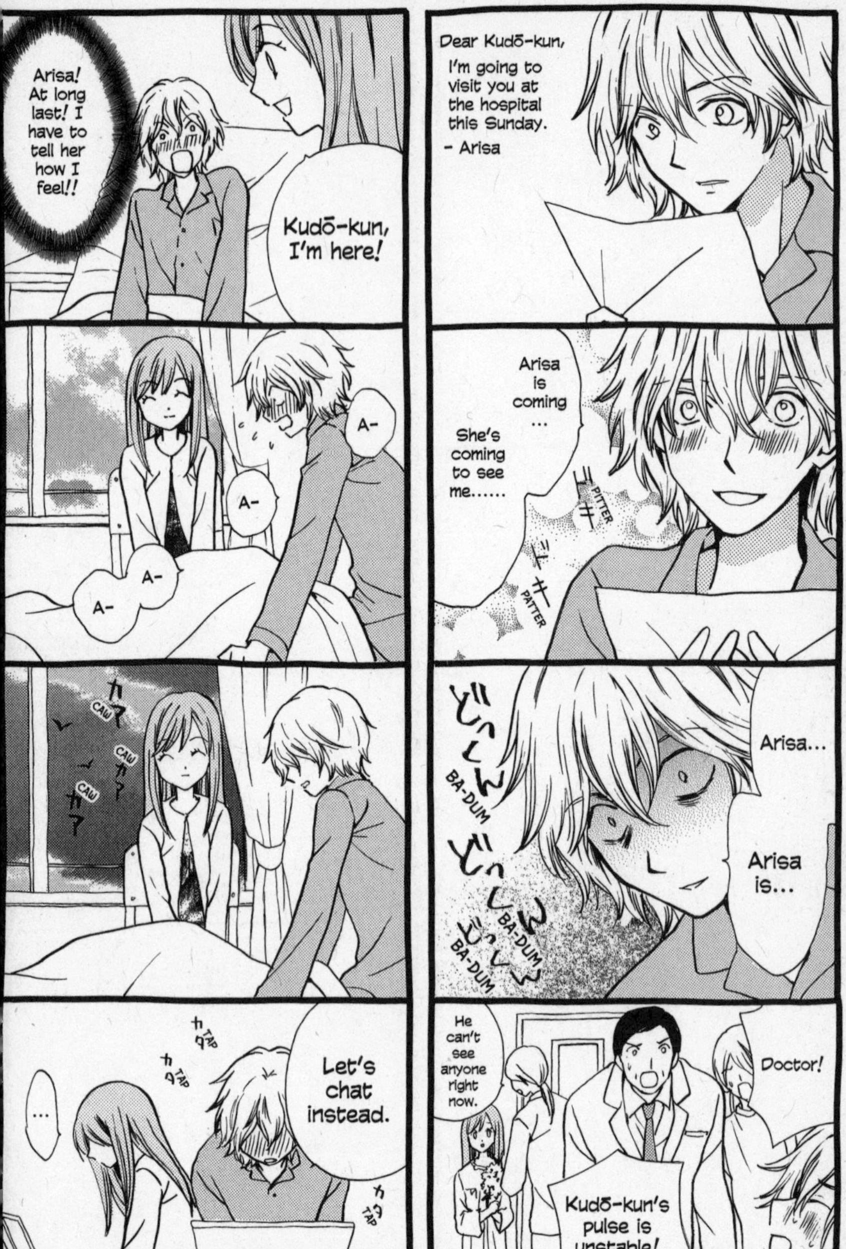
Dear Kudō-kun,
I'm going to visit you at the hospital this Sunday.
- Arisa
Arisa is coming ...
She's coming to see me......
PATTER
PATTER
Arisa...
BA-DUM
Arisa is...
BA-DUM
BA-DUM
Doctor!
Kudō-kun's pulse is unstable!
He can't see anyone right now.
Kudō-kun, I'm here!
Arisa! At long last! I have to tell her how I feel!!
A-
A-
A-
A-
CAW
CAW
CAW
Let's chat instead.
TAP
TAP
TAP
...

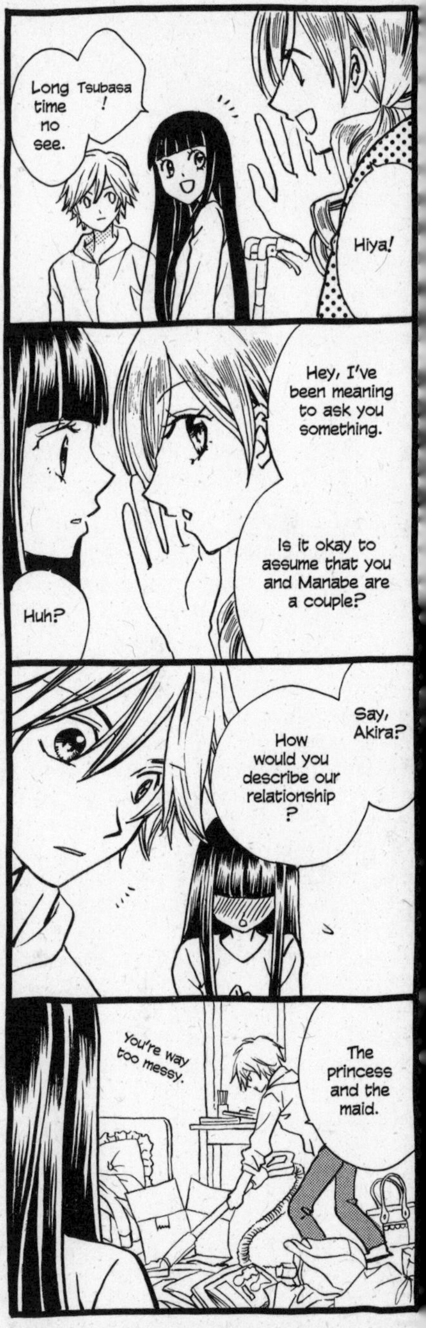
Hiya!
Tsubasa!
Long time no see.
Hey, I've been meaning to ask you something.
Is it okay to assume that you and Manabe are a couple?
Huh?
Say, Akira?
How would you describe our relationship?
The princess and the maid.
You're way too messy.

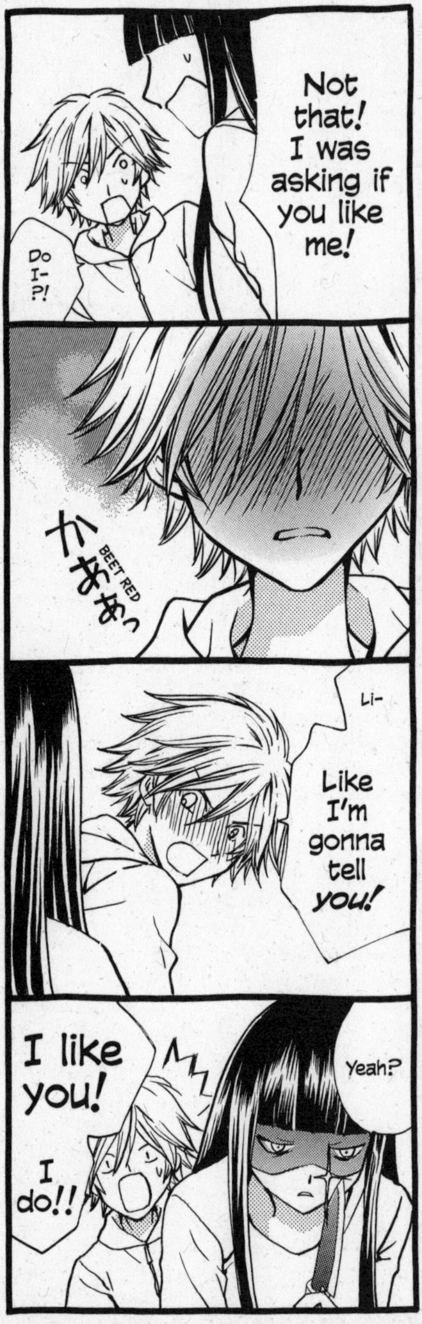
Not that! I was asking if you like me!
Do I-?!
かあぁっ
BEET RED
Li-
Like I'm gonna tell *you!*
Yeah?
I like you!
I do!!

While working on ARISA, I constantly asked myself, "What should happen next?" So I felt really relieved when I finished drawing that last page. I have all of my faithful readers to thank for making it clear to the finish line!!

At first I was a bit concerned about not giving the protagonist a love interest when this is supposed to be a girl's manga. But halfway through, I started to consider that a selling point.

Her lack of romantic relationships allowed me to fully direct Tsubasa's feelings toward Arisa. I think Arisa may be my favorite character in the series because I synchronized her with Tsubasa's feelings...

I actually drew the bonus story, "TSUBASA," which comes after the last chapter, shortly after I began working on the series. However, it didn't feel right to publish a story starring Arisa when the main series was undergoing so much drama while she was in a coma. It got pushed back until it ultimately became the concluding chapter. I guess it works as the final chapter. Why not?

Oh, right. While this was being serialized, I went through three different editors. That was a first, so it put me on edge. But all of my editors had a good understanding of the manga, so I really appreciated them all. And all three of them referred to "Tsubasa" as "Arisa" without fail...

At any rate, I am grateful for everyone who worked on this manga and offered their support! Thank you so much!!

Natsumi Ando 2012.7

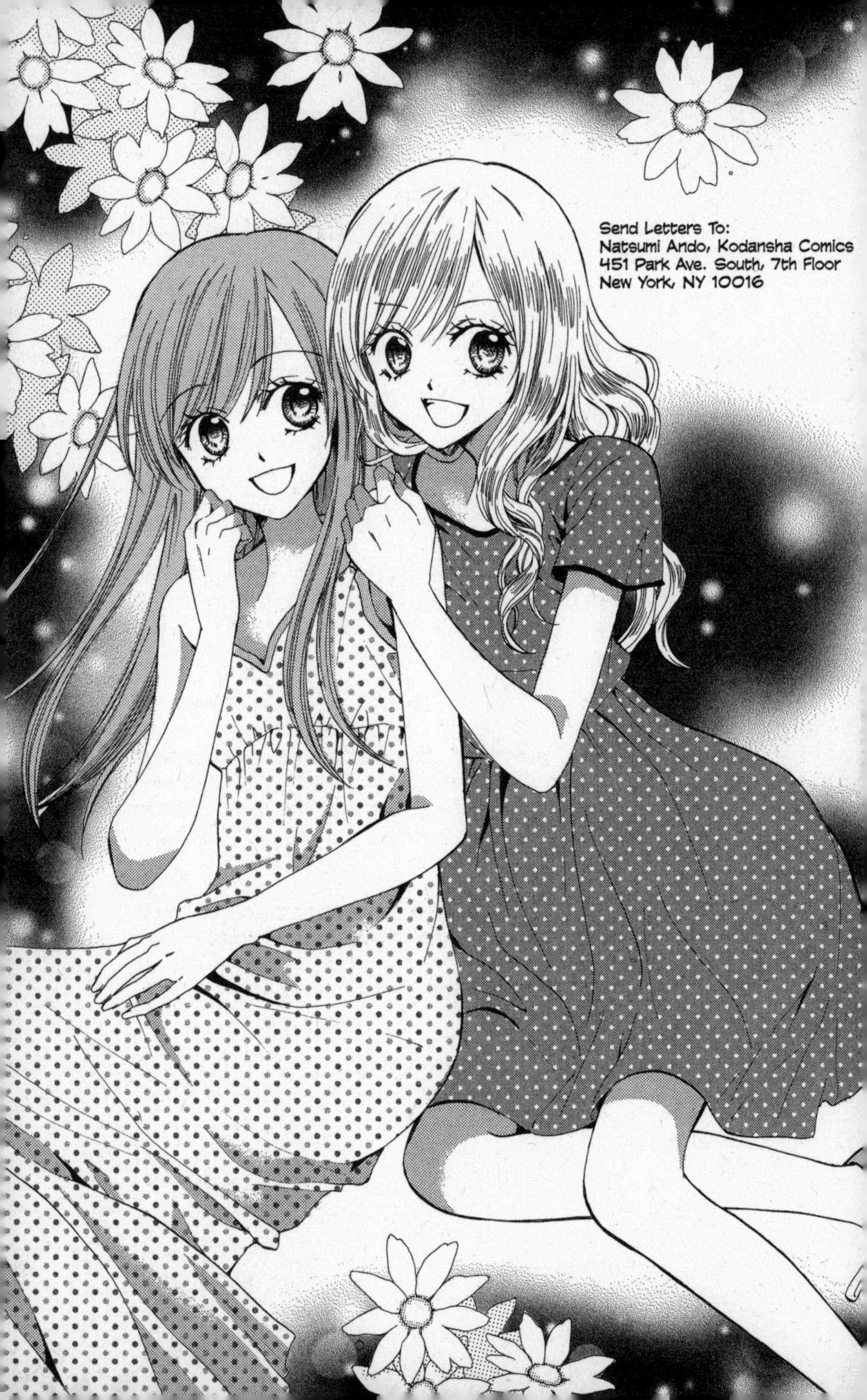

Send Letters To:
Natsumi Ando, Kodansha Comics
451 Park Ave. South, 7th Floor
New York, NY 10016

Arisa volume 12 is a work of fiction. Names, characters, places, and incidents are the products of the author's imagination or are used fictitiously. Any resemblance to actual events, locales, or persons, living or dead, is entirely coincidental.

A Kodansha Comics Trade Paperback Original.

Arisa volume 12 copyright © 2012 Natsumi Ando
English translation copyright © 2014 Natsumi Ando

All rights reserved.

Published in the United States by Kodansha Comics, an imprint of Kodansha USA Publishing, LLC, New York.

Publication rights for this English edition arranged through Kodansha Ltd., Tokyo.

First published in Japan in 2012 by Kodansha Ltd., Tokyo.

ISBN 978-1-61262-439-6

Printed in the United States of America.

www.kodanshacomics.com

9 8 7 6 5 4 3 2 1

Translation: Jackie McClure
Lettering: April Brown
Editing: Lauren Scanlan